Religion, Tradition, and Renewal

# Religion, Tradition, and Renewal

*Edited by Armin W. Geertz
and Jeppe Sinding Jensen*

AARHUS UNIVERSITY PRESS

Copyright: Aarhus University Press, 1991
Printed in Denmark by Rosendahls Bogtrykkeri, Esbjerg
Published with the financial support of the Danish Research Council for the
Humanities and the Aarhus University Research Foundation
ISBN 87 7288 213 1

AARHUS UNIVERSITY PRESS
Building 170, Aarhus University
DK-8000 Aarhus C, Denmark

Cover illustration:
M.C. Escher, Développement I (1937).
Woodcut, 43,7 x 44,6 cm. Photo courtery of the Gemeentemuseum,
The Hague.

# Preface

Most of the essays in this book consist of papers read at the second international conference of the Danish Association for the History of Religions, which coincided with the 5th anniversary of the founding of the association, and which took place at the University of Aarhus on May 14-17, 1987. The two exceptions are the essays written by Michael Pye and J.G. Platvoet. They both attended the conference but did not present papers. Fortunately for us, however, they graciously agreed to write essays specifically for this volume.

One of the goals of the conference was to nurture a dialogue between historians of religions and social anthropologists from various European countries. The 45 participants from Denmark, England, Finland, West Germany, the Netherlands, and Sweden demonstrated that such a dialogue was necessary and fruitful. The general discussions and concluding debate were intense, probing, and enlightening.

The study of historical processes is a fundamental issue in the history of religions. Not only do the requirements of contemporary society force the dichotomous issue of tradition and change, stagnation and renewal on us, but also the very essence of "tradition" and the way it works teases us with ephemera and challenges us to the very core of our methodologies and definitions. Religions undergo change but present themselves as unchanging realities, and yet the very idea of the apparent dichotomy between tradition and modernity is a misunderstanding. In fact, as most recent scholarship has shown, tradition is intimately bound up with a dialectic process of continuity and change.

The participants of the conference were asked to focus on one or all of three variables: the variables of religions and their correlations with presumed constants, the variables of the theoretical scrutiny of tradition and renewal, and, finally, the variables of the paradigms of the study of religion itself. The papers clearly demonstrated that careful scholarship reveals much that cannot be sufficiently explained in terms of the absolute dichotomy between tradition and change.

The costs of the conference were covered by the Danish Council for the Humanities and the Faculty of Theology at the University of Aarhus, and publication costs were covered by these two institutions

6

as well as by the Research Foundation of the University of Aarhus. We extend our grateful thanks for their support, and we also wish to extend our gratitude to the Publishers for their excellent assistance.

A.W.G.
J.S.J.

March 1991

# Table of Contents

8

*Theory and Method*

# Tradition and Renewal in the Histories of Religions: Some Observations and Reflections

*By Jeppe Sinding Jensen and Armin W. Geertz*

## The Enforcement of Tradition

In the histories of the religious traditions of the world, we meet many instances in which the values of the past are upheld. Child-rearing practices, rituals, and initiations are just a few of the myriad institutions and practices which preserve the ways of the past. Behind such practices lies the belief that the ways of the past are meaningful and appropriate and that past actions and beliefs form blueprints for future actions and beliefs. This is, at least, what we habitually think concerning these issues.

Such beliefs are widespread, not only among scholars, but perhaps even more so among politicians and the general public. A clear-cut example of how these views influence legislation is the so-called Holy Quran Bill which was unanimously adopted by the National Assembly of Pakistan in 1987. The proper name of the bill was "Holy Quran Elimination of Printing Errors (Amendment) Bill", and its purpose was to provide for the elimination of errors in cassette recordings of recitations of the Quran. However problematic this may sound, the even more astonishing fact is that the same bill introduced measures for the punishment

of a non-Muslim author who translates, interprets or comments upon an Ayah of the Holy Quran contrary to the belief of Muslims as also the printer or publisher of such translations, interpretation or commentary.[1]

The general idea, though, is clear: the Quran is a divine message, unaltered throughout eternity, and all human activities associated with it should equally forever remain uniform. The same attitude validates most indigenous conceptions of Islamic culture and learning: it is a fixed body of notions and actions definable to the smallest detail. The Pakistani bill fully illustrates the paradoxical fact that it is common-place in religion to accomodate new situations (social, cultural,

economical, etc.) by recourse to the undiluted truths of the most
ancient past. New tasks require ancient means. This is apparently how
it has always been. One may ask if this is just another way in which
religion is antithetical to reason, because from where we stand today
in secularized and historically-oriented cultures, we recognize that
religions and their related traditions do of course change through time.
This is most dramatically seen in the case of, for example, prophetic
movements where radically old solutions are being offered as new
messages. The dialectics of tradition and renewal, as we conveniently,
but misleadingly say, are complex, and it is not surprising that these
topics have received attention in recent scholarly investigations of the
histories of religions and other cultural manifestations.

## Some Recent Publications

Brief mention will be made in this section of a number of works,
which have appeared over the last decade or so, dealing with issues
related to the main theme of this book. Comprehensive coverage is
not the intention of this introduction. What is more important in this
connection is to present some of the issues involved in the various
kinds of interpretations offered. In 1976, Gunther Stephenson edited
a collection of essays by German scholars entitled *Der Religionswandel unserer Zeit im Spiegel der Religionswissenschaft*. The broad
scope of the book includes investigations of religions in various parts
of the world, past and present, along with two sections on reflections
and methodological problems. Of particular interest here is the critique
by Hubert Seiwert of the ways historians of religions have dealt with
the explanation of changes in religious systems, especially the
commonplace historical-genetical explanations. These explanations may
well answer questions about the origin and forms of change ("Woher"
and "Wie") but they do not answer the crucial question of the
"Warum" of change. The historian's task is not only to describe what
happened but also to explain it (Seiwert 1976).

A work which has aroused some interest among historians, sociologists, and anthropologists is *The Invention of Tradition* edited by
Eric Hobsbawm and Terence Ranger. The book is discussed eleswhere
in this volume, but it is important to note the general idea that tradition (here referring to the content and not to the act of transmission)
is perpetually recreated and not a given static as had been supposed
by earlier generations of scholars and tradition-bearers alike
(Hobsbawm & Ranger 1983). On the other hand, this kind of insight
should not really be new to either anthropologists or historians of

religions. Any fieldworker will know that tales about the past may readily account for present wishes, and historians of religions will recognize that myths about the rule of parrots at the beginning of time do not reflect historical events but legitimate the order in which the world now finds itself. Invention in this sense does not mean replacement as we tend to think.

Edward Shils, in his work *Tradition*, notes that the Enlightenment was antithetical to tradition, or:

At least its great spokesmen and its lesser interpreters thought it was. The success which the Enlightenment achieved was owed to its becoming a tradition (Shils 1981, 235).

The result was that emancipation from tradition became a tradition in itself. However ironical this is in Shils' view, it is none the less a "precious achievement of our civilization. It made citizens out of slaves and serfs" (234). Shils' book was written from the perspective of the history of European ideologies, but it retains a level of reflection worthy of attention by historians of religions working with non-European modes of thought.

Whereas most critical thought in Western intellectual history has been emancipatory in character, some historians of religions have advocated a personal and existentially relevant attitude to the world's religious traditions. Foremost among these is Mircea Eliade who presented modern man's estrangement from tradition as fundamentally detrimental to individual and social balance, hence the politics of nostalgia which seeks, on the basis of a universalist interpretation of religions, to restore Man as a complete and inherently spiritual being. However much such claims are derived from working with material from the history of religions, the outcome is pseudo-scientific and constitutes "worldview construction" in its own right, i.e., making sense in the modern world by old means. The same track is followed in a recent collection of essays by Charles A. Long devoted to the "restatement of the reality of the human" (Long 1986, 6).

A more subtle understanding must be applied. Traditions are not always pure and novel inventions, nor are they unaltered relics of primordiality attesting to the wisdom of the ancients and thus applicable as spiritual medicine against the ailments of modern life. The old and the new are fashioned in and by human agents in time and space. A sophisticated analysis of the complicated dialectics is offered by Roy Wagner in his book *The Invention of Culture*. Wagner expounds the relations between cultural convention and invention: conventions are only such because they are constantly invented, and invention is only possible and meaningful in relation to and on the basis of convention (Wagner 1981).

When applied to that specific aspect of human culture which historians of religions study, Wagner's stance casts new light on the role of religions in changing societal conditions. This perspective is elaborated in various ways in a collection of essays edited by Bruce Lincoln with the disquieting title *Religion, Rebellion, Revolution*. The essays originated from a conference held in Minnesota in 1981, partly prompted, in the words of the editor, by the public puzzlement over the events of the Iranian revolution, which seemed to challenge in a profound manner all tacit agreement on theses of secularization. As Lincoln states in the opening lines of his introduction:

To study religion and revolution is to consider two different classes of phenomena, both of them extreme types within their respective categories. On the one hand, revolution is the extreme form of socio-political action..... Similarly, religion must be understood - in part, at least - as the extreme form of ideology, whereby socio-political structures, attitudes and patterns of behaviour are provided not merely with abstract philosophical ration-alizations, but with sacred warrants and legitimation (Lincoln 1985, 3).

This basically functionalistic conception of religion as legitimation and conservation is then challenged because, in Lincoln's words, it is "denying to religion the full range of dialectic possibilities inherent in any ideological system" (8).

Not quite so theoretically inclined and dealing more descriptively with the changes of religious systems from 1945 to the present day, is the volume *Religion in Today's World* edited by Frank Whaling. The bulk of the essays treat various traditions in their contemporary settings in useful and easily accessible form for students and non-specialists in the respective fields. Of special interest is Jacques Waardenburg's contribution, "The Study of Religion in Today's World," because he not only refers to the intellectual side of the history of the study of religion but even more so to the institutional sides and to the crucial questions of how a study of religion depends on a host of societal and cultural factors (Waardenburg 1987).

Looking back on the past to help explain the present in the study of religion may also be supplemented with prognostic and programmatic visions of the future. One such discussion is particularly relevant to the academic situation in North America of the history of religions where the discipline is comparatively recent and independent of the continental European philological tradition (Alles & Kitagawa 1985).

## On Modernization and Tradition

Seen from a conventional Western perspective, no religious tradition was more antithetical to the ideas of the Enlightenment, modernization, and intellectual emancipation than Islam. Whether this view is a result of skewed and politically useful perceptions is not really the issue here, though one may no doubt attribute these views to the particularly sensitive position that Islamic culture has held in the historically Christian West. What has been said of Islam may equally well be said about any other traditional universe of discourse, religious or ideological. It is ironical that this religion and the cultures associated with it have taken the scholarly community by surprise and given impetus to renewed and critical investigations of theories of the relations between ideologies and political action, as we noted in connection with the volume edited by Bruce Lincoln.

Over the past decade there has been a steady flow of literature dealing with Islam in various forms and topics like "resurgence, upheaval, revolution, political change", etc., as surveyed by for instance Jerrold D. Green (1985) and Yvonne Y. Haddad (1986). And all this in relation to Islam as *the* religious tradition considered most impervious to modern (i.e., our Western) ideas. From within the Islamic tradition itself, it has been repeatedly maintained that the Tradition is inflexible and forever ordained by Allah. What discloses the Pakistani legislators' worldview as basically traditional is the fundamental belief in a transformation of society that hinges on the revival of a metaphysically validated original state of affairs. What is noted by the scholar, however, is that the "original condition" is a creation of contemporary interpretation by people who deny the very act of interpretation.

Such literalist readings are by no means restricted to Islam. Any variety of fundamentalism is based precisely on the idea that neither history nor interpretation exist or have any value. History is negated in the sense that it is the original state in *illo tempore* or the perfect model society that is the object of desire, and what happened since then is largely degradation and corruption. Interpretation is eschewed in favour of a literalist reading of the scriptures as revealed truths. Fundamentalism as such is more readily disclosed when it relates to ancient religious traditions, but it can, and does, influence political thought and discourse (Tapper & Tapper 1987). Advocates of fundamentalism have always seen threats to their thoughts or actions as coming from the outside, thereby sustaining the idea that idealogical and religious systems more than anything else are unchangeable entities, i.e., it is only external factors which generate changes or instability in the system.

Literalist readings of tradition have, as well, affinities with earlier theories of religion and culture where the prerequisite for a concept of culture was its lack of dynamics. It is still a common and not unpopular assumption in the West that modernization occurred "by itself" and that it will spread all over the world in similar ways, given time and the workings of reason. However much such a view can be shown to be evolutionistic and ethnocentric, it is probably impossible to extricate oneself completely from it, the "tradition" of modernity being so deeply enmeshed as it is in our epistemology. Some of the most valiant efforts to extricate scientific thought from the tradition of modernity are being made today by leading scholars of the very disciplines which have propagated the tradition, such as sociologist Anthony Giddens (1979).

## The History of Religions and Tradition

That modernization ideology is our basic intellectual framework in the humanities and in the social sciences (to say nothing about the technical sciences) is amply demonstrated by looking at past theoretization, whether it was concerned with political and institutional change or with secularization of religious systems. As long as social and political scientists concerned themselves with Western societies, the theories seemed plausible enough, but after the extended inclusion of non-Western societies within the scopes of research, many positions have become untenable. Historians of religions, traditionally more philologically than social scientifically oriented, were wary of theories of class stratification, urbanization, etc., because somehow the theories did not really fit and consequently were of little use to the topic. The malaise of the historians of religions was partly due to the negligence of their work on the part of the social scientists. A subject like the history of religions was allocated only marginal importance in the academy. But here, too, there seems to be a change in tradition, and our field may become more influential, given a wider scope of dialogue. Today, development projects also involve, e.g., anthropologists and not just technicians or economists in recognition of the fact that "indigenous" traditions actually have value and weight instead of being merely superfluous survivals of pre-rational thought. To understand what happens in Turkey, for example, it is of couse not enough to study Islam as it has developed in Turkey, but, on the other hand, no understanding will emerge from a study that ignores Islam and the specific cultural situation of that country (Eisenstadt 1984).

Historians of religions, more than any other students of intellectual history, should scrutinize their own arsenal of terms and ideas, simply because the adequate study of other traditions demands faithful interpretation. We may then ask if our modern epistemology with its emphasis on radical breaks and changes is not itself a product of such breaks and changes. We may have been brought up to believe, far more than we realize, in exaggerations of differences to the point where the relations between Them and Us can only be understood in a synthetic series of dichotomies.

Such notions as prelogical mentality are a case in point. Nothing wrong in itself, but when it is promoted to cover an entire spectrum of ideas that are viewed as essentially different than ours, then something is out of proportion. If there can be said to be such a thing as prelogical mentality, it can surely be found in our own midst and not just in Others. Lévy-Bruhl has long been discredited, but non-rationality is still considered mainly to be a major characteristic of non-Western modes of thought

Another contestable pair of concepts is that of religious affiliation and ethnicity, where ethnicity is considered as being stable and religious affiliation as varying with conversion, new religions, etc., because this is how things developed in the West. Other studies have shown that ethnicity and cultural forms may change but that religious affiliation is the more stable category (Barth 1983, Bentley 1987). What this means is simply that anything may change. What requires analytical explanation, then, is why people change their ways or how change is possible at all on the basis of tradition.

Among anthropologists and social scientists, it is commonplace to view symbolic and religious actions as goal-oriented, so, if traditions change or are interpreted in new ways, it is in order to cope with new situations and maximize what may be in the actor's own interests. A typical case is that of land claims that are based on genealogical or quasi-mythological terms. It is the will to power and wealth that explains action, and religious idioms and images may then shroud such intentionality in socially acceptable terms. This is an instrumentalist view of culture, ideology, and religion in essence. What is interesting from this perspective are matters of difference, changes, and breaks, because they disclose underlying social conflicts

that are the true objects of study. What religious people do and say
are cover-ups and social manipulation.

Many historians of religions object to this somewhat gloomy view
of humanity, partly for private religious and philosophical reasons, but
also because it is difficult to ignore the continuity of ideas and beliefs
that are not conducive to private gain or profit-maximization however
symbolic it may be. Scholars with a more intimate acquaintance with
the developments of religions in historical processes have certain
problems with the more mechanical views of religion. Not that their
view is necessarily anti-Marxist, but modes of thought and human
intellectual inventions cannot always be accounted for in terms of
"profane" conditions. Religions as realms or registers of discourse are
of course related to their historical settings, but no simple relationship
exists between material conditions, religious thought and action in
social life, and ritual - political or otherwise. A thought provoking
study of this problem is offered by David D. Laitin in his monograph
on religious differences and political divisions among the Yoruba of
Nigeria (Laitin 1986).

Historians of religions have a propensity to think in terms of
continuities and long durations, and they study ideas that may be
traceable over thousands of years. There are at least two dangers in
this, the first being that the long durations may be more or less our
own constructions which only serve to facilitate an alleged understanding of the distant cultural or religious expressions. The other
danger, obviously, is that one can be led to overlook the disruptive
and fragmentary elements. Certain historians of religions have fo-
cussed entirely on the primordial and the timeless, which is, of course,
highly questionable for a historian of any kind. Out of this kind of
perception of religion, any kind of change is equal to heresy or corruption of initial and ideal states.

## Tradition and Temporality

We have two conflicting explanatory frameworks, then: one which
claims that everything is invented for the occasion, and one which
claims that all meanings are bound to primordiality. The truth may be
discernible somewhere in between, the only problem is to account for
it in plausible and theoretically adequate terms, i.e., to explain the
relationship between ideology and practice when people are faced with
problems of change (Bentley 1987). If we allow for certain structural
similarities and analogies between religions and languages as systems
for creation and expression of meaning in social contexts, we will find

that both language and religion change over time notwithstanding the fact that they are felt and believed by the practitioners themselves to be continuous with the past. Retrospectively, the analyst is able to discern between epochs, periods, waves, and other forms of temporality which can be used to designate and identify changes. Some observed changes may then be considered as more radical breaks over shorter time-spans both from external and internal points of view, whereas others are first identified when viewed over longer periods, and only by the external observer who may come into conflict with a tradition's own interpretations. That external observers and internal participants have different interpretations of what is meaningful is hardly a novel conception, but the relations involved between these perspectives are sometimes more problematic than it may seem. An intriguing case was discussed by Ann Fienup-Riordan in her description of how an Alaskan Inuit community reacted to the production of a motion picture, based on one of their indigenous traditions, starring Robert Redford. The film-makers wanted to reach a contemporary Western audience, which meant that the contents of the Inuit narrative had to be completely inversed. The anthropologist had some objections to this at first, whereas the Inuit did not! What happened was that the film-makers' intentions had prompted radically new local reinterpretations and re-formulations of the indigenous narratives (Fienup-Riordan 1988).

## Time in Anthropology

In contrast to historians of religions, who have mainly dealt with the distant in time and space and produced intelligibility through the construct "religion", anthropologists have studied the distant in space, geographically, socially, and culturally. Classic ethnographic monographs were written in the style of "ethnographic present", thereby giving an impression of contemporality that is essentially false. Ethnographic present is really about the past, as Mary Louise Pratt wrote: "...trying to describe the culture as it was before Western intervention" (Pratt 1986, 42). Her extended critique of this paradigm is related to the ways anthropology has overlooked the historicity of people "without a history", in this case the Kalahari Bushmen (Pratt 1986, 42-50). But even aside from that, it is problematical enough to describe the present as it occurs, or, as Sally Falk Moore stated: "in the thick of fieldwork how is the anthropologist to distinguish the transitory from the durable, cultural change from cultural persistence?" (Moore 1987, 728). As a result of a heightened awareness of the

historical and processual, anthropologists are now "acutely conscious
of observing part of the cultural construction of part of a society at
a particular time", where they used to believe that they were studying
whole societies (735). George E. Marcus and Michael M.J. Fischer
pointed out another aspect of the problem:

In a sense, ethnographies that really report present conditions are future
historical documents, or primary sources, in the making. The challenge, then,
is not to do away with the synchronic ethnographic frame, but to exploit
fully the historical within it (Marcus & Fischer 1986, 96).

Historians of all sorts are increasingly becoming interested in anthropological approaches and anthropologists are turning to history, not
only of the remote places where anthropologists have roamed but also
of the Western past.
    One prominent figure actively participating in this shift in
anthropological research is Marshall Sahlins who summed up the con-
vergence of approaches in the following manner:

Practice clearly has gone beyond the theoretical differences that are
supposed to divide anthropology and history. Anthropologists rise from the
abstract structure to the explication of the concrete event. Historians devalue
the unique event in favour of underlying recurrent structures. And also
paradoxically, anthropologists are as often diachronic in outlook as historians
nowadays are synchronic (Sahlins 1983, 534).

Historians of religions have, as noted, been more interested in tracing
ideas and practices than in the unique event, but the orientation
towards contemporary issues and more synchronic system-oriented
analysis is now on the rise.

## Evolution: A Chain That Breaks

Originally, the concept of evolution was conceived as a framework
that could make sense of an atemporal diversity of human affairs:
social, cultural, religious, and other differences could now be located
and explained. Since its demise, the concept of evolution has been
much despised in most human sciences, though it is obvious that
much has changed in man's total history and that these changes
should be accounted for. This may not bother us much here, but one
point should be noted, viz., that no matter how earlier theories of
evolution were put forward, they were structured by "stages", in other

words, analytic constructs fabricated in order to render the flow of time intelligible. A famous (and much debated) concept like the "Neolithic revolution" fully discloses the problem: how can a change in subsistence forms that lasted thousands of years be thought of as a revolution with all the drastic connotations this word carries? For historians of religions and anthropologists alike, there is, furthermore, the deeply distressing question of how such changes in subsistence are related to changes in social organization, culture, worldview, and religion in general. Much of what even today characterizes research in certain fields is in fact "survivals" or "gesunkenes Gedankengut" derived from past generations of scholars with mechanistic conceptions of the relations between, e.g., subsistence forms and religious ideology. An example of how this works in practice may be found in research on ancient Greek religion, where such ideas have been consistently tied to theories of cultural diffusion in attempts to explain the peculiar character of Greek religion as scholars saw it. What the ancient Greeks themselves may have thought of their religion was less of a problem, and it has only recently surfaced in France among structuralist anthropologically minded classicists. What we have here is an example of research that strove to explain changes that were irrelevant to the religious community in question. We are not arguing that this kind of research should be completely abolished or shunned, but that its value has to be reconsidered. The paradigm is well known in the earlier phases of the history of religions that operated with a view of culture and religion as assembled from an array of discrete elements brought together more or less haphazardly but with constant meanings. When such elements were then thought to represent stages in evolution, everything could be explained, but the sense made is today seen as instances of scholarly myth-making and learned obfuscation.

## Form, Function, Structure, and Meaning

What is needed when investigating issues of tradition and renewal is an amplification of methodological awareness. And here the primary issue is whether the criteria and concepts used are internal to the tradition's own self-understanding or to the scholar's conceptual universe. The differences are often forgotten.

Change also makes a difference. No change would be noticeable if there was not a basis for comparison in some way. This means that the investigation of change and continuity is essentially the same as the investigation of any other kind of comparable difference when it comes to the more fundamental questions of epistemology. In the following, we shall briefly outline some of our own deliberations in this respect.

Whether an object of research is considered similar or dissimilar to any other object usually depends on a first quick glance at appearances, in other words, perceptions based on the scholar's intuition of what constitutes likeness. This is where the trouble begins, since the business of scholarship is then to explain appearances by referring to more than just similarities in form. However, simple likeness is what has made it possible for us to delineate the field of religion in general. All religions "look alike" in as much as they have rituals, gods, incantations, myths, etc., but from our studies we know that they are not the same. So the criterion of form is not a sufficient classificatory device, even though some religions or traditions may be demonstrated to include various combinations of form-based categories, such as polytheism or monotheism.

A different range of criteria are introduced by the concept of the function(s) of religions and traditions. It is evident that a break in or re-formulation of tradition may involve, e.g., a change in pantheon, but, however drastic such a change may be, the tradition in question may be said to fulfill the same sociological or intellectual functions as before. One can also find examples of functional changes where the form remains the same.

A third way to view changes in religious traditions is to consider the fundamental structure(s) of the relations between this and the other world, between humans and god(s). The following example should illustrate what is meant here. A change of tradition that involves the three criteria mentioned is the Lutheran Reformation which, on the formal level, rejected papal authority and introduced the indigenization of the scriptures; on the functional level, provided a different social status (though some remained the same) for the institutions of the church in the societies concerned; and, on the structural level, reordered the relations between, e.g., the individual and God in reference to the question of salvation.

Ultimately and perhaps most importantly, there are changes in meaning and interpretation. To give an example, we may think of various interpretations of the ideas of apocalypse in the eastern Mediterranean in the beginning of the Christian era (Kippenberg 1983). The ideas among the different religious communities were in some ways similar seen at the level of motives (i.e., form), but, when given different interpretations in varying contexts, they also assumed different functions by giving legitimation to various kinds of action in the mundane world. Yet, at the same time, they have the structural characteristic in common that they devalorize the mundane. The example illustrates just how complex a situation we may face when engaged in an explication of all the factors involved in change. One may be able to find examples where change is only brought about by a new interpretation of the same form, function, or structure, but it is hardly imaginable, because a change in one of these four registers is more likely to produce change in some or all of the others. Even more, it has to be remembered that these four registers of investigation are not fixed entities, but are flexible analytical contructs.

One may have objections to this seemingly rigid splitting into categories, but just as evolution was only thinkable in stages, so analysis of religions and other human activities is only possible through a range of concepts by which we can divide, split, and dismember the continuous so as to make it amenable to investigation and interpretation and thereby make it meaningful for us to talk about tradition and change at all in the scholarly study of religion which itself continually changes in the form, function, structure, and meaning assigned to it by its participants and the world surrounding it.

## Concerning the Essays in this Book

The essays in this book illustrate the complexities outlined here. Two of the papers are of a more general theoretical nature, and the rest deal with problems in specific areas of the world.

Historian of religions Michael Pye makes it clear in his paper that the very term "tradition" means, literally, the act of giving across or handing on, and he would reserve the use of the term in scientific discourse as covering the process and not the substance of being moved along. Furthermore, he sees the identification of the meaning of a tradition as a creative, interpretive act on the part of the exponent, and he suggests that the study of this process requires a great deal of sensitivity on the part of the observer. Focussing on the carrier of the tradition brings the student of religion directly into the realm of meaning and the production of meaning which not only makes his/her analysis relevant to us, but also to them, and, therefore, a theory of the dynamics of religious traditions must take account of both processes of reflection.

Anthropologist Yme B. Kuiper examines the significance and impact of Clifford Geertz' ideas on the history of anthropology. He analyzes Geertz' research programme for the anthropological study of cultures and argues that it is partly a continuation and partly a renewal of certain anthropological and sociological traditions. On the one hand, Geertz combines the culture and personality school of American thought with a further development of Parsons' action theory. His renewal of the study of cultures is particularly visible in his pragmatic approach to symbols, his study of public ritual as the reading of a text, and his integration of theoretical and methodological analysis with empirical study.

Historian of religions Lourens van den Bosch traces the migration history of the Surinamese Hindus and the transformation of Hindu ideas and practices first in Suriname and then in the Netherlands. In Suriname, the Hindus needed to define themselves to themselves in the new context. Old relations were reformulated against the background of traditional ideology. This process of reformulation was repeated in the Netherlands. It was especially due to the corrosion of the caste system that the migrants were forced to reflect on their identity. Thus, for instance, the rule of endogamy moved from caste to ethnic criteria. Another change was interest in new Hindu missionary groups which explicitly formulated the essentials of ideology. The situation in Holland remains, however, to be resolved.

In his analysis of suttee in Bengal in the early 19th century, anthropologist Poul Pedersen demonstrates how the frequency of this seemingly "traditional" practice was in fact a "modern" expression of status mobility which certain castes enjoyed due to regionally and internationally expanding trade. Thus, in paying attention to the strategic interests of individuals and groups "who are engaged in traditional behaviour", tradition is seen to be the contemporary dynamics of invention and reinvention.

Anthropologist Steven Vertovec takes his departure in Hobsbawm's definition of the "invention" of traditions as a process of formalization and ritualization which implies continuity with the past through repetition. Vertovec suggests that this activity is more likely to occur among religious minorities undergoing rapid social change. Describing the role of a recently created repertoire of religious practices known as *yagnas* in the Hindu renaissance among Hindus in Trinidad, the author illustrates the process of the invention of traditions. This process, it is pointed out, is only one of several alternatives open to religious people.

Historian of religions Pieter Goedendorp looks at the theoretical problems concerning the long accepted theory that the title *al-Qâ'im al-Mahdî* used by early Shiite groups has been transferred from a pre-Islamic environment. Diffusionist explanations can tell us much, but they neither pay attention to the literary denotations nor the institutionalization of the concepts. The approaches of the early philosophers suggest continuity with late antiquity, but *assume* primary meanings to terms that are characterized by many connotations. Turning to the symbol theories of Clifford Geertz and Sherry Ortner, the author argues that attention should be paid to the way in which secondary meanings are institutionalized by means of performances and scenarios.

Theologian Niels Peter Lemche provides an alternative interpretation of the history of Israelite religion than the one commonly promoted by more traditional research. Traditional research has generally restricted itself to the Old Testament as the sole source of information about the Israelite religion. In supposing that the Old Testament account is the result of human invention, the author presents a new reconstruction of the religious history of Israel. He concludes that the Israelite religion before the Babylonian exile in the 6th century B.C. was a polytheistic fertility religion almost identical to neighbouring religions. Similarly, the transition to a monotheistic religion between 800-500 B.C. did not occur in Israel alone. The Yahweh religion was given greater emphasis through a combination of a religious reform movement, the later Deuteronomistic school of thought, and the Babylonian exile.

The problem of the status of tradition in a culture ideologically opposed to the idea of change but which in fact is changing all the time is the subject of historian of religions Monica Engelhart's paper. By studying the incorporation of Western ideas and items in the Djuluru cult of Fitzroy Crossing, Australia, the author questions the applicability of such analytical categories as "syncretism" and "new cults". Her point is that the main characteristic of these cults is that they provide a cultural strategy for translating contact situations into the framework of indigenous religious institutions.

Viewing the dynamics of change from the point of view of cognitive dissonance, in which new cults or reformulations of traditions are necessary in the face of drastic changes, historian of religions Jan G. Platvoet suggests that the post-1874 Anokye traditions, which creatively reformulated earlier traditions, helped the Asante to withstand the dissonance of subservience to the Indirect Rule of the British Crown. In other words, "the Anokye traditions are a post-1874 retrospective 'renewal' of Asante religions.... By protologizing Asante identity at a time when it was severely shaken, they considerably strengthened it".

Historian of religions Hans Witte describes the possible conditions for renewal in the West African concept of person. In his opinion, renewal means change on the basis of continuity, and this can only occur if the idea of the community remains attached to that of the lineage in West African thought.

Anthropologist Durk Hak explains in his essay the explosive rise of new denominations at the Dutch fishing village of Urk since the 1930's. The author introduces a demographic explanation which views religion in Urk as a way of taking issue and a way of establishing prominence and distinction. Furthermore, the recurrent religious fissions are explained by means of Fokke Sierksma's neurosis theory. Hak is of the opinion that religion is the steering mechanism of culture but also that economic modernization has a determining influence on the religious sphere.

Sociologist of religion Margit Warburg asks whether the introduction of a religion into a new area is parallel to the founding of a religion, in other words, whether the relationship between a missionary and his/her converts is parallel to that of the founder and his/her disciples. After tracing the history of the Bahá'í movement in Denmark, the author concludes that the parallel does exist, albeit from a sociological point of view, since the adherents of the religion consider the two situations to be fundamentally different.

## Notes

1. Quoted from *The Pakistan Times Overseas Weekly,* September 27, 1987.

## Bibliography

Alles, Gregory D. & J.M. Kitagawa, 1985: "Afterword, The Dialectic of the Parts and the Whole: Reflections on the Past, Present, and Future of the History of Religions", in: J.M. Kitagawa, ed., *The History of Religions, Retrospect and Prospect,* New York.

Barth, Fredrik, 1983: *Sohar, Culture and Society in an Omani Town,* Baltimore.

Bentley, G. Carter, 1987: "Ethnicity and Practice", *Comparative Studies in Society and History* 29 (1), 1987, 24-55.

Eisenstadt, S.N., 1984: "The Kemalist Regime and Modernization: Some Comparative and Analytical Remarks", in: J.M. Landau, ed., *Atatürk and the Modernization of Turkey,* Boulder, 3-15.

Fienup-Riordan, Ann, 1988: "Robert Redford, Apanuugpak, and the Invention of Tradition", *American Ethnologist* 15 (3), 1988, 442-455.

Giddens, Anthony, 1979: *Central problems in Social Theory. Action, Structure and Contradiction in Social Analysis.* Berkeley.

Green, Jerrold D., 1985: "Islam, Religiopolitics, and Social Change, A Review Article", *Comparative Studies in Society and History* 27, 1985, 312-322.

Haddad, Yvonne Y., 1986: "Muslim Revivalist Thought in the Arab World, An Overview", *The Muslim World* 76 (3-4), 143-167.

Hobsbawm, Eric & T. Ranger, 1983: *The Invention of Tradition,* Cambridge.

Kippenberg, H.G., 1983: "Diskursive Religionswissenschaft", in: B. Gladigow & H.G. Kippenberg, eds, *Neue Ansätze in der Religionswissenschaft,* Munich.

Laitin, David D., 1986: *Hegemony and Culture, Politics and Religious Change among the Yoruba,* Chicago.

Lincoln, Bruce, 1985: "Introduction", in: idem, ed., *Religion, Rebellion, Revolution,* New York.

Long, Charles, 1986: *Significations: Signs, Symbols and Images in the Interpretation of Religion,* Philadelphia.

Marcus, George E. & Michael M. J. Fischer, 1986: *Anthropology as Cultural Critique. An Experimental Moment in the Human Sciences,* Chicago.

Moore, Sally Falk, 1987: "Explaining the Present: Theoretical Dilemmas in Processual Ethnography", *American Ethnologist* 14 (4), 1987, 727-736.

Pratt, Mary Louise, 1986: "Fieldwork in Common Places", in: James Clifford & G.E. Marcus, eds., *Writing Culture. The Poetics and Politics of Ethnography,* Berkeley, 27-50.

Sahlins, Marshall, 1983: "Other Times, Other Customs: The Anthropology of History", *American Anthropologist* 85 (3), 1983, 517-544.

Seiwert, Hubert, 1976: "Religiöser Wandel: Alternativen religions-wissenschaftlicher Fragestellungen und Erklärungsmodelle", in: G. Stephenson, ed., *Der Religionswandel unserer Zeit im Spiegel der Religionswissenschaft,* Darmstadt, 309-322.

Shils, Edward, 1981: *Tradition,* London.

Stephenson, Gunther, ed., 1976: *Der Religionswandel unserer Zeit im Spiegel der Religionswissenschaft,* Darmstadt.

Tapper, Nancy & Richard Tapper, 1987: "Thank God We're Secular!" Aspects of Fundamentalism in a Turkish Town", in: Lionel Caplan, ed., *Studies in Religious Fundamentalism,* London.

Waardenburg, Jacques, 1987: "The Study of Religion in Today's World", in: F. Whaling, ed., *Religion in Today's World. The Religious Situation of the World from 1945 to the Present Day,* Edinburgh, 335-364.

Wagner, Roy, 1981: *The Invention of Culture,* Chicago.

Whaling, Frank, ed., 1987: *Religion in Today's World. The Religious Situation of the World from 1945 to the Present Day,* Edinburgh.

# Religious Tradition and the Student of Religion

## By Michael Pye

It is a remarkable fact that the nature of tradition, which in one way or another is crucial for the understanding of so many religious situations, has not been the subject of sustained analysis on the part of specialists in the study of religion. The word itself is frequently used, but all too often it is allowed to suggest something static, left over from the past and subject to the strains and stresses of a present which is thought to be different and new. At the same time aspects of religion which are evidently dynamic are considered under other headings such as interaction, renewal, or change. It is salutary, however, to recall the underlying meaning of the word "tradition", namely, "giving across", deriving ultimately from latin *trans* and *dare*. This is clearly brought out in the German equivalent *Überlieferung*, which literally means "handing over". Admittedly, the term *Überlieferung* is also sometimes used unthinkingly, just as "tradition"is used in English, to refer to a cultural entity which has been handed down from the past but which in itself remains static and unchanged. The form of the word *Überlieferung*, however, does suggest the activity or process of handing on. It is desirable not to lose sight of this aspect when using the English term "tradition". Thus while people sometimes speak of "a tradition", by which they mean a more or less precisely fixed cultural element, the more interesting usage in the study of religion is "tradition" understood as the act of handing on, which implies process and movement. In fact, the specific cultural elements sometimes referred to as traditions can also be designated in other ways, e.g., as a ritual or a belief complex. Thus the word "tradition" is hardly required to specify such elements in themselves. For theoretical purposes, therefore, it is better to reserve the word tradition as far as possible for a whole stream of such elements regarded from the point of view of the process of handing on or transmission, with all the attendant features which this implies.

The movement spoken of here is movement from a time which

the participants or actors in the process of tradition regard as the past (though for the observer it is only a past) into a time which for the participants or actors is a present bearing a presumed future (not yet available for the observer among the socio-cultural data at his disposal). Thus the participants or actors bear an existential responsibility which the observer does not directly share but which, if he seeks understanding, he dare not ignore.

While what has been said so far may be considered valid for tradition in general, we are concerned here, above all, with religious tradition. Religious tradition cannot be treated in isolation from the wider field of tradition in all its forms. Thus, a theory of religious tradition must be held wide open to the stimuli of various disciplines, especially, but not only, social anthropology. As a special case in the wider field, however, religious tradition displays some characteristics which cannot easily be reduced to or assimilated under a general theory of tradition. This is because the truth claims or value claims raised by at least some religious traditions pose, or at least imply, questions of meaning, sometimes critically, for the cultures in which they are carried forward. In this respect, the appraisal which the observer might independently make of such truth or value claims is (for the discipline of religious studies) not of any great significance. The existential questions to which such claims are ultimately addressed, even if only implicitly, persist within the human situation regardless whether any particular religion is deemed by the observer to be true or false, valuable or worthless. Moreover the articulate bearers of religious tradition, whether they are shamans, bishops, or Buddhist monks, are conscious of this existential and sometimes critical dimension to a greater or lesser extent.

In view of the above, it is not surprising that an interest in tradition as an aspect of culture and especially of religion has arisen both among social anthropologists on the one hand and among the exponents of various traditions, that is, theologians and their equivalents in non-theistic religions, on the other hand. Social anthropologists are in principle not concerned with truth claims (unless it be in their spare time), whereas the theologians and other exponents of tradition are actively concerned with them, even if only implicitly, for their very task lies in the projection of meaning. The latter aspect further attracts its own type of scholarly literature which may have little to do with anthropology. This point may be illustrated by juxtaposing two well-known works, which deal in their different ways with the destiny of major religious traditions, Islam and Buddhism, in far-flung cultural contexts, namely: Clifford Geertz' *Religion in Java*

(1960) and Alicia Matsunaga's *The Buddhist Philosophy of Assimilation* (1969). These two works are rather dissimilar in their approach while both are widely recognised to be excellent. The former is explicitly anthropological, and seeks to understand the relations between complementary aspects of a sociocultural system of which Islam forms a part. The latter assumes a more or less Buddhist standpoint while reflecting on the relations between Buddhist teaching and other religious beliefs in India, China, and Japan. The analysis is aided by concepts which are themselves Buddhist-derived.

An integrative theory of religious tradition is, therefore, required which is able to mediate between these different tendencies, and such a theory must be considered the responsibility of those who specialise in the historical and comparative study of religion. Why is this? How does such an intermediary role arise? On the one hand, the specialist in religious studies, like an anthropologist, aligns himself with the experience and the self-understanding of the people whose religious tradition is under study. His goal is the understanding of the tradition in question, an understanding which, in the first instance at least, should be phenomenological or, to use another terminology, emic. On the other hand, precisely because it is a religious tradition and not, for example, a question of pottery technology, this very activity leads him into that area of interpretation which under ordinary circumstances is the responsibility of the articulate exponent of the tradition.

It may be noted in passing that there is not any particular requirement for the student of religion, at least, to limit attention to non-literate or small-scale societies. Indeed, interesting questions arise precisely in the shift to literacy (which can ultimately lead to nostalgia for a non-literate time) and in the interaction between small-scale societies and relatively differentiated ones. The shift to literacy can be considered over a very long period in the case of the Japanese religion Shinto which may be regarded as an "adjusted primal religion" (Pye 1984) with a high nostalgia quotient in modern times. A more short-term example is the conscious cultivation of Maoriness (Maoritanga) in recent New Zealand history, which means that Maori religion is accepting distance from a perceived past in the interests of self-conservation (c.f., Schlang 1988). The constant shift into complexity is important for the student of religion, for, within this shift, tradition is never static but always in some respects dynamic.

At any one time a religious tradition is never quite what it was before, or never bears quite the same meaning which it bore before, even if the changes which it undergoes or the development of its meaning are in a strong sense consistent with its past and possibly

profoundly loyal to it. Thus the exponents of religious tradition bear
a responsibility which is in part creative. This too must be understood
by the observer, not just abstractly, but in terms of the specific case,
and this means that to achieve the understanding mentioned above, he
has to move so closely to the heart-beat of the tradition under study
that he is aware of how its meaning is put into question in the given
situation. By this is not meant, necessarily, an intellectual questioning.
There may be such, but on the whole, admittedly, religious tradition
under observation more frequently appears to go unquestioned. Nevertheless, that the meaning is put into question is something which is
sensed by the responsible exponents who are aware of the danger of
non-tradition and the consequent loss of social and existential meaning. The very force of tradition is an indication of its fragility. Con-
versely, the fragility demands creative responsibility. If the very identification of the meaning of tradition in a particular situation demands
a creative act on the part of the exponent, this, in turn, has to be
followed through imaginatively by the observer. If this is not understood, the observer will always turn aside at the very point where the
reception of the past becomes intense for the participant, that is to
say, wherever the meaning is subject to or threatened by change and
thus takes on critical significance. If the observer is fully sensitive to
the fragility of the situation and hence to the perceived need for the
process of tradition to be carried through, he will realise that at one
and the same time both the future and the past are at stake.

This principle may be summed up in what is probably the short-
est sentence in the extensive works of Ernst Troeltsch, namely
"Wesensbestimmung ist Wesensgestaltung" (Troeltsch, 1922, 421; cf.,
Morgan & Pye 1977, 162), the import of which may be paraphrased
as: to define the tradition is to reshape it. The thrust of Troeltsch's
argument at that point was to stress the inevitablility of interpretative
change with a view to the present situation and presumed demands of
the future. But the presupposition of such an interpretation is itself a
view of the nature (or in his terms, essence, "Wesen") of the perceived tradition, of which, however, alternative views are possible.
Thus, in the act of tradition, to put it provocatively, the past is subject
to change. Notice that this point is not quite the same as the idea that
traditions may be invented, semi-consciously, in retrospect, to fulfil a
perceived need, which is worked out most interestingly in recent essays entitled *The Invention of Tradition* (Hobsbawm & Ranger 1983).

A polarity between anthropologists, on the one hand, and theologians, or those who look over the shoulders of theologians, on the
other hand, was noted by Robert Redfield in his well-known lectures

published as *Peasant Society and Culture*. Writing of the adjustments made between Islamic tradition and local tradition, he comments, "Here the Islamist comes to meet the anthropologist. Professor von Grunebaum, discussing the interaction between local saint and Islamic orthodoxy, sees from the top, so to speak, the same interaction that Westermarck, studying local saints in Morocco, saw from the bottom" (Redfield 1956, 85, cf., von Grunebaum 1955 and Westermarck 1926). However, in the light of what has already been said, this polarisation would seem to be not quite adequate. Redfield was concerned, as an anthropologist, with the relations between the cultural elements of a small-scale community, or peasant culture, and an incursive tradition with wider and socially different foundations. Hence arose his frequently cited and, indeed, illuminating distinction between "the great tradition" and "the little tradition", which is set out preeminently in a chapter bearing the significant title "The social organisation of tradition" (Redfield 1956, 67-104). The social basis of this distinction is that a little tradition is carried unreflectively by a peasant or village society whereas a great tradition is cultivated by a class of professional exponents. It is important to note here that the two kinds of tradition fall within identifiable socio-cultural parameters, which are presumed to be distinct. It is by assuming these two distinct areas that reference could be made, painlessly, to the Islamist, on the one hand, (who deals with the great tradition) and the anthropologist, on the other hand (who deals with the little tradition).

While Redfield saw that the two should somehow be brought together, he tried to do so by defining each of the two sides more decisively. But is this the right approach? If an Islamist and an anthropologist in fact come together in the field at a point where the great and the little tradition meet, there is a third party in the conversation, who does not appear prominently in Redfield's account, except as a social object. This is none other than the carrier of tradition himself, whose task it is to cope with the interaction of diverse cultural elements in a situation where the meaning for the time is still to be established. The carrier of tradition is responsible both to the past and to the future, and, as was argued above, the identity of tradition is therefore always at risk. To appreciate this critical openness at any one time, it is necessary to be something more than, or at least slightly other than, either an anthropologist or a philologically oriented cultural historian (i.e., in this case, an Islamist), at least in a restrictive sense of these terms. The student of religion has to be, under these circumstances, a kind of tradition carrier by proxy. To put it more provocatively, he is required to be, by imagination, or by almost participant observation, a theologian with interchangeable gods.

The delicate responsibility of the carriers of any tradition, which is to be entered into imaginatively by the student of religion (the *Religionswissenschaftler*), leads on to the requirement of a special complexity in the overall theory of religious tradition, a complexity which is not always evident in limited case-studies, excellent and useful though they may be in themselves. A theory of tradition must include both an understanding of the dynamics of religious change as an observable socio-cultural process, which has taken place up to the present of the observer, and a hermeneutical openness in which the participant's responsibility for the handing on into the future is adequately reflected. On this basis some misunderstandings can be removed. As was said at the outset, "tradition" does not refer to what is old or left over from before. Hence it is not quite appropriate to speak of "tradition and renewal" as if these were opposites, for the act of tradition, in the sense of handing on, itself implies a renewal. A renewal is a recapitulation of what was, in a world which is no longer what it was. Similarly, it is not quite appropriate to speak of "tradition and interpretation" as if these were opposites, for there is no handing on without interpretation. The only way to avoid interpretation is to forget. Admittedly, forgetting has a healing power of its own, but it does not set tradition in motion. Tradition is always in motion.

Although it is quite beyond the range of this short statement to set out a detailed or fully systematic theory of religious tradition, a few words may be added on one more crucial feature, namely, the relation, sometimes tension-laden, between the unreflective and self-conscious forms of tradition. This feature is particularly important because the existence of both unreflective and self-conscious religious traditions demands a widely extended theoretical perspective, which is by no means easily achieved, especially if the main argument above is not to be allowed to lose its force.

Unreflective tradition, that is, tradition which takes place without the participants engaging in reflection on the process in which they are engaged, may be oral only, but may equally have a strong written component. This is not to deny that, as Vansina wrote, "Oral traditions are historical sources of a special nature" (Vansina 1965,1), but it does imply the need to look for the decisive features of an overall theory of religious tradition in a slightly different framework than that addressed in his important work *Oral Tradition*, which, as the subtitle says, is "A Study in Historical Methodology".

In so far as the student of religion reflects upon unreflective tradition, he will seek to develop a coherent image of the dynamics of religion, that is, of religion in terms of its movement. Thus, he will seek to understand the shifting correlations (syncretism, synthesis, assimilation, etc.) between religious and other cultural elements of diverse origin and to understand innovation, growth, decline, and disappearance. All of these are themes which have been treated with such a diversity of approach, and above all in the context of so many different cultural areas, that the provision of bibliographical details on a small scale here would be quite misleading. It is clear, however, that the distinction between oral and written tradition is a subordinate question in this perspective.

What is important for a theory of religious tradition is that all of the aspects of the dynamics of religion, which are frequently played out without selfconscious reflection, are marked with uncertainty. Thus, it is not surprising that the participants in the process of tradition themselves begin to indicate the landmarks of coherence. Above all, they create the symbols of·authority, such as creeds; but they also permit deviation and ambiguity in varying degree. A ritual may be abbreviated without loss, for a while. When uncertainty' sets in, continuity is called for, then reformulation, then innovation. Many a prophet is the final prophet. But the last prophet is continually set in context in accordance with later needs. Since the participants themselves notice this, and even debate it, the unreflective form of religious tradition is always giving way to the self-conscious form.

The observer is true to the participants and moves with them. He does not proudly restrict himself to a meta-language, invented by his profession, as if the world were inhabited by a combination of savages and scientists. He is aware that reflection on the process of tradition emerges both haltingly and controversially within religion itself. He is stimulated by the notions pertaining to consensus (only made necessary by the threat of divergent tradition, which could mean loss of tradition) developed in Judaism and Islam. He notes the rationalised adaptive tactics in the Buddhist books of discipline. He follows through the emergent theories about the status of previous prohpets, and even of other revelations. Thus, upon a theory of the dynamics of religions, there has to be built a coordinated view of the self-conscious reflection on those same processes as developed by the participants themselves.

It is to be expected that there should be some relationship between these two levels. While pursuing these considerations together with the participants in religious tradition, the student of religion must refrain (in accordance with his discipline, though not necessarily in his spare time) from identifying himself finally with the normative requirements of the participants. Only in this way can he remain free to achieve that one further level of abstraction and coordination which will eventually be required to work out a comprehensive theory of religious tradition.

## Bibliography

Geertz, Clifford, 1960: *The Religion of Java*, Chicago.

Grunebaum, G. von, 1965: *Unity and Diversity in Muslim Civilization*, Chicago.

Hobsbawm, E. & T. Ranger, 1983: *The Invention of Tradition*, Cambridge.

Matsunaga, Alicia, 1969: *The Buddhist Philosophy of Assimilation. The Historical Development of the Honji Suijaku Theory*, Tokyo

Morgan, R. & M. Pye, 1977: *Ernst Troeltsch: Writings on Theology and Religion*, London.

Pye, Michael, 1984: "The Place of Shinto in the Typology of Religion", in: Y. Yamamoto, ed., Proceedings of the Thirty-first International Congress of Human Sciences in Asia and North Africa, Tokyo, 1055-6.

Redfield, Robert, 1956: *Peasant Society and Culture. An Anthropological Approach to Civilisation*, Chicago.

Schlang, Stefan, 1988: Religiöse Aspekte von Maoritanga, (Diss.) Marburg.

Troeltsch, Ernst, 1922: *Gesammelte Schriften II*, Tübingen (reprinted Darmstadt 1962).

Vansina, J., 1965: *Oral Tradition. A Study in Historical Methodology*, London. (English translation of *De La Tradition Orale, Essai De Méthode Historique*, 1961).

Westermarck, Edward, 1926: *Ritual and Belief in Morocco*, London.

# Person, Culture, and Religion: Clifford Geertz' Revitalization of Traditional Anthropology[1]

## By Yme B. Kuiper

About twenty years ago Clifford Geertz published his famous essay "Religion as a Cultural System" (Geertz 1973b). Inspired by the German sociologist Max Weber, Geertz characterized the anthropological study of religion as a two-stage operation: in the first place, an analysis of the system of meanings embodied in the symbols which make up religion, and, in the second place, the relating of these systems to social-structural and psychological processes. According to "meanings-and-symbols anthropologists" like Geertz, the importance of religion consists in its capacity to serve as a source - for the individual as well as for the group - of general, yet distinctive conceptions of the world, the self, and the relations between them. Religion provides its believers with a world view. At the same time, Geertz argues, this model of reality indicates how people have to behave in certain situations. Geertz calls this programme for action an ethos. The term "ethos" also refers to the tone, character, and quality of people's lives.[2]

Geertz ended his essay, however, in a rather skeptical tone: "My dissatisfaction with so much of anthropological work in religion is not that it concerns itself with the second stage - social-structural and psychological analysis of religion - but that it neglects the first"; in other words, the cultural analysis of significant symbols and meanings in various religions; an analysis that also avoids the pitfalls of a complete reduction of culture (or religion) to social structure, political ideology, economic systems, and the like. According to Geertz, anthropology (and especially the anthropology of religion) needs models for analyzing symbolic action.

Today, twenty years later, Geertz' reflections seem to have been prophetic. In my view, his plea for a symbolic, interpretive approach in the anthropology of religion has turned out to be self-fulfilling (Ortner 1984; Boon 1982). There are few students of present-day anthropology who are not acquainted with Geertz' seminal essay. No

doubt most specialists in the anthropology of religion are likely to
have read also some of Geertz' monographs and articles on religious
phenomena in Morocco and Indonesia (see among others, Geertz
1960; 1968; 1973d-g; 1979; 1980; 1983a). Over the past few years,
Geertz seems to have become a kind of ambassador for cultural
anthropology: his works are being discussed by many non-anthropolo-
gists as well. Among his public, one can find historians - including
historians of religion - sociologists of religion, sociologists, psycho-
logists, philosophers, linguists, and theologians (Morgan 1977; Walters
1980; Hofstee 1986; Moore & Reynolds 1986, ch. 1-3). Sometimes
his works are received with approval, sometimes with severe criticism
or mixed feeling - but they are at least being read and discussed.

In this article I will analyse Geertz' programme for the anthropological study of cultures. I will argue that this programme is
partly a continuation and partly a renewal of some well-known anthropological and sociological traditions. In order to characterise the
relationship between these respective traditions and the Geertzian
research programme more adequately, I will give a brief summary of
Geertz' studies of a seemingly universal systems of symbols, viz., the
concept of person. I will, furthermore, discuss some of the fundamental criticism Geertz' approach has stimulated.

## An Anthropological Universal? The Concept of Person

According to Geertz, the task of a cultural anthropologist is to map
out systems of symbols. A difficult problem arises when doing this:
how do we select the most important systems of symbols of a given
society? This task is somewhat simplified by the fact that some
systems are universal systems that embody a means of orientation that
is indispensable to human beings, or, as Geertz nicely puts it: "the
problems, being existential, are universal; their solutions, being human,
are diverse" (1973h, 363).

One of these means of orientation is the "concept of person": the
cultural characterisation of individual human beings (or the cultural
part of the self). Every society has the disposal of systems of symbols
in terms of which persons are conceived as representatives of certain
distinct categories of the person, specific sorts of individuals.[3]

Geertz makes a sharp distinction between the individual and the
person. An individual is a living, biological being that is born, grows
to maturity, grows old, and dies. The person is a vehicle of meaning,
a representation of a kind of individual. In one of his essays, Geertz

sketches a plurality of symbol systems which can define concrete classes of determinate persons:

And the symbol systems which define these classes are not given in the nature of things; they are historically constructed, socially maintained, and individually applied... Some, for example, kinship terminologies, are ego-centered; that is, they define the status of an individual in terms of his relationship to a specific, social actor. Others are centered on one or another subsystem or aspect of society and are invariant with respect to the perspectives of individual actors: noble ranks, age-group statuses, occupational categories. Some - personal names and sobriquets - are informal and particularizing; others - bureaucratic titles and caste designations - are informal and standardizing (Geertz 1973h, 363-364).

Even though the starting point of Geertz' view on "the concept of person" is a very general one, he is, above all else, interested in a) the intracultural concept of person in a specific society, and b) differences between actual conceptions of the person in various societies. In the range of the world's cultures, the Western concept of person is a rather peculiar idea. The Western person is "a bounded, unique, more or less integrated motivational and cognitive universe". A Western person is a dynamic centre of awareness, emotion, judgment, and action. It would be a categorical mistake to place the experience of person of other cultures within this Western framework. Understanding other people demands setting aside this Western conception and interpreting their experiences within the framework of their own idea of what selfhood is.[4] Besides, Geertz' own analyses demonstrate that the Javanese, Balinese and Moroccan concepts of person differ markedly, not only from a Western conception but, not less clearly, from one another.

Characteristic of the Javanese concept of person is the sharp separation between inward feelings and outward actions. These two sets of phenomena are not regarded as functions of one another but as independent realms of being. In both realms, a Javanese individual tries to be, or to act, or to think "pure", "refined", "polished", "subtle", and "civilised" - to use our terms. In the inner world, this is to be achieved through religious, mostly mystical, discipline. In the outer world, it is to be achieved through etiquette, even if its rules are not extremely elaborate. The result is, then, an inner world of stilled emotion and an outer world of shaped behaviour. To illustrate this, Geertz tells the touching story of a young informant whose wife had died suddenly. The reaction of the informant was to approach his neighbours with a smile on his face and laboriously apologize for the absence of his wife.

The Balinese concept of person is quite different. What philosophy is in Java, theatre is in Bali. Balinese society and culture, Geertz argues, are an enactment of hierarchy, a theatre of status. The Balinese see their life as a play. Not the actors, but the parts they play will last. This play is about status and hierarchy. The staging of hierarchy is a recurrent aspect of Balinese culture. In his book *Negara*, Geertz analyzes the Balinese theatre-state in the nineteenth century. In those days, mass-rituals (e.g., cremation of kings, princes, or lords, pilgrimages, temple dedications) did not serve to legitimize the Balinese state. It was exactly the other way round: the state existed to make mass-rituals possible. Ceremony was not form but substance, or, to quote a well-known passage from one of Geertz' articles: "Power served pomp, not pomp power" (Geertz 1973f, 335).

Present-day Balinese culture is, to a certain degree, still characterized by the principles of status and hierarchy. Given this situation, one specific emotion is very central to Balinese life. The Balinese term for this emotion is *lek*. Geertz points out that this term is often mistranslated by our term "shame". According to Geertz, "stage fright" would be a much better translation. The core of this emotion is the fear that, for want of skill or self-control or perhaps by accident, the illusion will not be maintained - the fear that the actor will show through his part. When this happens, a Balinese person feels naked. Consequently, the behaviour of the Balinese aims at preventing this.

Characteristic of the Moroccans, Geertz wrote, is their hyper-individualistic behaviour in public relationships. The so-called mosaic system of organization in Morocco has two important implications: a) the behaviour of individuals is constantly contextualized, and b) in public behaviour, participants are continuously searching for information about one another. This does not mean, however, that the specifically Moroccan concept of person will always change essentially in accordance with the context of behaviour. Central to the Moroccan idea of self is the confidence that one can rather be pragmatic, adaptive, and opportunistic in one's relations with others, or, as Geertz puts it, "a fox among foxes, a crocodile among crocodiles". Interaction with others, then, is usually no threat to the person or the self.

## Geertz and the Tradition of American Anthropology

The foregoing sketch of Geertz' analyses of the Javanese, Balinese, and Moroccan concepts of person serves to illustrate the main thesis of this article: that Geertz' approach to the study of cultures is partly a result of and partly a deviation from a certain tradition within classical American anthropology. I am referring to the so-called "Culture and Personality" approach of anthropologists such as Ruth Benedict, Margaret Mead, Abraham Kardiner, Cora Dubois, Clyde Kluckhohn, and Ralph Linton. This approach was especially popular in the thirties and forties of this century (see de Waal Malefijt 1974). These American anthropologists gave the concept of culture a meaning that differed from earlier definitions. In 1934, Ruth Benedict wrote in her famous study *Patterns of Culture*: "...a culture, like an invidual, is a more or less consistent pattern of thought and action". The comparison she made between culture and individual, was certainly not accidental. Benedict, as well as some of her colleagues, assumed that the typical features of a culture as a whole are expressed by the personality of each individual representative of that culture. Within the "Culture and Personality" approach the idea of personality was conceived in different ways.

On the whole, three main variants of classical anthropological research on "personality" can be distinguished: 1) psychological and individualistic research on 'personality traits', 2) more interactionist research on interpersonal dispositions, and 3) research on the ways in which an individual's experience and behaviour are integrated, wherein the cultural context then serves explicitly as the framework of research (Bock 1980, chapter 3). Geertz' work represents the third variant; he criticized the first variant in several articles.

With their fieldwork data, collected among American Indians, in the Far East, and in Oceania, the "Culture and Personality" anthropologists attempted to trace the relationship between culture and personality within relatively simple societies. During the Second World War this programme was extended to encompass the more complex societies of Japan, Germany, and the Soviet Union, and research was focused on the concept of "national character".

Once again, these American anthropologists considered culture as an important factor in the development of personality, and they held individuals to be the ultimate locus of culture. Given these presuppositions and their affinity to psychoanalysis, one can understand the emphasis they placed on processes of socialization and enculturation.

I already stipulated that the work of Clifford Geertz can be understood in connection with the third variant of the "Culture and Personality" tradition. I would like to illustrate this assertion by referring to a study published by the couple Gregory Bateson and Margaret Mead, called *Balinese Character* (1942). It is remarkable that this elegant, rich study with hundreds of photographs, contains a large number of concepts and ideas which can be found as well in Geertz' kind of anthropology and in his ethnographic studies on Balinese culture, thought, and action. Just as Geertz would do later, Bateson and Mead focused their research on the ethos-aspect of Balinese culture, that is, they tried to describe the way the emotional life of the Balinese was organized in culturally standardized forms. As with Geertz, they were quite aware of the fact that in doing research an anthropologist needs his own concepts and abstractions, or, as Bateson and Mead put it in their introduction to *Balinese Character*:

This is not a book about Balinese custom, but about the Balinese - about the way in which they, as living persons, moving, standing, eating, sleeping, dancing, and going into trance, embody that abstraction which (after we have abstracted it) we technically call culture (Bateson & Mead 1942, xii).

Geertz' kind of anthropology was also profoundly influenced by two important guides of twentieth century sociology: Max Weber and Talcott Parsons. The latter introduced the work of Weber in the United States and became Geertz' teacher (Peacock 1981).

In his co-called "action-theory", Parsons approached culture as one of the three interdependent systems which regulate human behaviour, the other two being society and the individual. Parsons tried to develop a model that could integrate the perspectives of Durkheim, Weber, and Freud. Geertz, however, does not use Parsons' model altogether. What he adopts is Parsons' conception of culture within that model of systems (Geertz 1979: "I tried to develop it from where he had left it"). Geertz combines this notion of cultural system with Weber's insight that the behaviour of individuals always consists in "meaningful action". One may summarize Geertz' synthesis of Weber and Parsons as follows: a major task of the anthropologist is, in the first place, to understand behaviour in terms of the meanings that participants ascribe to it. As I already pointed out, the next step is to relate that behaviour to a configuration of the ideals, values, and attitudes it reflects.

## Geertz' Work as a Renewal of the Study of Cultures

Given the anthropological and sociological traditions I have sketched above, the question arises concerning what the innovating trait of the Geertzian view on culture might be. In what respects does his vast *oeuvre* provide a renewal of the study of cultures?

In the first place, I would like to draw attention to the fact that according to Geertz, culture has a rather objective and autonomous character. As culture is a complex consisting of systems of symbols, it should be conceived not in a mentalistic or psychological but rather in a pragmatic way. Symbols should be looked for not in the heads of people, but in their public and collective actions. To put it differently: meaning is a public fact. Geertz considers, e.g., the behaviour of people in visible, complex rituals as a kind of busy traffic of symbols. These symbols he then calls "vehicles of meanings". Geertz borrowed the metaphor of traffic and vehicles from Wittgenstein's and Ryle's "ordinary language philosophy" - a kind of philosophy he appreciates very much.[5]

Another analogy cherished by Geertz is the characterization of the anthropological analysis of, e.g., crucial religious rituals as the reading of a text containing various messages. In the cremation of a Balinese prince, he identifies the following messages: a certain consciousness of the divine, the invocation of a sacred atmosphere, societal prestige and the public imposition of a feeling of togetherness.

The most striking and valuable feature of Geertz' work, however, is the integration it shows of theoretical and methodological analysis, as well as empirical data (see Bakker 1988, 92-98). Geertz does not pretend to construct grand, all-encompassing theories. Nor does he deliberately collect exotic facts - "the stranger the better" - to destroy universal theories of sociologists and the like. He even detests the so-called "Bongo-Bongo attitude" of many of his colleagues: "what you assert may be true, but it does not apply to my tribe of the Bongo-Bongo". Geertz' kind of anthropology rather consists of specific research (e.g., on public, religious ritual) in a specific context (e.g., a village in Bali, a small town in Morocco) in order to gain an insight into a culture or a religion (the Balinese, Moroccan, etc.). It is therefore that many of Geertz' case-studies also offer a general understanding of culture or religion - to put it in Geertz' words: "All ethnography is part philosophy" (Geertz 1967).

According to Sherry B. Ortner, Geertz' cultural approach marks an important shift in the anthropology of the eighties to a new theoretical orientation which she has labelled "practice" (or "action") anthropology:

For the past several years, there has been growing interest in analysis focused through one or another of a bundle of interrelated terms: practice, praxis, action, interaction, activity, experience, performance. A second, and closely related, bundle of terms focuses on the doer of all that doing: agent, actor, *person*, *self*, individual, subject (my italics).

A crucial point is that "the study of practice is not an antagonistic alternative to the study of systems or structures (e.g., 'society' or 'culture'), but a necessary complement to it". Besides, Ortner remarks,

....this theoretical movement appears much broader than the field of anthropology alone; recent linguistics, sociology, history and literary studies have also been influenced by this new trend. In anthropology there is a growing body of literature which explores the variable construction of self, person, emotion, and motive in cross-cultural perspective (Ortner 1984, 127, 144-147 and 151).

## The 'Culturological' Temptation

I already mentioned Geertz' sympathy for a specific variant of British philosophy. Most British anthropologists, however calling themselves, *nomen est omen*, "social anthropologists" do not appreciate Geertz' work. In their opinion, Geertz is much too little of a sociologist. Moreover, they think that Geertz depicts the cultures he studied (Java, Bali, Morocco) in a much too homogeneous way, as if these were simple, "primitive" cultures. This criticism can be illustrated by quoting the comment Sir Edmund Leach has given on Geertz' ethnographic studies of Bali:

Geertz makes the categorical, but quite unverifiable assertion that 'all Balinese share the same general beliefs, the same broad ideas of how their society is or should be arranged'. Geertz is here writing about Balinese 'culture' as the counterpart of Balinese 'society'. This style of argument makes axiomatic that every 'society' ('social group') is culturally homogeneous. But from a sociological point of view this is totally misleading. Almost all empirical societies are socially stratified and each stratum in the system is marked by its own distinctive cultural attributes - linguistic usages, manners, styles of dress, food, housing etc. (Leach 1982, 43).

Sir Edmund does make a point, but what his criticism mainly refers to is a difference in theoretical point of view. With his various essays, Geertz has succeeded in starting debates not only on ethnograpic details but also on fundamental theoretical problems.

One of these problems has been discussed with respect to Geertz' approach to religion "as a cultural system". His work has been criticized for being too culturological and too a-historical; some critics state that Geertz' approach does not leave enough room for specific research into the social and political conditions and forces that generate and change cultural systems like religion (Bax 1987). According to Talal Asad, Geertz' definition of religion "omits the crucial dimension of power, ignores the varying social conditions for the production of knowledge, and its initial plausibility derives from the fact that it resembles the privatised forms of religion so characteristic of modern (Christian) society, in which power and knowledge are no longer significantly generated by religious institutions" (Asad 1983, 237).

In his *Anthropological Studies of Religion*, however, Brian Morris gives a fine evaluation of this criticism:

Given his stress on religion as a symbol system and his tendency to see religion as an inner state - a 'faith' - Geertz never *fully* explored the social forces that produced the religious beliefs and practices. Geertz's whole outlook remained close to the German idealist tradition.... But in attempting to understand religion within a *specific* sociopolitical context, Geertz certainly provides a more dynamic approach to religion than that evinced by anthropologists who have not been influenced by Weberian sociology - Douglas and Turner, for example. His studies of the religious systems of Java and Bali, in fact, indicate the pervasive influence of Weber, and though Geertz accepts the notion that his own approach is one of cultural hermeneutics, these studies go beyond that of simply interpreting the religious symbolism. As with Durkheim and Weber, there is a discrepancy in Geertz between his theoretical intent, specified in general programmatic statements, and his substantive analyses. (Morris 1987, 316, 319; my italics).

## Some Concluding Remarks

Notwithstanding some possible, relevant criticism of his approach to culture(s) and religion(s), Geertz has developed a fruitful, *cultural*-anthropological research programme. Geertz' notion of culture as systems of meanings embodied in symbols implies a circumscript task for anthropologists: they have to map out the relevant symbol-systems of specific cultures. According to Geertz, they should do that step by step, using the method of induction: from "directly observable modes of thought" to theoretical statements, and, next, using the latter to improve the original interpretations of empirical data:

The analysis of culture comes down therefore not to an heroic 'holistic' assault upon the 'basic configurations of the culture', an overarching 'order of orders' from which more limited configurations can be seen as mere deductions, but a searching out of significant symbols, clusters of significant symbols, and clusters of clusters of significant symbols...and the statement of the underlying regularities of human experience implicit in their formation (Geertz 1973h).

By comparing these cultures one can also trace the characteristic aspects of certain systems of symbols. A Geertzian comparison of, e.g., Javanese and Balinese concepts of person does not aim at constructing a general anthropological theory, but rather at showing differences and resemblances. The contrasts between them give an insight into the character of both cultures. Diversity is Geertz' real concern, universality - e.g., the "category of the person" - is mostly used as a merely strategic starting point.

This research strategy, however, does not imply that Geertzian ethnography would fall back into a sort of "descriptivism". As another American anthropologist, James L. Peacock, recently put it:

Ethnography generalizes...in some respects more akin to literature than to science. Ethnography reveals the general through the particular, the abstract through the concrete.... Ethnography is unlike literature and like science in that it endeavors to describe real people systematically and accurately, but it resembles literature in that it weaves facts into a form that highlights patterns and principles. As in good literature, so in good ethnography the message comes not through explicit statement of generalities but as concrete portrayal (Peacock 1986, 83; see also Geertz 1988, ch. I).

In spite of Geertz' assertion that systems of symbols - e.g., concepts of person - are expressed in actual, visible behaviour, these conceptions are not easy to pick up. An anthropologist is not a vacuum-cleaner. He has to make elementary - methodological and theoretical - decisions (cf. Shweder & LeVine 1984, 1-24).

Globally speaking, Geertz regards systems of symbols as relatively stable, durable products of culture. Culture, Geertz once wrote, moves like an octopus. But, of course, symbols have a historical dimension. To what degree can the genesis of, e.g., concepts of person be described and interpreted in terms of continuity and durability? Geertz' kind of anthropology and his interpretation of religion have been labelled as an a-historical perspective - unjustly, I think: Geertz' approach is not *per se* hostile to historical questions. For instance, Geertz' research on the process of religious modernization in Bali shows his talent as a cultural historian (Geertz 1973e).

Finally, the work of Geertz is an excellent starting-point for a debate on relativism. Geertz himself is certainly not an *extreme* relativist. He explicitly rejects the idea that our scientific, anthropological models should never be applied to the analysis of other cultures. He once called this sort of relativism an "academic neurosis". "Relativist" is not an adequate term to characterize Geertz' work. In my opinion, "pluralist" is a more appropriate term. Geertz values the differences between peoples, cultures, and societies. In his research on concepts of person, Geertz tries not so much to find an answer to our (or his) deepest questions but rather to gain access to answers other peoples have given.

## Notes

1.  I wish to express my gratitude to David Bos and Armin Geertz for their stimulating comments.
2.  See Geertz 1973c, 126-127: "In recent anthropological discussion, the moral (and aesthetic) aspects of a given culture, the evaluative elements, have commonly been summed up in the term 'ethos', while the cognitive, existential aspects have been designated by the term 'world view'. A people's ethos is the tone, character, and quality of their life, its moral and aesthetic style and mood: it is the underlying attitude towards themselves and their world that life reflects. Their world view is their picture of the way things in their sheer actuality are, their concept of nature, of self, of society. It contains their most comprehensive ideas of order".
3.  In a way, social anthropology has its own research programme for the concept of person. This starting point was Marcel Mauss's essay "Une Catégorie de l'esprit Humain: La Notion de Personne, Celle de moi" (A Category of the Human Mind: the Notion of Person, the Notion of Self), published in 1983, in the *Journal of the Royal Anthropological Institute*. Some recent results of this more social anthropological research programme can be found in: Carrithers, Collins, and Lukes 1985. The book is dedicated to the memory of Marcel Mauss. None of the twelve authors refer to the work of Geertz.
    In the conclusion of this book, S. Lukes states: "What preoccupies

Mauss, and the contributors to this volume, is...'the notion or concept
that different men in different ages have formed' of the person in the
narrow sense more particularly 'according to their systems of law,
religion, customs, social structures and morality'. What is this wider
'notion or concept' or structure of thinking concerning the person that
is held to be fundamental, universal and necessary?... Mauss, and most
contributors (see) the category of the person...as a structure of beliefs"
(op. cit., 285).

4.   Geertz 1983b, 59. My summaries of Geertz' analyses of Javanese,
     Balinese, and Moroccan concepts of person were also derived from this
     essay.
5.   Cf. also Geertz' use of Ryle's notion "thick description"; Geertz 1973h.
     With respect to the philosophical analysis of symbols and meanings,
     Geertz has also been influenced by the works of the American philo-
     sopher, logician, and art critic Susanne Langer; cf. Jeunhomme 1986.

## Bibliography

Asad, T., 1983: "Anthropological Conceptions of Religion: Reflections on
     Geertz", *Man* 18, 237-259.
Bakker, J.W., 1988: *Enough Profundities Already. A Reconstruction of
     Geertz's Interpretive Anthropology,* Utrecht.
Bateson, G. & M. Mead, 1942: *Balinese Character. A Photographic Analysis,*
     New York Academy of Sciences, vol. 2, New York.
Bax, M., 1987: "Religious Regimes and State Formation: Towards a Research
     Perspective", *Anthropological Quarterly* 60, 1-11.
Bock, P. K., 1980: *Continuities in Psychological Anthropology. A Historical
     Introduction,* San Francisco.
Boon, J.A., 1982: *Other Tribes, Other Scribes. Symbolic Anthropology in the
     Comparative Study of Cultures, Histories, Religions, and Texts,*
     Cambridge.
Carrithers, M., S. Collins, & S. Lukes, eds., 1985: *The Category of the Per-
     son. Anthropology, Philosophy, History,* Cambridge.
Geertz, C., 1960: *The Religion of Java,* Glencoe.
Geertz, C., 1967: "The Cerebral Savage", *Encounter* 4, 25-32.
Geertz, C., 1968: *Islam Observed. Religious Development in Morocco and
     Indonesia,* Chicago.
Geertz, C., 1973a: *The Interpretation of Cultures,* New York.
Geertz, C., 1973b: "Religion as a Cultural System", in: Geertz 1973a, 87-
     125 (orig. in: M. Banton, ed., *Anthropological Approaches to the Study
     of Religion,* London 1966, 1-46).
Geertz, C., 1973c: "Ethos, World View, and the Analysis of Sacred

Symbols", in: Geertz 1973a, 126-127.

Geertz, C., 1973d: "Ritual and Social Change: a Javanese Example", in: Geertz 1973a, 142-169 (orig. 1959).

Geertz, C., 1973e: "'Internal Conversion' in Contemporary Bali", in: Geertz 1973a, 171-189 (orig. 1964).

Geertz, C., 1973f: "Politics Past, Politics Present: Some Notes on the Uses of Anthropology in Understanding the New States", in: Geertz 1973a, 327-341 (orig. 1967).

Geertz, C., 1973g: "Deep Play; Notes on the Balinese Cockfight", in: Geertz 1973a, 412-453 (orig. 1972).

Geertz, C., 1973h: "Thick Description: Toward an Interpretive Theory of Culture", in: Geertz 1973a, 3-30.

Geertz, C., 1973i: "Person, Time and Conduct in Bali", in: Geertz 1973a, 342-411 (orig. 1966).

Geertz, C., 1980: *Negara. The Theatre State in Nineteenth-Century Bali*, Princeton.

Geertz, C., 1983a: "Centers, Kings, and Charisma: Reflections on the Symbolics of Power", in: *Local Knowledge. Further Essays in Interpretive Anthropology,* 121-146 (orig. 1977), New York.

Geertz, C., 1983b: "From the Native's Point of View': On the Nature of Anthropological Understanding", in: *Local Knowledge. Further Essays in Interpretive Anthropology,* 55-70 (orig. 1974), New York.

Geertz, C., 1988: *Works and Lives. The Anthropologist as an Author,* Stanford.

Geertz, C., H. Geertz, & L. Rosen 1979: *Meaning and Order in Moroccan Society. Three Essays in Cultural Analysis,* Cambridge.

Hofstee, W., 1986: "The Interpretation of Religion. Some Remarks on the Work of Clifford Geertz", in: H.G. Hubbeling & H.G. Kippenberg, eds., *On Symbolic Representation,* Berlin/New York, 70-83.

Jeunhomme, J.M.P., 1986: "The Symbolic Philosophy of Susanne K. Langer", in: H.G. Hubbeling & H.G. Kippenberg, eds., *On Symbolic Representation,* Berlin/New York, 84-101.

Kuiper, Y.B., 1986: "Religion, Symbols, and the Human Condition. An Analysis of the Basic Ideas of Jan van Baal", in: H.G. Hubbeling & H.G. Kippenberg, eds., *On Symbolic Representation,* Berlin/New York, 57-69.

Leach, E., 1982: *Social Anthropology,* Oxford.

Moore, R.L. & F.E. Reynolds, 1986: *Anthropology and the Study of Religion,* Chicago.

Morgan, J., 1977: "Religion and Culture as Meaning Systems: A Dialogue between Geertz and Tillich", *Journal of Religion* 57.

Morris, B., 1987: *Anthropological Studies of Religion,* Cambridge.

Ortner, S., 1984: "Theory in Anthropology Since the Sixties", *Comparative Studies in Society and History* 26, 126-166.

Peacock, J.L., 1981: "The Third Stream: Weber, Parsons, Geertz", *Journal of the Anthropological Society of Oxford* 12, 122-129.

Peacock, J.L., 1986: *The Anthropological Lens: Harsh Light, Soft Focus,* Cambridge.

Pinxten, R., 1979: "Clifford Geertz", in: idem, *On Going Beyond Kinship, Sex and the Tribe. Interviews on Contemporary Anthropology. Its Philosophical Stands and Its Applicability in the U.S.A.,* Gent.

Shweder, R.A. & R.A. LeVine, 1984: *Culture Theory. Essays on Mind, Self, and Emotion,* Cambridge.

Waal Malefijt, A. de, 1974: *Images of Man. A History of Anthropological Thought,* New York.

Walters, R.G., 1980: "Signs of the Times: Clifford Geertz and the Historians", *Social Research* 47, 537-556.

# Hindus:
# Traditions at Home
# and Abroad

# The Development of a Hindu Identity among the Hindustani in Suriname and the Netherlands

*By Lourens P. van den Bosch*

This paper focuses on certain aspects of the development of Hinduism as practised by Hindustani migrants in Suriname and in The Netherlands. This development is a very complex one. Therefore, a lot of research has to be done before a clear picture can be drawn of this religious minority in the Netherlands, and a good understanding is only possible if one reviews its situation in Suriname as well. For those who are not very well acquainted with the geography of Suriname, it is a former Dutch colony on the northeast coast of South America and is often regarded as belonging to the Caribbean area.

I shall restrict myself to a few remarks which may throw some light on the construction of a Hindu identity in Suriname and its gradual transformation in the course of time, both of which will fit in with the theme of this conference: "Religion, Tradition, and Renewal".

The first part of the theme refers to religious tradition, which implies in the case of the Surinamese Hindus, the traditional religion as found in their original country Hindustan in the north of India, or to be more precise, the area which today is called Uttar Pradesh and Bihar. In the course of my paper, I shall present information on the history of their migration between 1873 and 1916 from India to Suriname and their incorporation as an ethnic group with specific characteristics.

The second part of the theme has to do with the idea of the renewal of a religion or, as I would prefer to call it, with the idea of its transformation. In our case this concerns the transformation of Hinduism, its religious ideas and practices in Suriname, and later on in Holland, under the influence of the new natural, social, and cultural environments. In the field of interaction between Hindustani migrants and this new environment, a development took place in which their traditional dominant institutions such as the joint-family and the caste were weakened and even disappeared. In this process of transformation, teachers with new religious doctrines from the original homeland sometimes found a sympathetic hearing among the migrants, because their ideas better fitted the new situation. One of them was Svāmi Dayānanda Sarasvatī, leader of the *Ārya Samāj*, the congregation of the nobles. He proclaimed a return to the original Aryan religion and a purification of Hinduism from later accretions. His ideas can be regarded as an attempt at "renewal" or "renaissance" of what he supposed to be the true Aryan religion. As a result of the successful missionary activities of his followers in Suriname, the traditional Hindu priests were also forced to organize themselves and to elucidate their principal doctrines within the context of the new society.

The migration of the Hindustani to Suriname initially led to a disorientation and an identity crisis. In the original homeland, their position in society was clearly defined within the context of the traditional ideology and especially the practice of Hinduism, but in Suriname the ways in which the migrants had to define themselves to themselves and to one another were not self-evident. The mutual relations between the migrants had to be reformulated. This reformulation was a gradual process which took place against the background of the traditional ideology in consideration of the new environment. Moreover, they had to define their position as an ethnic group in the presence of other ethnic groups in Suriname, especially the Creoles. A repetition and a continuation of this development took place, as well, in their migration to Holland where they number at the moment about 85,000 and should increase in the coming decades due to expected high birth rates.

## The Hindustani in Suriname

The migration of Hindustani to Suriname is closely linked with the abolition of slavery in the Dutch colonies in 1863 (De Klerk 1953, 35 ff.). In the law dealing with this question, a temporary measure was included that the liberated slaves had to work on the plantations as indentured labourers for a period of ten years. In the meantime, a solution to the problem was found in consultation with the British government, which had had similar problems in her colonies in the Caribbean. This resulted in the right to recruit Indian labourers on contract by officials of the Dutch government. These labourers were obligated to work five years on the plantations in Suriname. In their contracts, "penal sanctions" were included which enabled the planters to take legal action against them in the case of laziness, negligence, or desertion.

In 1870, an emigration agent and a recruitment depot were established in Calcutta. The first indentured labourers left Calcutta for Suriname in 1873 with the sailing ship *Lalla Rookh*, presently the name of the most important organisation of the Hindustani community in the Netherlands, but also the name of its periodical. Until 1916, sixty-three ship-loads followed with a total number of about 34,000 migrants. The recruitment came to an end on account of sharp protests by the Indian Nationalists against indentured labour. About 80% of the migrants were recorded at their arrival as Hindu and 17% as Muslim. A representative sample has been made in the registers of the immigration office in Paramaribo after the composition of the Hindu group of migrants which resulted in a list of 81 castes (De Klerk 1953, 98 ff.). It is shown that the indentured labourers did not only belong to the low and depressed castes, but also to the higher and middle ones. Nevertheless, it becomes clear that the brahminical castes are not proportionally represented but are much lower, when one compares their percentual numbers with the situation in their homeland, viz., the United Provinces and Bihar. In 1931, about 5% of the Hindustani population in Suriname gave as their original caste a brahminical one. This comparatively low number is often explained by the fact that orthodox Hindus were not allowed to travel abroad for religious reasons. Moreover, it is argued that the authorities of the recruitment depot would have been quite critical with respect to brahmins. They were often regarded as double-faced agitators and unfit for plantation labour, because they preferred to have the heavy and dirty labour done by members of the lesser castes. As a group, however, the brahmins had an important share in the gradual organization of the religion of the Hindus in Suriname.

The Hindu migrants were especially contracted for work on plantations, irrespective of persons. Therefore they had to carry out, at least initially, the same tasks in the fields. This implied that the traditional division of labour based on the caste system was no longer valid in the new situation. The criteria applied for the selection of labourers on the various plantations were not derived from those of castes. Only families were kept together as far as possible, but the majority of the migrants came without their families. In the beginning, they had few possibilities to marry and to raise a household, because there were many men among the migrants and relatively few women. Generally, they did not show an interest in marrying outside their own ethnic group because of the difference in language and culture. The disproportion between the sexes was corrected in the course of time, when male labourers returned to their original country to find wives who were willing to marry and migrate to Suriname (De Klerk 1953, 146).

It will be clear that disorientation and frustration were great among the Hindustani in the first period of their migration. It took considerable time to found a new religious community in Suriname, which was adapted to the new situation. The structure of this new community in some respects differed from that in their original country where the caste system was the basis of society.

## The Caste System and Its Disintegration

A few words should be said in this context about the caste, because it forms as it were the smallest unit in the hierarchical organization of traditional Indian society. It is essential for a good understanding of how the Hindu people perceive themselves and each other. The caste can be broadly defined as a corporative closed group, the members of which share a common name and a supposed remote ancestor. It is traditionally distinguished by craft-exclusiveness and governed under the authority of an own committee by rules of endogamy, food, the sharing of meals (commensality), mutual intercourse and other social-religious customs. The hierarchical ranking of castes takes place on the basis of the purity and pollution dichotomy (Dumont 1980, chapter II). The members of a caste are supposed to be hereditarily tainted with a certain amount of impurity because of their traditional caste occupation.

In this system, the brahminical castes form as it were the top while the sweeper and tanning castes are at its basis because they are connected with the dead and decaying substances, the main agents for pollution. It is of no importance whether individual members actually follow their traditional caste profession. This separation between castes on the basis of the dichotomy of pure and impure has its opposite in the *jajmāni* system which regulates the division of labour. This system stresses the interdependency between the castes on account of the allotment of specific tasks to members of specific castes. Each caste fits in the whole and is classed according to the pollution scale (cf. also Harper 1964, 151ff). It goes beyond the scope of this paper to go into detail, but the division of labour takes place on the basis of these ideas. Members of brahminical castes, for instance, are not allowed to wash their own clothes. Its defiling effects makes them unfit for communication with sacred reality. For this reason they have it done by members of the washermen caste. This last mentioned caste is unfit for sacred functions on account of its impurity and needs the help of other specialists in such situations.

The caste situation was fundamentally changed for the migrant workers in Suriname. The crimps in charge of the recruitment of indentured labourers in India took no account of caste distinctions. They looked for healthy labourers fit for field work. This implied that migrants of various castes were thrown together in the recruitment depot and in the ships to Suriname, irrespective of caste. They had to share the same room and the same food and participated in the same impure activities. In this "pressure-cooker" they came "betwixt and between" their traditional roles (cf. Turner 1969, 94ff.), which were characteristic of the hierarchical society in India, and had to form a new community. This situation continued in Suriname where the migrants had to do the same menial duties during the period of their contract side by side. The corrosion of caste system led to a new reflection on their identity and to a reorientation. This development should, however, be seen against the background of their specific settlement patterns in Suriname. In the first period, they lived as comparatively isolated groups on plantations in the countryside. They had their own language, presently called Sarnami, and their own cultural and religous traditions. The colonial government restricted itself to certain regulations with respect to marriage, education, and name-giving without enforcing them, but did not interfere in their way of living (see De Klerk 1953, 180 ff. and Speckman 1965, 54-55). The Marriage Regulation Act for Asiatic People of 1941 implied a change in this policy, but by this time the Hindustani had become a well-knit group among the other groups in Suriname.

One of the main differences between the Hindu population in India and that of Suriname is the absence of the caste system as an institution which regulates social intercourse between persons and groups of persons. The caste as a corporative group with an own caste committee does not function any more. The caste rules with respect to marriage have fallen into disuse. The same applies for the purity regulations concerning various kinds of food, beverages, meals and intercourse. Hindus belonging to different castes can marrry and eat together (De Klerk 1953, 167 ff.). This means that persons are no longer primarily judged in connection with their former caste. In other words, caste identity is no longer decisive for the way in which the Hindus perceive themselves and each other in various situations. The individual is no longer subordinated to caste and attributed with qualities derived from that group.

In 1916, the colonial government introduced a new system of

name-giving on a voluntary basis which made it possible for Asiatics
- Hindustani, Javanese, and Chinese - to adopt new names according
to the pattern which was current among the other inhabitants of Suriname. This implied that the Hindus could give up their traditional
names which were often connected with their original castes, but in
the course of time it became clear that families once belonging to
brahminical and warrior (*kṣatriya*) castes attached much value to
expressing their former caste identity in their family name. Brahmins
choose traditional names like Śarma ("prosperity"), Sukul ("bright"),
Dube ("he who knows two Vedas"), Misier or Miśra ("honoured"),
and the like. Also the *kṣatriya* families had their own traditional stock
of names, like Varma ("protection"), Singh ("lion"), and Thakur
("lord") (De Klerk 1953, 182-184). In this way they tried to preserve
their former prestige connected with this caste. The conclusion seems
to be justified that the notion of caste still stands firm among some
groups, but the caste system as a social institution has disappeared.

One of the main characteristics of the caste system is endogamy.
Two marriage partners should belong to the same caste, but they
should not be related too narrowly (Dumont 1980, 109 ff.; Kapadya
1947, 46 ff., and 1966, 117 ff.). With the fading away of this system
in Suriname, the rule of endogamy was transposed to the ethnic group
as a whole. The main criterium was that the parents in their choice
of a marriage partner for their child always should confine themselves
to the Hindustani community. As such, they followed a policy of
separation with respect to other ethnic groups in Suriname. This rule
was so strict that Indian boys who went for study to Holland received
the injunction: "You are to marry an Indian woman, not a Dutch one"
(Speckman 1965, 70). However, in some specific cases, the marriage
rules were even more strict. Orthodox brahmins who functioned as
priests (*paṇḍits*) had to keep their lineage pure. For this reason, they
only used to marry brahminical girls in order that their offspring
would be fit for contact with sacred reality and could follow their
tracks.

## Hindu Organizations in Suriname: Ārya Samāj and Sanātan Dharm

The disappearance of the caste system had clear implications for the
formulation of a new religious identity. In traditional Indian society,
the Hindus were mainly interested in ritual activities, while their
religious ideology often remained implicit (Babb 1975, 31 ff.). These
ritual activities were also regarded as important by the Hindu

migrants. Among the rites of the life-cycle (*saṃskārās*) the solemnization of marriage and the wedding feasts were, e.g., seen as manifestations of crucial importance for Hindu group consciousness. The same applies to the great festivals of the year cycle such as *Dīvālī* and *Holī*. Nonetheless, the changed situation in Suriname required a more explicit reflection upon the essentials of Hindu ideology. The *Ārya Samāj*, a modern Hindu organization in India with missionary activities among the Indians in the Caribbean area, fulfilled in this need. The organization was founded in 1875 by Svāmi Dayānanda Sarasvatī who proclaimed a return to the norms and values of the ancient Vedic scriptures. He protested against child-marriage, the practice of suttee, the caste system and against all kinds of superstition and exploitation. He proclaimed the sole authority of the Vedas and a pure monotheism (Gonda 1963, 308 ff.; Klimkeit 1981, 171 ff., esp. 192-193; Speckman 1965, 47 ff.). He took a stand against later accretions in Hinduism and was against each form of idolatry. Sacrificial woreship of God should take place by means of *homa*, a sacrifice to the fire (cf. De Klerk 1951, 50-57). This ritual could be performed in the open air, and no temple was required. Sarasvatī stressed the importance of knowledge, truthfulness, love, and justice (Soekhlal 1986, 81 ff.). Though his ideas obtained only a small hearing in India, they found fertile ground among the Hindu migrants in the Caribbean area. The first ardent followers of the *Ārya Samāj* were found in Suriname in 1912. The movement grew in a constant tempo, and, in 1930, an official organization, the *Ārya Dewaker* (Aryan Sun Society), was founded to promote activities in Suriname. It especially attracted the younger intellectual Hindus because of its more rational and social bias (De Klerk 1953, 154 ff. and 193 ff.).

With its message of a return to the true belief of the Vedas and its claim of purification of the tradition, the *Ārya Samāj* adapted quite well to the situation of the Hindu migrants in Suriname. Its teaching formed, as it were, a justification for the non-observance of the purity rules regulating the caste system. Moreover, it put a high premium on individual development with its educational ideas on own knowledge, understanding, and responsibility. It proclaimed that individual human life is determined by actual behaviour, by personal inclinations, and natural abilities and not by the observance of caste rules. In consequence of this view not only brahmins could officiate as priests in ritual sessions, but also all other Hindus, regardless of sex. The sole condition was the possession of the required ritual knowledge.

The more traditional Hindus were compeled by the success of the *Ārya Samāj* to organize themselves and to formulate answers to burning questions. In 1929, they founded an association called *Sanātan Dharm (Sanātana Dharma)*, which is closely linked with the *Bhārata Dharma Mahāmaṇḍala* (The Great Association of Indian Religion). This umbrella organization of traditional Hindus was founded in India in 1902 (De Klerk 1951, 21). The main object of the *Sanātan Dharm* was the promotion of social welfare among the inhabitants of Suriname and the propagation and preservation of the Hindu religion among them (De Klerk 1953, 193). For that reason, its followers call themselves *Sanātanis,* followers of the *sanātana dharma*. Unlike the *Āryas*, they do not attach much value to education and instruction in the doctrines of their religion. They are mainly interested in the right performance of the rites by their priests (De Klerk 1951, 29). Nonetheless, there is a clear trend among them to stress the monotheistic elements in their religion. The god Viṣnu is especially worshipped. In a recent leaflet, he is described as the highest unity and truth; the other gods are only viewed as manifestations of him (Stichting Lalla Rookh n.d., 28-29). This orientation on Viṣnuitic doctrines becomes comprehensible if one bears in mind that the original homelands of the migrants were of great importance in the sacred geography of Viṣnuism.

The caste system, with its hierarchy based on the opposition of pure and impure, is in India reflected in the cult of the gods (cf. Harper 1964, 151 ff.). Each caste has its own religious traditions and its own deities, but this hierarchical inequality is supplemented by religious communities in which the equality of people is stressed before the one omnipresent God. These devotional (*bhakti*) groups developed more egalitarian theologies which threw new light on the religious identity of man. In the attribution of names, this identity is often expressed, e.g., in names like Rāmdās, "slave of Rāma", etc. These communities with their own theological and ritual traditions form as it were the counterpart of the caste system (cf. Turner 1969, chapter 5: "Humility and Hierarchy; The Liminality of Status Elevation"). In Suriname, however, these devotional groups did not develop because of the absence of their raison d'être. Disintegration of the caste system made additional *bhakti* movements actuallly superfluous. This development resulted in a brahminical re-orientation with a vague monotheistic ideology in which equality is proclaimed. This ideological change in Suriname is not only expressed in the religious teachings of the *paṇḍits*, but also in the organization of their ritual tasks. The brahmins have no ritual specializations which are valued according to the purity scale. They are involved in all kinds of ritual activities, even in the funeral rites which are shunned by high caste brahmins in India on account of their extreme pollution (see Van der Burg & Van der Veer 1984, 163, and Dumont 1980, 58, on the *mahābrāhman*).

## The Joint-Family

Besides the caste system, the joint-family forms the other essential pillar, characteristic of traditional Indian society. In Suriname this also has been corroded. Traditionally it was composed of three or more generations living together in the same compound, cooking in the same kitchen, owning property in common, and pooling their incomes for common spending (Ross 1961, 34). The oldest male member of the group is usually the head of the family and the adminstrator of its joint property. The members are closely bound together by mutual rights and obligations. It has been remarked that the joint-family system "strongly limits social mobility and social change because it binds the individual to others on the basis of birth, forces him to contribute to the support of a large group independently of his ability, introduces nepotism into both business and politics, and assures the control of the younger generation by the elders" (Ross 1961, 14, quoting Kingsley Davis). In such a system, there is no place for liberalism and individualism, but the traditions of the community and the family are decisive. The individual is regarded as part of the whole and derives its identity from its position in the family. As such, there is a similarity to the caste system in which the individual is also subordinated to the whole.

As is mentioned above, it was initially impossible for the Hindustani migrants in Suriname to reconstruct the joint-family as an institution, but the notion was kept alive. In the course of time, they organized their families along the lines of the joint-family. The sons were associated with the household group of their father. Usually they lived together in the same compound or under the same roof. The father was head of the family and in that capacity responsible for a respectable marriage of his sons and daughters. He had to uphold the honour of the family by marrying off his daugher(s) before puberty to a suitable party, according to traditional "law" (*dharmaśāstra*) (see, e.g., Manu IX.4; transl. Bühler 1886, 328). Until 1930, child-marriage was a rather common affair, especially in the country-side (Speckman 1965, 74 ff.). After the consummation of marriage, the young couple moved into the house of the groom's father, because it was often dependent upon his household for subsistence. As a result of this, the younger generation usually remained subject to a strict social supervision and, consequently, bound to the customs and traditions of the Indian community.

The notions with respect to the joint-family have been important in the reconstruction of the Indian household in Suriname, but also other trends can be observed. Since the forties, a clear orientation towards the nuclear family has taken place (Speckman 1965, 79 ff.). The main reasons for this development are the improved education of the younger generation and a resistance to child-marriage, especially on the part of the government. In the Asiatic Marriage Decrees of 1941, a minimum age of thirteen years for girls and fifteen for boys was decreed by the government for the validation of marriage. The compulsory service in the army, which detached many boys from their old environment, was another factor which undermined the cohesion of the joint-family. The boys were influenced by the European and Creole society and developed a higher measure of individual self-reliance. They objected to the traditional authority relations in the joint-family. Moreover, many young Hindustani came into a closer contact with the town on account of the great demand for labour in Paramaribo. All these developments gradually resulted in a changed perception by the younger generation of their own individuality and their place in society. The self was no longer primarily viewed in relation to caste and the traditional household, but seen as a relatively independent entity which could make autonomous decisions.

The new notions with respect to individuality worked on in religious traditions. In this context it may be useful to devote a few words to the institution of marriage in India and Suriname. Traditionally marriage was regarded as a consecratory rite which could not be dissolved because of its religious character (see, e.g., Kane 1974, II, 619 ff. and Kapadya 1966, 167 ff.). The choice of the suitor was carefully arranged by the family of the bride according to a whole series of prescriptions. The negotiations on the bride-wealth were a concern of both families. Marriage was not seen as an affair between two individuals based on personal choice, but it was essentially a matter between two families. The father met his religious obligations by marrying his nubile daughter in time to a suitable party, and, by this act, he upheld the honour of the family. The boy's family was mainly interested in the continuity of its own household and lineage. This could be guaranteed by the consummation of marriage and by male offspring. After marriage, the wife was defined in terms of her husband and his family. In the beginning, she had a subordinate position and had to accomodate herself to the mistress of the house, mostly her mother-in-law, and to the other older persons, but her position bettered as she presented more sons to her husband.

In Suriname, the gradual shift in the perception of individuality has resulted in a changed view on marriage and the household. Marriage is no longer primarily regarded as a matter between two families, but also as the choice of two individual persons for each other. The religious idea that marriage is a consecratory rite which cannot be dissolved is no longer generally acknowledged. The introduction of the Asiatic Marriage Decrees in 1941 enabled the official registration of marriage and divorce. Since that time, the idea has taken form that marriage is an agreement of will between two persons which can be dissolved. Notwithstanding these developments, many Hindustani are attached to the performance of the traditional wedding rites because it is felt that their Hindu identity is expressed by means of them. The traditional notions with respect to the idea of the social person underlying these rites are no longer regarded as essential. The transition from the joint to the nuclear family follows quite naturally from this changed vision on the self and marriage.

The gradual integration of the Hindustani migrants in Surinamese society since the beginning of the forties also has led to an increased awareness of their ethnic identity. As long as they lived as peasants in separate economic and cultural niches the religious differences in the group were regarded as important, but with their migration from the rural areas to the city they entered the same niche as the Creoles and had to compete with them. This development produced "a strong tendency within the Hindustani group to neglect the internal socio-religious differences and to stress the fact that Hindustanis were a group originating in India, having a common history and therefore a common identity" (Van der Burg & Van der Veer 1986, 520). This reorganization along ethnic lines worked on in the formation of the Hindustani Political Party in 1949.

## Hindus in Holland

The second migration of a great number of Hindustani to Holland has led to a new crisis in the Hindu community and to a reflection upon its position and identity in Dutch society. In Suriname, the Hindustani had organized themselves as a solid ethnic group with political influence alongside with other ones. The trends towards a greater measure of individuality and a more egalitarian ideology resulted in Suriname in specific forms of Hinduism. In Holland the situation is quite different. The government policy to distribute the Hindustani migrants over the whole country, the disintegration of traditional authority and the weak religious organization of the Hindu *pandits* form an important impediment for the reorganization of the religious community along traditional lines. The developments with respect to individuality have been intensified among the Hindustanis who are no longer a well-knit group. The religious leaders of the *Sanatānis* and *Āryas* in Holland feel themselves often incapable to deal with the crisis of their followers. They try to find solutions to present problems by pursuing the realization of traditional religious provisions as those known in Suriname. Besides this development, also a new reorientation to India and its religious traditions takes place in an attempt to reconcile their religious views with the new natural, social, and cultural environment. In the present situation the great rites of the lifecycle such as the birth, marriage, and death rites, and the great rites of the year cycle, especially *Holī* and *Dīvālī*, are still regarded by most Surinamese Hindus as important means for the expression of their religious identity, but the traditional ideology underlying these rites does not go along with the new trend. Therefore it remains to be seen whether and, if so, how an new articulation of tradition can be realized which is adapted to this changed society and the changed perception of the self.

Religion, tradition, and renewal: the Surinamese Hindus in Holland find themselves in a process of interaction between these two poles. The question to be investigated is whether and, if so, which form of Hinduism will be developed in Dutch society.

## Bibliography

Babb, L., 1975: *The Divine Hierarchy: Popular Hinduism in Central India*, New York/London.
Bühler, G., 1886: *The Laws of Manu*, Oxford (SBE XXV).
Burg, C.J.G. van der, & P.T. van der Veer 1986: "Ver van India, ver van Suriname: Hindoestaanse Surinamers in Nederland", in: C.J.G. van der Burg, ed., *Surinaamse Religies in Nederland*, Amsterdam, 23-36.
Dumont, L., 1980: *Homo Hierarchicus, The Caste System and Its Implications*, Chicago (Complete Revised English Edition).
Gonda, J., 1963: *Die Religionen Indiens II, Der Jüngeren Hinduismus*, Wiesbaden.
Harper, E., 1964: "Ritual Pollution as an Integrator of Caste and Religion", in: E. Harper, ed., *Aspects of Religion in South Asia, Journal of Asian Studies* 23, 1984, 151-197.

Kane, P.V., 1974: *History of Dharmasâstra*, vol. II, Poona (2nd ed.).

Kapadya, K.M., 1947: *Hindu Kinship,* Bombay.

Kapadya, K.M., 1966: *Marriage and Family in India*, Oxford (3d ed.).

Klerk, C.J.M. de, 1951: Cultus en Ritueel van het Orthodoxe Hindoeïsme in Suriname, Amsterdam (thesis, Leiden 1951).

Klerk, C.J.M. de, 1953: *De Immigratie der Hindostanen in Suriname,* Amsterdam.

Klimkeit, K.J., 1981: *Der politische Hinduismus, Indische Denker zwischen religiöser Reform und politischem Erwachen*, Wiesbaden.

Soekhlal, T., 1986: "De opkomst van de Arya Samaj in Suriname", in: C. J.G. van der Burg, ed., *Surinaamse Religies in Nederland*, Amsterdam.

Speckman, J.D., 1965: *Marriage and Kinship among the Indians in Surinam,* Assen.

Stichting Lalla Rookh, *Plechtigheden en Gebruiken bij Huwelijk, Geboorte en Overlijden van Hindostanen*, Utrecht (Uitgave Stichting Lalla Rookh).

Turner, V.W., 1969: *The Ritual Process, Structure and Anti-Structure*, London.

Veer, P.T. van der, & C.J.G. van der Burg, 1984: "Religieuze autoriteit en identiteitvorming bij Surinaamse Hindoes in Nederland", in: D.C. Mulder, ed., *De Religieuze Gezagsdrager,* Amsterdam.

# Ambiguities of Tradition: Widow-Burning in Bengal in the Early Nineteenth Century

*By Poul Pedersen*

Widow-burning, or *suttee*, is one of the fascinating horrors of the world. Missionary propaganda and traveler's tales from India have always had their chapters on the cruel superstitions of the Hindus, and this has created an exaggerated impression of the prevalence of widow-burning, as if it were a daily experience. In fact, many Westerners spent a whole lifetime in India without ever seeing a widow being burnt.

We have reason to think that the number of suttees culminated in the early nineteenth century, shortly before 1829, when it was virtually stopped by the British. It was most frequent in Bengal where it probably never exceeded one thousand cases annually. Compared to the total population of Bengal Presidency, this amounts to 20 cases for every 1,000,000 people. Outside Bengal, in Madras and Bombay Presidencies, the frequency was even lower: 2 cases for every 1,000,000 people.[1]

In this paper, I will discuss the uneven distribution of suttees in India and the uneven distribution within Bengal itself. In my concluding remarks, I will raise a few points on the concept of tradition.

## The Faithful Wife

The most common term for widow-burning is suttee, which is the anglicized version of the Sanskrit word *sati*, which means virtuous and faithful wife. Suttee existed in two forms: one called *sahamarana*, where the widow ascended the funeral pyre of her deceased husband and was burned alive with his corpse, and the other called *anumarana*, where the widow was burned alone, since her husband had died and been cremated elsewhere (Sharma 1976).

One can only speculate on the origin of suttee (cf. Pedersen 1984). The Vedas say nothing about it, so it was probably unknown in the early period of Indian civilization. The earliest historical record of suttee is from Punjab in the fourth century BC., and, from later times, we have scriptural and epigraphic evidence, which is supplemented by later eyewitness reports of Western travelers in India (Sharma 1976).

Widow-burning was outlawed in Bengal in 1829 and the year after in the rest of the British territories (Seed 1955).[2]

After that time, only a few cases were reported each year - and reports still come in.[3]

Western reactions to suttee were dominated by missionaries' and liberal reformers' disgust of what they considered to be a fanatical and inhuman custom, and they used it as an argument for extended British interference in Indian affairs.[4] A minority of Westerners interpreted suttee in romantic and sentimental terms as an expression of the highest ideals of love and devotion.[5]

Hindus and Westerners have always agreed that suttee is a religious custom or institution. Hindus have rationalized the burning of widows in two different ways, which nevertheless share the same ideal of womanhood: that the wife must regard the devoted service of her husband as her greatest duty (Srinivas 1956, 484). One interpretation of this duty is that the wife should become a *sati*. By following her deceased husband in the flames of his funeral pyre, she frees him and herself of all sin, and the couple will experience eternal bliss in Heaven (Colebrooke 1837). This is based on a relatively simple idea of Heaven and Hell and the way to salvation.

The other interpretation is founded on the much more complex ideas of metempsychosis. Here it is stated that for a woman there is no way out of the cycle of rebirth as long as she is born a woman. Her only hope of advance towards liberation is if she is reborn as a man. By becoming a *sati*, she will become a man in her next life (Winternitz 1920, 60 ff.).[6] To become a *sati* was one of the two ideal possibilities prescribed for widows, but it was the one chosen by only a few. The alternative was to endure widowhood in a state approximating social death. This was the more common choice.

## The Caste System

From a sociological point of view, suttee should be seen within the framework of the caste system. This I shall define minimally as a hierarchical order of endogamous and competitive status groups. It is highly significant that inter-caste relations are power relations, i.e., that claims to a specific status by one caste must be negotiated against claims to status by other castes. Another important aspect of the caste system is that behaviour and norms of behaviour are caste or, perhaps more precisely, status specific. High caste behaviour is clearly distinguishable from intermediate and low caste behaviour. These distinctive types of behaviour are most easily observed in dietary rules, marriage regulations, treatment of women, and worship. For example, a high caste person will be vegetarian, abstain from drinking alcohol, his women will be secluded, widow remarriage will be prohibited, and he will be served by Brahmins. Intermediate and low castes will differ from this in such a way that the intermediate castes are closer to high caste ideals of behaviour than the low castes.

A third aspect which I wish to emphasize is the process which Srinivas has called Sanskritization (Srinivas 1956). This is a dual process of upward social mobility and downward spread of high caste ideals of behaviour. A caste which has gained economic and political power can force its way up the status hierarchy by adopting the behavioural norms of the higher castes if - and I emphasize if - it can make other castes accept its claims to a new status. And to do so takes negotiation and persuasion. In short, it takes power.[7]

Suttee was unevenly distributed among the castes. It was more prevalent among the higher castes, especially among the priestly and warrior castes, Brahmins and Kshatriyas. But it was also, though rarely, practised among the intermediate and low castes, in particular among those who engaged in trade.

## The Prevalence of Suttee in Bengal

Now, with this background I shall try to answer two important questions. First, why was widow-burning more common in Bengal than elsewhere in India in the early nineteenth century? Second, why do certain intermediate and low castes in Bengal burn their widows contrary to expectation?

In my answers to these questions, I shall point to three important differences between Bengal and the rest of India. These are differences in female property rights, in the prevalence of polygamous marriage practices, and in relation to colonial power and the world market.

### Differences in Female Property Rights

There never was any single body of traditional hindu law. Two variant schools held sway over Hindu society in different parts of India. The dominant law in Bengal was the Dayabhaga school, but in the rest of India, it was the Mitakshara school (Tambiah 1973). Here

I shall only outline the main differences between these law schools regarding the property of women and the rights of the widow.

According to the Mitakshara school (i.e., outside Bengal), the members of the joint family are divided into two parts: between co-parceners (who are agnates owning joint property) and other members (the women, i.e., in-coming wives and daughters of the joint family) who are entitled to maintenance, which includes residence, food, clothing, medical attention, education, etc. The in-coming wives have these rights even if widowed (Tambiah 1973).

In the Dayabhaga school, which prevails in Bengal, the legal position of the widow is different in regards to property rights. Here a widow of a sonless member of the joint family is "entitled to practically the same rights over joint family property which her deceased husband would have had" (Kane 1941, II, 1, 635). Kane sees here an evident connection between the property rights of the widow and the higher incidence of widow burning in Bengal: "This must have frequently induced the surviving members to get rid of the widow by appealing at a most distressing hour to her devotion to and love for her husband" (Kane 1941, II, 1, 635).

A variant of this opinion was expressed by at least two contemporary observers. In a letter dated 18-11-1818, Mr. Ewer, the acting Superintendent of police in the Lower Provinces, stated to Mr. Bailey, the Secretary to the Judicial Department, that it was the desire of the male relations of the widows to appropriate the properties left by the husbands of the latter which greatly encouraged the practice of suttee (Mukhopadhyay 1957).

Lord Minto, who was Governor-General from 1807 to 1813, said that the many cases of widow-burning were caused among other things by the greed of the heirs of the widow (Potts 1967, 147).

Altekar saw the widow's rights to property in Bengal as progress compared to the rest of India, where the Mitakshara school held sway (Altekar 1957, 261). From our point of view, it seems that the many Bengali *satis* paid a high price for that.


*Polygamous Marriages in Bengal*

The peculiar Brahmin hypergamous marriage arrangement in Bengal is called *Kulinism* and is unique in its extreme consequences.

The Rahri Brahmins of Bengal were organized into three ranked groups, with Kulins at the top, Bansaj in the middle, and Srotriya at the bottom. Between these three groups there existed hypergamous marriages relations so that Srotriya daughters could obtain a husband from their own group as well as from Bansaj and Kulin. Bansaj daughters could obtain husbands from their own group and from Kulin. Kulin daughters could only marry Kulin sons.[8] Seen from the top, this made it difficult for Kulin families to find a Kulin husband for their daughters since they were competing with Bansaj and Srotriya families. If the Kulin family would avoid being degraded in the caste hierarchy, it was necessary for it to have its daughters married before puberty. These two circumstances, the widespread demand for Kulin bridegrooms and the Brahmin practice of child marriage, created the enormous dowries that went along with a Kulin son's marriage to a Kulin or non-Kulin daughter. This again meant that for the Kulin father in search of a bridegroom for his daughter, any Kulin man would do: he could be a child or an old man, married or not.

This system of hypergamy caused severe misery for the women. Female infanticide and the suicide of daughters were its logical consequences.[9]

Such an important manifestation of status as marriage was supposed to be expressed publicly, and, when the groom died, his (often) many widows were expected to express their family status even if none of the widows had cohabited with the deceased. They did so by following the dead body of their husband on his funeral pyre as *satis*.

We have no exact information on the magnitude of these polygamous widow-burnings, but, as the Kulin hypergamy was by far the most extreme case of polygamy in India, it must have added something to the numbers of suttees in Bengal.

We have Ward's observations of Kulin-suttees from the years around 1800: in 1789, near Kalighat, 4 women on the same pyre; in 1799, 37 women on the same pyre, "the fire was kept burning for three days"; in 1812, 12 women on the same pyre. Ward also reports an instance about the same time where 18 widows of the same Kulin Brahmin mounted his pyre and were burned to death (Ward 1817, I, 96-115).

## Widow Burning, Colonial Power and World Market

The British were active in many places in India. In the seventeenth century, they had factories at Surat, Bombay, Madras, and Calcutta, but, in the late eighteenth century, the logic of conquest made Calcutta and Bengal the center of colonial economic and political activity. When the British defeated the Mughal governor at the battle of

Plassey in 1757, they held *de facto* power in Bengal. In 1765, they secured from the Mughal emperor the right to collect revenue in Bengal, Bihar and Orissa. From this position of *Diwan*, there followed a continuous expansion of the British domain in Bengal (Misra 1961, 73 ff.).

Here I shall only mention two important consequences that followed the british dominance in Bengal. Land was capitalized as revenue rights that were bought and sold, and new groups in society became owners of land and revenue rights. Among the new groups investing in land were those Indians who had profited form the trade with the British. They had owned their fortunes as agents or brokers to mercantile and banking houses (Misra 1961, 132 ff.). This was not confined to the privileged natives of the metropolis of Calcutta but reached out into the countryside via the network of markets where local traders dealt in wheat or other agricultural products which were exported from Calcutta to overseas markets such as England (Crawfurd 1838).

With these changes, new groups could build a strong economic basis for claims to a higher status in society, by their newly acquired access to the fortunes of land and trade. Bengal was to experience widespread and determined efforts at Sanskritization, where the burning of widows was one way of expressing the feeling of, or wish for, a new and higher status.

Kalikinkar Datta provided a compilation of suttee cases in the area between Kazimbasar (Murshidabad District) and the mouth of the Hugli River during May and June 1812. The caste background of the deceased husbands is also provided: 13 were Brahmins, 5 Oilmen, 4 Carpenters, 4 Kaiasthas, 4 Kivarthas, 3 Blacksmiths, 3 Gardeners, 3 Goldsmiths, 3 Barbers, 2 Rajputs, 2 Weavers, 1 Merchant, 1 Brazier, 1 Husbandman, 1 Potter, 1 Bagdee (Datta 1936, 79 ff.).

We cannot say whether these cases represent a trend in the prevalence of suttee among the different castes. But we can use them to ask some strategic questions about the character of social mobility in the caste system. We can ask if these 51 cases suit our expectations of the social distribution of suttee.

They do, more or less, since the Brahmins are the highest and the Bagdees, for example, among the lowest castes in Bengal. But another thing about these cases is the remarkable high score of the Oilmen. How can we explain that a low ranking caste like the Oilmen were such eager widow-burners?

A closer look at the castes and caste ranking in Bengal reveals some interesting information on the Oilman caste. The castes in

Bengal are conventionally grouped as follows: 1. Superior castes (Brahmins, Kaiasthas, etc.); 2. *Sat* (clean) sudras (Barbers, Blacksmiths, Sadgops, etc.); 3. Intermediate castes (Kivarthas, Washermen, etc.); 4. Low castes (Chamars, Doms, etc.) (Hunter 1875-77; Majumdar 1971, I, 573 ff.). Where do we find the Oilman caste in this ranking scheme?

We find it in two places: among the *sat* Sudra castes under the name of Teli and among the low castes under the name of Kalu.[10] Telis are rich and Kalus are poor. Teli seems to have the same history in the districts of Bengal. Its members have grown rich and influential and have given up their original profession of pressing and selling oil and have turned to agriculture and trade in grain, and they have forced their way up the caste hierarchy.[11] It is reasonable to believe that Teli in its long Sanskritizing march upward in the caste hierarchy took to burning their widows in imitation of the high castes and thus adding to the numbers of suttee.

Let us look at this from another point of view. If we are right in assuming world market and colonial forces as the background for some Sanskritizing and widow-burning castes, then we should expect the highest incidence of suttee where these forces were felt most strongly in Bengal. We should expect to find a higher incidence in Calcutta Division than in the remoter divisions of the Presidency. And that is exactly what we find. Of the 8,134 cases of suttee that took place in Bengal between 1815 and 1828, 5,119 (or 63%) were in Calcutta Division alone (Mukhopadhyay 1957, 105 ff.).

Amithaba Mukhopadhyay provided these data, but without noticing what was going on in Bengal in early nineteenth century. He wrote that:

Calcutta and the neighbouring districts were the areas where Europeans had personal intercourse with the most enlightened and influential classes of the Hindu community and where the chief efforts of Government, of societies and of individuals had been directed to the spread of knowledge and to the improvement and extension of education (Mukhopadhyay 1957, 105 ff.).

From this we should expect that Calcutta Division showed the lowest incidence of suttee. As it actually did not, Mukhopadhyay falls back on the "traditional" understanding of tradition: "The only explanation we may offer for the high incidence of *sati* in Calcutta Division is perhaps the strong hold of the *sati* tradition on the people of this locality for a long time" (Mukhopadhyay 1957, 105 ff.).

Thus, with such an idea of traditon we have a paradox. When

Bengal came under the modernizing influence of colonialism and the world market, we saw traditional behaviour being extremely modern. Such a paradox is confusing because of the teleological and evolutionistic assumptions of much historiography. An historical anthropology should know better.

I will finish my argument by extending it. In *Statistical account of Bengal*, there are hints that Teli is a splintergroup of Kalu, which holds a very low position in the Hindu community. It seems that very few Telis have their original occupation of oilpressing and selling, but that they were then (ca. 1870) engaged in agriculture and trade. All Kalus were oilpressers and sellers. I suggest that Teli has Sanskritized its way from Kalu. The ambiguity of the high ranking position of Teli is illustrated by the fact that

Some years ago before 1872 the question arose as to whether a Teli could legally perform all the religious ceremonies which the Nasabak, or one of the nine superior castes, can. The question was referred to the Pandits of Nadiya, who decided that the Telis were Nasabak: but it appears probable that this decision was influenced by the wealth and general importance to which the caste has attained (Hunter 1875-77, I, 61).

The earliest published material on the Oilman caste that I have found is from Montgomery Martin's *The History, Antiquities, Topography, and Statistics of Eastern India* from 1838. The data Martin compiled in his 3 volume work were collected by Francis Buchanan in the years 1807-1813 (Cohn 1968, 14). So we are now much closer to the events of the early 19th century.

Martin has some extremely important data on Teli in Bihar from Patna City District and Dinajpur District (Martin 1838: I, 341, 545; II, 569). Where Martin (or his observer) found Teli, the caste was economically differentiated into three groups. The first group was poor oilpressers who hired their oilmill and their labour power to grovers of oil seed. They were paid with part of the pressed oil and the oil cake, which they fed to the oxen that drew the oil mill.[12]

The oilpressers of the second group were wealthy enough to buy seed and sell the oil on the market and were thus relatively independent of the growers of seed.

The third group was "not only able to purchase seed which they squeezed but had also some good carriage oxen with which they traded in other grain; the oil cake giving them a facility in feeding the cattle" (Martin 1838, I, 341).

Here we see how the economic differentiation distributes advantages unevenly within the Telis. Those with many oxen could go into trade with oil, grain, and other commodities and prosper. Eventually they could change profession, habits, and caste position. Those with few oxen would be as they always were: clients of the agricultural castes or small dealers in oil, because of lack of funds for Sanskritization.

Thus we must think that if the Oilman caste once was one endogamous group, then there would, along the lines of the economic differentiation, arise hypergamous marriage relations between poorer and richer groups; or the marriage relations would break down completely, the caste split in two, and we shall end up with two castes occupying different positions in the caste hierarchy, one at the top, the other at the bottom (Martin 1838, I, 341).

The data on the Oilman caste are unfortunately not from the districts around Calcutta. So I cannot prove that all this happened, but one can take the argument as a model for what was going on in Bengal at that time. So further empirical research must prove or disprove the value of the model for the events in Bengal in early 19th century.

## The Dynamics of Tradition

In this paper, I have tried to combine certain aspects of Indian civilization in order to produce an explanation of the high incidence of widow-burning in Bengal in the early 19th century. I have argued that since the form taken by social mobility within the Indian caste system results in the spread of high caste behaviour, we should expect that other than high castes also engaged in high caste behaviour. Substantially, this means that intermediate and low ranking castes should practice child marriage, the prohibition og the remarriage of widows, and widow-burning to some extent. The preconditions for such cultural strategies for changing status are not to be found within the Indian culture itself, but are historically provided changes in economic and political relations. So one can explain local variations of cultural expressions by referring to the different and changing relations each locality has to its wider regional and global contexts. More specifically, I have argued that colonialism and world market forces provided the Oilman caste of Bengal with the resources for caste climbing. The Oilmen were privileged in relation to the historical development. Their combination of production and trade gave them enormous advantages in the regionally and internationally rapidly expanding trade. The riches they earned showed themselves in their Sanskritization and in their *satis*.

This argument is based on a dynamic conception of tradition. The high incidence of suttees in Calcutta Division confronted Mukhopadhyay with a paradox he could not solve. His invocation of tradition was of no help because tradition alone explains nothing. On the contrary, tradition itself is in need of explanation.

Tradition is activity, and tradition is always somebody's tradition. I have deliberately avoided any reference to tradition as explanation in this paper. Instead, I have pointed to the dynamics of tradition, to the strategic interests of individuals and groups, who are engaged in traditional behaviour. From such a perspective of practice, tradition is something which is invented and reinvented, something which is kept alive and insisted upon in daily use, and something which is forgotten or left to die when people stop caring about it.

All in all, tradition is part of a cultural strategy, a set of tools for the creation of meaning, and as such is always contemporary. Understood in this manner, tradition is no less modern than "modernity".

## Notes

1. These figures are given with reservations, since they contain little recorded fact and some creative speculation on my part. The population figures have been calculated from Census of India 1881 and projected backwards in time with the help of the growth rates estimated by Das Gupta 1972. The number of suttees have been recorded in *Parlamentary Papers on Sati* and cited in Mukhopadhyay 1957. These figures are for several reasons not immediately comparable, and my calculations probably only point to differences in magnitude.
2. On *suttee* in the native states, see Bushby 1855 and Thompson 1928.
3. See the reports in the German magazine *Stern*, November 26, 1981, and in *Far Eastern Economic Review,* October 8, 1987. I am grateful to Michael Gravers for this last reference.
4. Two examples are Johns 1816 and Peggs 1828.
5. It is interesting that Ananda K. Coomaraswamy adopted this interpretation. See Coomaraswamy 1956, 115 ff.
6. It is important that there is no corresponding idea of widower-burning.
7. An example of successful Sanskritization is given in Bailey 1957, and, for a failure, see Sinha 1965.
8. This hypergamous system has been discussed by Beteille 1977, 34 ff.
9. These consequences have been noticed by many observers at different

times during the nineteenth century. See the several contributions to the contemporary Calcutta weekly *The Reformer*, cited in Chattopadhyay 1978, Hunter 1875, I, 53 ff., and Bose 1883, 232 ff. Similar hypergamous relations were also found, though to a lesser degree, among the Kayastha, see Datta 1961, 37. and Dumont 1970, 162 ff.

10. The existence of these two Oilman castes can be demonstrated for almost any district in Bengal, see Hunter 1875-77.

11. Hunter 1875-77, I, 61; II, 47; III, 53, 287; V, 49, 191 f., 404; VI, 51, 225, 230; VII, 45, 217, 378; VIII, 44, 175 ff; IX, 50; X, 82, 257; XI, 248 ff; XIII, 45, 244; XIV, 66 f., 71; XVIII, 74, 275; XIX, 37.

12. For a description of oil pressing techniques see Bose 1975, 73 ff.

## Bibliography

Altekar, A.S., 1957: *The Position of Women in Hindu Civilization*, Benares.

Bailey, F.G., 1957: *Caste and the Economic Frontier*, Manchester.

Beteille, Andre, 1977: *Inequality Among Men*, Oxford.

Bose, N.K., 1975: *The Structure of Hindu Society*, New Delhi.

Bose, Shib Cunder, 1883: *The Hindoos as They Are*, Calcutta.

Bushby, H.J., 1855: *Widow Burning*, London.

Chattopadhyay, Gautam, ed., 1978: *Bengal: Early Nineteenth Century. Selected Documents*, Calcutta.

Cohn, Bernard S., 1968: "Notes on the History of the Study of Indian Society and Culture", in: Milton Singer & Bernard S. Cohn, eds., *Structure and Change in Indian Society*, Chicago 1968.

Colebrooke, H.T., 1837: "On the Duties of the Faithful Hindu Widow" in: H.T. Colebrooke, *Miscellaneous Essays*, London, vol. 1.

Coomaraswamy, Ananda K., 1956: *The Dance of Shiva*, Bombay.

Crawfurd, John, (1838) 1971: "A Sketch of the Commercial Resources and Monetary and Mercantile System of British India with Suggestions for their Improvements by Means of Banking Establishments", in: K.N. Chaudhuri, ed., *The Economic Development of India Under the East India Company*, Cambridge, 1971.

Das Gupta, Ajit, 1972: "Study of the Historical Demography of India", in: D.V. Glass & R. Revelle, eds., *Population and Social Change,* London 1972.

Datta, Kalikinkar, 1936: *Education and Social Amelioration of Women in Pre-Mutiny India*, Patna.

Datta, Kalinikar, 1961: *Survey of India's Social Life and Economic Conditions in the Eighteenth Century (1707-1813)*, Calcutta.

Dumont, Louis, 1970: *Homo Hierarchicus*, London.

Hunter, W.W., 1875-77: *Statistical Account of Bengal*, vol. I-XX, London.

78

Johns, William, 1816: *A Collection of Facts and Opinions Relative to the Burning of Widows*, Birmingham.

Kane, P.V., 1941: *History of Dharmasastra*, vol. II, pt. 1, Poona.

Majumdar, R.C., ed., 1971: *The History of Bengal*, vol. 1, Delhi.

Martin, Montgomery, ed., 1838: *The History, Antiquities, Topography, and Statistics of Eastern India*, London.

Misra, B.B., 1961: *The Indian Middle Class*, London.

Mukhopadhyay, Amitabha, 1957: "Sati as a Social Institution in Bengal", *Bengal Past and Present* 76.

Pedersen, Poul, 1984: "Hamlet og enkebrænding", *Antropologiska Studier*, 35-36.

Peggs, J., 1828: *Suttee's Cry to Britain*, London.

Potts, Daniel, 1967: *British Baptist Missionaries in India 1793-1837*, Cambridge.

Seed, Geoffrey, 1955: "The Abolition of Suttee in Bengal", *History*, October.

Sharma, Arvind, 1976: "Suttee: A Study in Western Reactions", *Journal of Indian History* 54.

Sinha, Pradip, 1965: *Nineteenth Century Bengal*, Calcutta.

Srinivas, M.N., 1956: "A Note on Sanskritization and Westernization", *The Far Eastern Quarterly* 15.

Tambiah, S.J., 1973: "Dowry and Bridewealth, and the Property of Women", in: Jack Goody & S.J. Tambiah, *Bridewealth and Dowry*, Cambridge, 1973.

Thompson, Edward, 1928: *Suttee*, London.

Ward, W., 1817: *A View of the Literature and Religion of the Hindoos*, vol. II, London.

Winternitz, M., 1920: *Die Frau in den indischen Religionen*, Leipzig.

# Inventing Religious Tradition:
# *Yagnas* and Hindu Renewal in Trinidad

*By Steven Vertovec*

In *The Invention of Tradition*, an admirable book edited by Hobs-bawm & Ranger (1983), there appear a number of important examples of how ideologies and socio-cultural practices have been formulated and institutionalized among certain groups or nations in order to "use history as a legitimator of action and cement of group cohesion" (Hobsbawm 1983, 12). The title of the book is explained as follows:

'Inventing Tradition' is taken to mean a set of practices, normally governed by overtly or tacitly accepted rules and of a ritual or symbolic nature, which seek to inculcate certain values and norms of behavior by repetition, which automatically implies continuity with the past. In fact, where possible, they normally attempt to establish continuity with a suitable past (1).
Inventing traditions...is essentially a process of formalization and rituali-zation, characterized by reference to the past, if only by imposing repetition (4).

The articles in the book demonstrate this process: Welsh and Scottish Highland traditions, aspects of the British monarchy, and colonialism in Africa and India are shown to have been created to legitimate so-cial systems and to consolidate social groups by creatively making reference to the past. Surprisingly, examples of "invented religious tradition" are scarcely mentioned in the book, though such a process is doubtless widespread around the world and throughout the history of religions. Many facets involved in the institutionalization of cha-risma, which Weber (1963, 1968) analyzes, can be described as making use of "invented religious tradition". Further, the "cargo cults", "nativistic endeavors", or "revitalization movements" studied by anthropologists are perhaps the best examples of how new religious beliefs and activities can become ritualized through repetition along with the invocation of the historical - or mythical - past (see Linton

1943, Aberle 1962, Worsley 1968). Doubtless many forms of sectarian fission or religious revival have contained elements of "invented tradition" as well.

It is particularly among religious minorities in contexts of rapid social change where the "invention of religious tradition" is likely to occur. Religious groups, who are perceived by others as socially or morally inferior and who also perceive themselves to be socially or materially deprived, may experience high degrees of stress and disorganization particularly during periods of social and economic change (cf. Wallace 1956). Increased secularization and communal fragmentation can occur, or, alternatively, some form of renewal can bolster communal sentiments and religious fervor. Local historical circumstances, structural characteristics of the wider society, and the role of dynamic individuals are foremost among the factors which can come into play in conditioning the course of religious minorities in such situations.

The following description of some modern developments among Hindus in Trinidad, West Indies, shows this kind of process at work. There, a recently created repertoire of religious practices collectively known as *yagnas* have contributed dramatically to religious renewal among Hindus. Fifteen to twenty years ago, Hindus in Trinidad claimed to have experienced a demise in group religiosity which accompanied their generally poor economic and political condition of the time; this situation was followed by a period of tremendous socioeconomic change. Subsequently, a "Hindu renaissance" has occurred and *yagnas* are perhaps its most central institution. Yet the current range and practices of *yagnas* were not in evidence in the island fifteen years ago. Among Hindus in Trinidad, an "invented religious tradition" has contributed to renewing the community's religious commitment and activity.

## Hinduism in Trinidad: Socio-religious Ebb and Flow

Hindus have lived in Trinidad for over one hundred and forty years. After the abolition of slavery in the West Indies (1834-1838), sugar planters sought reliable reservoirs of cheap labour. They tried schemes to import Chinese, Madeiran, and Portuguese, and freed African workers, but none of the schemes proved successful. But in 1845 the planters of Trinidad, together with British colonial administrators, initiated a system for recruiting labourers in India and transporting them to the island to serve five-year contracts of indenture.[1] The bulk of indentured labourers to Trinidad came from a vast area within the

Gangetic plain, from Calcutta to the Punjab, with a lesser number from the vicinity surrounding Madras in South India. The greatest number of migrants from any single area were from what is now eastern Uttar Pradesh and Bihar. Between 1845-1917, over 143,000 Indians came to Trinidad and laboured on colonial plantations. After the expiration of their contracts of indenture, more than three-quarters of these migrants chose to stay on the island, continuing to labour on the estates, acquiring land of their own, and gradually becoming the backbone of Trinidad's sugar industry. Numerically, they have grown to comprise over 40% of Trinidad's current population of some 1.25 million (alongside 40% people of African descent, 16% people of racially mixed descent, and 4% Whites, Chinese, and Others).

Social and cultural practices of Hindus in Trinidad have been fundamentally transformed through their experience in diaspora (cf. Vertovec 1987). This transformation includes: the creation of an Indian *lingua franca* by means of an amalgamation of numerous linguistic forms (based on Bhojpuri Hindi), the attenuation of the caste system due to, among other things, the inability to recreate local caste hierarchies among the diverse array of Indian migrants (such that today only the extreme categories of Brahman and Chamar continue to be of any real social significance), and the "homogenization" of religious beliefs and practices through the creation of a single, orthodox set of beliefs and practices out of the heterogeneous set brought by villagers from throughout India. This has produced an essentially Vaishnavite, Puranic, congregational and *bhakti*-centred religion which is formally and centrally organized (see Vertovec 1989; see also Niehoff & Niehoff 1960 and Klass 1961).

Hindu religious activity in Trinidad has ebbed and flowed within varying social and historical circumstances. In the 1930's, fierce debates between Arya Samaj (Hindu reformist) missionaries from India and local representatives of Sanatan Dharma (the consolidated and homogenized form of Hinduism in Trinidad) led to a heightening of religious consciousness and the rise of concerted efforts to organize and promote Hindu culture (Forbes 1984, 1987). The dynamism stemming from this internal conflict coincided with attempts by Hindu leaders to gain legal recognition of Hindu marriages, efforts which proved successful in 1946. Following the independence of India, the first "Hindu renaissance" occurred in Trinidad as Hindu cultural traditions of all kinds were celebrated. Significantly, a single national Hindu organization was founded in the early 1950's. This organization, the Sanatan Dharma Maha Sabha, rapidly put to work a programme of constructing Hindu temples and schools. Moreover, the

Maha Sabha became practically indistinguishable, in leadership and goals, from the nascent People's Democratic Party (later to become the Democratic Labour Party). Hinduism in Trinidad became inherently politicized.

Since their introduction to Trinidad, Hindus have been relegated to the lowest position in the island's social hierarchy (Braithwaite 1953, Crowley 1957, Malik 1971). Their seemingly alien cultural ways, religion, and language - together with their relatively isolated rural settlement and agricultural livelihoods - helped bring about the low status attribution by urban Africans and elite whites. Such a hierarchy served to create Trinidad's notorious pattern of racial politics, pitting an African-dominated party against a mostly Hindu Indian one; this pattern characterized the island from the mid-1950's, through its independence in 1962, and up until recent years (see Ryan 1972). Hindu communal sentiments were inextricably linked with their party's political plight.

Most Hindus in Trinidad today see the 1960's as a period of social, political, and religious collapse within their community. During this time, the African-dominated political party obtained virtually complete power, and the Indian-backed party gradually suffered demise. Dire economic conditions were felt most by the rural Hindus. The Maha Sabha came under grassroots criticism for being overly Brahmanic and corrupt. Hindu religious activity diminished while fundamentalist Christian evangelicals made serious incursions into the Hindu community, converting numerous individuals who were finding little strength in their own traditions.

Beginning in 1973, however, Trinidad experienced an unprecedented economic shift which would have important consequences for the Hindu community. Trinidad has been a modest oil producer since the turn of the century, but this never significantly advanced the island's development. Yet, with the quadrupling of world oil prices by OPEC in 1973-74, Trinidad's oil brought the small island a sudden injection of wealth. Through spinoff industries like construction and transport, even rural villagers gained considerable financial benefits almost overnight (see Vertovec 1990). Interestingly, new socio-religious forms among Hindus were facilitated by the economic influx.

Hinduism in Trinidad - like in India - has always been essentially a family-based religion in terms of most rites, and an individually-based one in terms of devotion to a particular deity (*ishtdevata*). The chief religious event in the family's routine was an annual, three day set of rites: Hanuman *rot puja*, Satya narayan *katha*, and Suruj narayan *puja* (each consisting of a standardized set of offerings to the specific deities). Occasionally, families would host the fortnightly or monthly *Ramayan satsang* (gathering of family and friends to recite the Ramayana) which rotated among households in their immediate vicinity in the village. Little else was sponsored by individuals and their families, aside from infrequent rites of passage for family members.

The mid-1970's saw a great proliferation of religious events which were organized and financed by individuals throughout the village. Cane farmers, truck drivers, shop owners, and work crew supervisors were foremost among those who began to host elaborate ritual functions to which extended kin and fellow villagers were invited. Much of their newfound wealth was poured into Hindu religious activity at the same time it was invested in tractors, taxis, and TVs. For some, it must be said, sponsoring large sets of rites, with accompanying decorations and feasts, was primarily a show of affluence: by hosting an elaborate religious event, certain individuals hoped to gain secular prestige more than spiritual merit. But for many, hosting a *yagna*, series of *pujas*, or *satsang* has become a genuine form of devotion. "You mus' do it wit' a free mind", says one *yagna* sponsor, "for no special gain". "I sacrifice myself", says another, who purposely keeps no financial account of the enormous expenses extended for the seven-day celebration. He is not concerned with the amount he spends, and declares, "Ya not bargainin' wit' God, you know".

*Yagnas* are perhaps the single most important socio-religious institution in Trinidad Hinduism today, for they are the most common congregational activity where a sense of communality is bolstered at the same time an ethical and devotional message is promulgated.

## *Yagnas:* Social Organization and Ritual Practice

Since the turn of the century, at least, the week-long series of *pujas* and readings from the *Bhagavata Purana*, an institution colloquially known as the *Bhagwat*, has been a key public event among Hindus in rural Trinidad.[2] Now the *Bhagwat* is classed by pundits as one type of *yagna*[3] (or *yagya* or *jag*, a large-scale sacrificial rite), but in earlier years was the only religious celebration of its kind. (Klass never came upon the term *yagna* during his fieldwork in the late 1950's; personal communication). *Bhagwats* were group-sponsored (*panchaiti*), involved little preparation or decoration, were publicized by word of mouth, and provided little food - usually only *prasad* (food offerings to deities). Now, the basic structure of *Bhagwat*-like institutions (week-

long series of *pujas*, scripture readings, music, *prasad*) has been maintained under a general rubric of *yagna*, while the nature of sponsor-
ship, organization, texts, setting, and scale of these practices have all
changed dramatically.

The first modification or addition to the category was the *Ramayan yagna*. Its roots can be traced to the *Ramayan satsang* in which
all individuals sang *dohas* (verses) and *chowpais* (stanzas) of Tulsidas'
epic, while accompanying themselves with small cymbals. It was a
fundamental transformation of this *satsang* itself which eventually led
to the institutionalization of *Ramayan yagnas*. With the growing popularity of Hindi film music in Trinidad through the 1950's - thanks to
a famous contemporary radio programme and an increase in the number of Indian cinemas - the music and instrumental techniques then
used in many social and religious contexts changed rapidly. Professional recordings of devotional songs became more accessible at this
time also, leading to the growth of various, so-called "classical", types
of music. *Durpat, ghazal, turi, tilana*, and other South Asian styles
were heard increasingly throughout the island at a variety of religious
occasions. *Ramayan satsangs* were no exception to the ongoing transformation of religious music, a shift from one long-standing style of
rendering the *dohas* and *chowpais* (with a rigorous beat, communal
singing with cymbals) to another, more "modern", style resembling
"classical" songs or Hindi film music (played with a melodious
rhythm, a central singer with musicians playing *dholak* drum, har-
monium, *majira* cymbals and *dhantal* percussion piece).

The new style of singing the *Ramayana* became so popular that
by the 1960's it altogether replaced the former style of domestic
*satsang*. Also, whereas prevously the participants sang the text continuously from beginning to end, the modified *Ramayan satsang* provided pauses for a lay leader to interpret the scripture (usually in
English). Such an addition facilitated greater understanding among
younger, third and fourth generation Hindus, most of whom possessed
few Hindi language skills. This innovative and popular "musical
*Ramayan*" inspired a few local temple groups to promote a new
*Ramayan yagna*, to be conceived as a kind of extended *satsang*. A
temple in southern Trinidad boasts the first *Ramayan yagna* on the
island in 1963; members claim over 1000 people were in attendance
through each of its seven days, flocking to witness the novel event.
Until the 1970's *Bhagwats* remained the predominant type of *yagna*,
but *panchaiti Ramayan yagnas* (organized and sponsored like the
former by local communities) gradually gained in frequency.

This opened the door for further innovations. In some places

*(Bhagavad) Gita yagnas* were performed in the mid-1960's, as were *Devi yagnas* for *Nav ratri*. Neither of these types, however, became regular events in Trinidad villages.

The 1970's saw the creation of a number of new *yagna* types, and their frequency multiplied significantly as well. But instead of being community-sponsored, individuals - with their newly obtained wealth - came to donate nearly all of the several thousand dollars needed to hold a *yagna*. Sponsors literally spared no cost in making their *yagna* the most ornate, with the best food, best *bhajan* (devotional hymn) group, best pundit, and "best vibration". Moreover, in attempting to ensure a unique and well-attended event, some individuals organized *yagnas* with reading of less familiar texts. Regardless of type, an essential structure dominated each *yagnas*.

All *yagnas* in Trinidad are of at least seven days' duration. Some *Bhagwats* can be fourteen days long, if the sponsor has the means to maintain such a marathon celebration. Calendrically-fixed *yagnas* vary in length depending on the occasion.[4] Each night a *puja* must be conducted, a text recited and interpreted, *hawan* (fire oblation) and *arti* (homage by waving light) performed, *prasad* distributed, and a feast supplied. In *Bhagwat yagnas*, this must be done three times each day, thus considerably adding to the expense. *Bhajan* singing by a group of musicians occurs before, intermittently during, and after the recitation and *hawan*; the musicians also accompany the presiding pundit (honorifically called the *vyas*, after Vyasadeva, a legendary sage and purported compiler of the *Puranas*) during his sung recitation. They also play specific songs for *arti*, depending on the main deity worshipped. Usually on a particular night during any *yagna*, a special *puja* is performed relative to the type of *yagna* event (see Table). *Yagnas* may also be scheduled to coincide with a certain holy day (especially *jyanam ashtami* or the birth of Krishna with *Bhagwats*, *Ram navami* or the birth of Rama with *Ramayan yagnas*, *Maha Shivratri* or "the great night of Shiva" with *Shiv Puran yagnas*, and *Durga ashtami* or the birth of Durga with *Devi yagnas*).

The individuals who have sponsored *yagnas* are men who acquired fairly large amounts of capital during the years of national economic prosperity. Most held their *yagnas* with the expressed purpose of religious praise and devotion, though a few did so in fulfillment of some promise made to a deity, or to seek some personal boon. In either case, the ideal goal is to host *yagnas* for three to five years consecutively, although the richest seek to make it an annual event.

The amount of organization required to stage a seven-day *yagna* is enormous, and worth detailing to indicate important social aspects

## *Yagnas* and Associated Features

| Type | Focus of Worship | Special Rite |
|------|------------------|--------------|
| Bhagwat | Krishna | Gobardhan puja |
| Ramayan | Rama | Rameshwar puja |
| Shiv Puran | Shiva | Shiva puja |
| Gita | Krishna | Gobardhan puja |
| Devi or Durga | (Divine Mother) | Shakti puja |
| Garud Puran | (ancestors) | pitra puja |
| Vedic | (One God) | homa (hawan) |
| Kabir | (Sat Guru) | chowka |
| Ganesh | Ganesha | Ganesha puja |
| Sai Charitr | Sai Baba | (none) |
| Mahabharata | Krishna | (unknown) |

of such undertakings. The essential tasks to accomplish, regardless of *yagna* type, are as follows:

(1) Some three to six months prior to a proposed *yagna*, the sponsor must first choose and contact a pundit to act as *vyas*. Quite often an individual chooses his (or his wife's or children's) *guru* or "godfather" to fulfill this role. The same *vyas* pundit may serve year after year, or the sponsor may wish to obtain a different one each year in order to receive a variety of styles and discourses (many people complain that certain pundits say the same thing whenever they serve as a *vyas*). Also, *vyas* pundits are often chosen because of their humorous anecdotes, unique religious knowledge, renowned singing voice, or simply because they arrive with their own group of musicians (saving the sponsor extra organizational effort). They are almost invariably Brahmans (while pundits who perform ordinary family *pujas* may often be non-Brahmans). Once contacted, the pundit must consult his diary.[5] More importantly, he must consult the *patra* (astrological almanac) to make sure the proposed *yagna* dates are auspicious.[6] Once the dates are set with the *vyas* pundit, further organizational measures can proceed.

(2) Usually around three months prior to the *yagna*, the sponsor and his family begin to "fast". In Trinidad, where vegetarianism is not

a norm for Hindus, this means abstinence from alcohol and flesh (chicken, goat, and pork; beef is never eaten). Sex is ideally (but not always successfully) avoided as part of this fast. The essential idea is to "make oneself clean". This is done prior to any *puja* as well. Such abstinence indicates one of the few vestiges of the personal dimension of the purity-pollution complex so pervasive in India. An essential requirement of this preparation is to consume *satwic* food (such as fruit, nuts, and unspicy vegetables), referring to the purest and most subtle of the three *gunas* (forms of energy). No specific length of duration is actually set or agreed upon: some say fasts prior to *yagnas* should be for three months, some say sixty days, others say forty days. The point is that fasting is considered an act essential to prepare oneself to undertake a *yagna*. One must purify oneself physically and mentally, one sponsor stresses, "to get de real salvation an' de right t'ing" from the *yagna*.

(3) At least one month before the *yagna*, publicity is arranged. The rapid modernization of Hindu social institutions is evident here. Personal invitations are printed and delivered by car, while handbills announcing the *yagna* have become perhaps the most common form of Hindu ephemera. These are usually deposited at most local shops throughout the area. Moreover, announcements are submitted to national newspapers, to Indian radio shows, and to television programmes. Thus massive audiences are sought for any *yagna*. The actual attendance is drawn most of all (50% or more) from the host's village, then from adjacent areas (30-40%), with the balance from a wider region of the island. The notification of, and attendance by, people from areas outside the immediate vicinity not only tends to create new external networks but also act to establish a sense of communality in Hinduism more than in the past, when all activity was familial or local. Village Hindus presently know what religious activity is taking place within the region, know exactly what is going to happen there, and know that they can attend at any time and be treated as welcome guests.

(4) Within three to five weeks of the *yagna*, the sponsor must arrange for the performance of *bhajan* groups (four to ten musicians and singers of religious songs). The same group may be present throughout the week, but the ideal is to have a different group each night to provide a greater array of entertainment. Often, upon hearing of a forthcoming *yagna* through advance publicity, it is the *bhajan* group which contacts the sponsor, seeking to perform at his event. They will receive some pay (usually TT$50-$100),[7] but it is the chance to play and sing itself which motivates them. The last night

of any *yagna* is the engagement sought by most groups for, it is when the largest numbers (500 up to 1000 persons) are in attendance, and the post-ritual singing can last until the small hours of the morning. Also, sponsors often invite well-known "classical" Indian singers, whose inclusion can add considerable prestige to the event.

(5) One week before the *yagna*, a large enclosure in which to hold the ceremonies must be constructed adjacent to the sponsor's home. A group of men (usually sons, extended kin, and close neighbours) cut a large quantity of bamboo from the forest and transport it to the site. There, it is trimmed and lashed or nailed together to form a large structure surrounding the base of the house (most village houses are on poles; thus the area beneath the sponsor's home becomes part of the *yagna* setting). Galvanized corrugated iron is rented and attached to the bamboo frame to form a roof and walls. Inside, then, a centrally located *sinhasan* or raised stand is constructed for the *vyas* pundit, where he will sit cross-legged to deliver his recitation. To the side, a platform is built which will be occupied by the *bhajan* groups at night and by sleeping *sadhus*, or holy men, during the day (the latter often stay at the site for the entire duration of the *yagna*).

(6) The inside of the structure is decorated soon after being constructed. Wall-sized paintings of deities are rented and placed around the inside. Lengths of paper cuttings are bought or rented, to be hung in rows from the ceiling, thereby creating a very colourful and festive effect. (Sometimes the purchased paper decorations include shiny Christmas tree shapes and other Christmas ornaments!). Flashing lights are often mounted around the *sinhasan*. Immediately in front of this stand, a *vedi* (floor-level altar) is set-off by small railings and a white awning with dangling mango leaves; it is an area which will be considered sacred space once the *yagna* commences. For the most traditional sponsors, the *vedi* itself (its structure, designs, and ritual trappings) must be created by a member of the Nao or barber caste. However, significantly, the greater trend is to have any creative person fulfill this role, for which they are simply given the title of "the Nao". A special *hawan* pit is dug to the north of the *vedi*, while a triangular box is built to the east to house the *chowsat yogani* or sixty-four powers (these are two adjuncts to the *vedi* which are only found in *yagnas*). The Nao must remain for the entire duration of the *yagna*, each day cleaning and preparing the altar and general *vedi* area.

(7) Within a few days of the *yagna*, hundreds of chairs are rented and delivered to the site. Long tables and benches for feeding large numbers of people are also borrowed or rented, as are huge pots for

cooking. Portable gas stoves and gas must be obtained, and sometimes *chulhas* or earthen, wood-burning stoves are constructed. It the latter are used, a great deal of wood must be procured to provide sufficient fuel for the massive quantities of food to be freshly cooked each day. Loudspeakers, microphones, and amplifiers are rented too, and arrangements are often made with professional companies to videotape the forthcoming proceedings. Large tanks of water must be filled for cooking, drinking, and washing; in the dry season, water may take a good deal of effort to find and transport.

(8) All materials necessary for daily *puja* are obtained within a day or two of the event, including huge amounts of ingredients for *prasad* distributed after any Hindu rite. A small quantity of this is always offered in *puja*, then mixed-in with the larger mass, bagged, and distributed so that all who receive it gain the blessing of the food offering. While an entertaining and charismatic *vyas* and a talented *bhajan* group are commonly recognized as important features, another primary criterion for judging the success or popularity af any *yagna* is whether the food served each night is considered very good. Obtaining enough food to feed several hundred people each night for seven days is another necessary task to accomplish in organizing any *yagna*. An open credit account is normally established with some local grocer, which allows needed ingredients to be purchased at the last minute, as well as in advance. Donations of food are regularly made by kin and neighbours, sometimes well into the *yagna* week; many food items (such as rice and potatoes) can be returned to the grocery following the *yagna*, if donations have offset the amount originally purchased. Several hundred large banana leaves, from which individuals eat the feast with their hands, must be cut from the nearby forest on a daily basis throughout the *yanga* week. If these are not fresh or not available, it means many participants will go without eating - a worrisome prospect for any *yagna* sponsor!

Throughout the course of the *yagna*, many things need to be monitored or restocked. Foodstuffs, *prasad* ingredients and the small paper bags for its distribution, water parts for the lighting and sound systems, *puja* offerings, fuel, and other items must be checked and possibly replenished at a moment's notice. Labour, as well as paraphernalia, need to be managed effectively to maintain a smooth event. Of course, the sponsor and his immediate family cannot fulfill all of these organizational and managerial tasks, although they are always at the core of the supervision. A reliable network of extended kin (most of whom, on the husband's side, reside nearby) and neighbours has to be called upon to furnish help at all stages. The requirements for setting-up and carrying-out a *yagna* are now known well enough to most village Hindus that they can undertake the necessary tasks without much instruction. Many men know how to fell bamboo and build a tent; by the age of ten or so, boys know where to obtain leaves for plates and how to lash them together for carrying; small girls gather bunches of flowers and all women, young or old, know how to cook for huge numbers (morever, *yagnas* and weddings represent perhaps the only two social occasions on any scale in which men also help in the kitchen). All volunteers, whether kin or friends, believe they will derive benefits from lending such assistance: reciprocal aid will be one certain function, but spiritual merit is believed to accrue, too. Rather than merely aiding a sponsor and gaining his favours, one young helper comments, "It's God's work - He go bless me".

On the first day of the *yagna*, the kitchen bustles with activity throughout the morning and afternoon. It is a makeshift setting, a place under the tent in a far corner from the *sinhasan* and *vedi* area. Food preparation must be well timed so that all items are ready before the early evening, when the *yagna* will get under way. In the main area, young men set up hundreds of chairs in rows and make final adjustments to the lighting and sound systems. A stereo tapedeck is usually plugged into the loudspeakers, so that Hindi film music or tapes of professional *bhajan* singers can be played loudly all day. The mood among all the ten to fifteen helpers at this point is jovial, and they joke or play tricks on each other while making their more serious preparations.

During the day, a few participants begin to arrive, particularly relatives from other parts of the island (usually these are the host's affines, owing to norms of village exogamy). Other early arrivals may be *sadhus* from within the village and region.[8] In the late afternoon, the *vyas* pundit arrives. He is greeting with much veneration, and tradition-minded hosts will wash his feet and receive his blessing. The pundit who is to perform the *puja* each day also eventually comes, and although he is greeted with honour, it is not on the same scale as that accorded to the *vyas*. The pundits inspect the setting and arrangements, and casual conversation with the sponsor and his family ensues until the rites begin.

By 6:30 p.m., the *puja* (ritual offerings to deities) segment of the *yagna* begins. The sponsor and his family sit around the *vedi*, males dressed in white *dhotis* (loincloths) and *kurtas* (shirts), women in their best *saris* (wrapped dresses). While one pundit conducts the rite, the *vyas* eventually takes his place on the *sinhasan* and silently begins to prepare his discourse. On the first night of any *yagna*, the *puja* takes somewhat longer than usual since specific ritual items, which will be used the entire week, must first be "installed" and venerated: these include nine small flags on the *vedi* for the *Nawgra deotas* (nine planetary deities), sixty-four small flags in the triangular structure next to the *vedi* for the *chowsat yogani*,[9] *Jhandi* raised outside the tent, and certain symbolic articles relative to the type of *yagna* undertaken (including a coconut for *Durga devi yagnas*, *murti* (image) of Ganesha for *Ganesh jyanti yagnas*, *Shiva linga* for *Shiv puran yagnas*, and a model of Mount Goberdhan for *Bhagwat yagnas*).

Few people are in attendance during the early phases of *puja* on any night. As participants gradually arrive, they pay little attention to the *puja*, preferring instead to greet friends, look at the decorations, and chat. Men, women, and children immediately segregate themselves upon arrival, and usually stay separate throughout the course of the night. Young men most often stand by the door or just outside, acting "cool" and watching girls. Older men joke with each other in Hindi, occasionally going outside for a smoke. Children are remarkably well behaved: though acting silly in their little groups, they rarely have to be reprimanded by adults. Young single women gossip in sets of three or four (very aware of the watchful eyes of the young men). It is only the older women, most wearing their *oronhis* (white head veils), who tend to become absorbed in the ongoing religious rites. The *bhajan* group also arrives at some undetermined point, unpacking their instruments, tightening their *dholak* drums, and arranging their microphones. While the sponsor and his family concentrate on spiritual devotion, they are surrounded by the loud murmur of pleasant social activity.

On most nights, the *puja* is finished by 8:00 p.m., by which time the tent is almost overflowing with hundreds of people. The final *arti* of the *puja* is performed, then, while all in attendance stand and the *bhajan* group plays the requisite song. The *vyas* follows immediately with an invocation in Hindi, sings a *mantra* or prayer in which all join in,[10] and always finishes with a series of calls in Hindi to praise various deities (or *sanatan dharma* itself): to each call, the entire congregation responds with a collective shout of *"jai!"* ("victory!").

The *vyas* gives a welcome in English and asks the musicians to begin with a few *bhajans*. He then commences his Puranic recitation: singing a few lines of the given text, pausing to elaborate in Hindi, then interpreting and digressing in English.[11] Some sermons address concepts like *dharma* and *karma* and their play in everyday life. Far more often, however, the lesson concerns devotion to God (*bhakti*) and right behaviour towards fellow humans. Stories from the Puranas and other Hindu lore tell of certain mythical characters whose actions are meant to be exemplary. The sacred tales also legitimize present forms of practice: one *vyas* described a *yagna* held by an ancient king and attended by gods, where all the characters built a tent, did *puja*, listened to sacred texts, and ate a communal meal, "just like in Trinidad". Most *vyas* pundits are also sure to lace their sermons with humorous stories or "present-day examples", often concerning relationships between husband and wife or mother-in-law and daughter-in-law. To these, there is a response of loud laughter. A good *vyas* can hold the crisp attention of all for well over an hour and a half, including the casual young men who stand at the back or just outside the tent. Periodically, throughout his readings and interpretations, the *vyas* will call on the musicians to render more *bhajans*.

By 9:30 or 10:00 p.m., the *vyas* end his discourse. A final *hawan* and *arti* are performed by the sponsor and his family, who have remained seated in the *vedi* area throughout the evening. Again, all in attendance stand for the *arti*, and the *vyas* closes proceedings with a *mantra* and series or calls for praise, to each of which the response *"jai!"* is shouted by the crowd. Participants are asked to remain in their seats while children come around to all with *chandan* and *bhabut* (sandalwood paste and *hawan* ashes to anoint the forehead), perfume and sweet milk, and a tray with oil lamp and flowers (onto which individuals may make cash donations, or simply make a gesture of collecting the *arti* fumes on their hands and transferring them to their heads). Young men distribute bags of *prasad*, and all are invited to eat their fill at the long tables in the rear of the tent. It is the young men who delight in dishing-out the food, for they use the role to flirt with the young girls.[12] People gradually leave after eating and further chatting, though by midnight there are still perhaps two score remaining (even more so on the final night).

Each day, this process is repeated, from the first set of kitchen tasks in the morning to the last few *bhajans* at night. The food and flower offerings made at each night's *pujas* are collected and kept until the day after the *yagna's* close, when they are taken to a river or the sea and respectfully laid in and allowed to float away (a simultaneous offering to the goddess of waters, Ganga mata, and a conceived dissipation of elements back to the cosmos). The dismantling of the tent, decorations, *sinhasan*, and so on must be organized and carried out by a set of volunteers (often harder to assemble than in the stage of preparation). Borrowed and rented items are returned, and the credit accumulated at the grocery store is tabulated and settled. Many of the hosts will continue to fast for about a week; otherwise, within a day or two, life is back to normal for the sponsor, his family, and the village.

Over the week, the *yagna* will have cost from TT$6000-$8000. This may include TT$1000 for the *vyas* pundit alone, TT$400 for the *puja* pundit, TT$150 each night simply for the *prasad*, up to TT$400 for vegetables, flour, and other food items, TT$100 for lighting and sound equipment, TT$200 for chair rental, and perhaps TT$400 in offerings to *sadhus*, visiting pundits, and the local needy. But again, the sponsors, donors, and volunteers believe their investments of time, money, and effort are well worth it. For them - and the participants as well - *yagnas* represent "somet'in' to be proud of, somet'in' to preserve", "unity", "education", and a will to create "a devotional-type vibration", "a nice li'l *shakti* (energy)", and a revived "sense of community". The process of the proliferation and elaboration of *yagnas* since the mid-1970's has brought together people in a variety of ways, all deemed by Hindus as positive benefits for the perpetuation of their religious tradition and the strengthening of their religious identity.

A deep economic recession has troubled Trinidad since around 1982, when world oil prices tumbled. Hindu villages have come to feel the downturn severely: not only have extra-village jobs become few, but the long-ignored agricultural base now provides little financial input. None the less, the current "Hindu renaissance", begun in the mid-1970's with the aid of institutions like *yagnas*, has continued with a strong momentum. *Yagnas* are less frequently sponsored by individuals, but local groups of all kinds now engage in fund raising activities in order to conduct these events.

So central have the rites become, that young Hindus in Trinidad do not realize that *yagnas* are a recent creation within their religious corpus. Older Hindus attest to the contemporary inception of *yagnas* (noting both its similarity to and difference from earlier *Bhagwats*), but they believe it is essentially a welcome return to a religious form expounded by sacred scripture and long practiced in India. In their sermons, pundits themselves declare that such an institution is Hinduism's proper mode of worship. A technical legitimation for *yagnas* is ultimately of little concern for Trinidad Hindus. Its significant role in the renewal of Hindu religiosity on the island is cause enough for its widespread acceptance.

## Conclusion

Invented religious traditions are not "less authentic" religious phenomena than traditions proved to be extant through centuries. The fact
that adherents attest to an unbroken link between current practices
and those of ancient times provides all the legitimation that is necessary to place the former on an equal par. The importance of recently
institutionalized orientations and activities is further strengthened when
they are amalgamated with longstanding beliefs and activities (such as
*hawan, puja*, and *arti* in the Trinidad *yagna*). Socio-religious innovation is the heart of religious renewal: new rites, new relationships,
new perspectives are produced to stimulate a community towards engaging in spiritually and socially rewarding action. Through the
process of the "invention of tradition", the new is utilized for the sake
of, or in the name of, the old. This separates the category of religious
renewal from that of new religious movements, in which a radical
break with the old is called for (examples of sectarianism may contain
elements of both citing and condemning the old in the name of the
new). Any study of religious movements or religious change must
bear in mind such ways in which historical patterns of belief and
practice are used, broken with, invoked, and invented.

## Notes

1.  This method of gaining a workforce had been maintained by sugar
    planters in Mauritius since 1834 and in British Guiana since 1838; the
    indenture system would later bring Indians to other Caribbean colonies,
    Natal, and Fiji.
2.  Angrosino (1983, 380) thoroughly misreads Klass (1961, 173) to claim
    that Bhagwats in Trinidad require animal sacrifice to Kali. The two
    practices are associated in no way.
3.  In the early Vedic religion in India, *yagnas* were the central rituals of
    sacrifice (see Danielou 1964, 64-78). In Trinidad they have taken on a
    meaning of their own, associated wholly with the socio-religious
    activities described in these pages.
4.  *Garud puran yagnas* span the period of *Pitra Paksh*, fourteen days
    devoted to ancestors; *Ganesh jyanti yagnas* take place over eleven days,
    from the birthday of Ganesha to the next full moon (marking the
    beginning of *Pitra Paksh*); and *Devi yagnas* or *Durga yagnas* are
    celebrated over the full nine nights of *Nav ratri* (one such period around
    March, another in October).

5. It should also be noted that many pundits in Trinidad have other full- or part-time occupations, as teachers, insurance brokers, engineers, and so forth; rarely are they manual labourers.

6. Bitter allegations are sometimes made that some pundits interpret the *patra* in relation to their personal diaries: that if the proposed dates conflict with prior engagements, they tell the *jajman* (client) that the planets are in poor aspect (until they actually have an open date, thus ensuring the lucrative *yagna* appointment). This is an allegation made regarding the arrangements for *puja* dates as well.

7. At the time of fieldwork in 1984-'85, TT$2.40 = US$1.00.

8. These are usually retired men who are strict vegetarians and well-versed in sacred lore. In India, most *sadhus* are landless and wandering ascetics, most of whom belong to religious orders. This is not the case in Trinidad. However, here many have been invested with a *kanthi* (cotton cord worn round the neck, bearing a bead of tulsi wood), a Vaishnavite symbol likely stemming from the Ramanandi *panth*. Though living comfortably with their children or grandchildren, Trinidad *sadhus* devote much of their time to attending various ritual functions and are generally well respected throughout the village outside of religious contexts (even by non-Hindus).

9. Most village Hindus are unclear as to what the sixty-four *chowsat yogani* flags actually represent. Some say they are all the planets, referring to the many astrological influences over one's life; other villagers believe they are aspects of *shakti*. Another general idea is that the *chowsat yogani* are symbolic of the entire pantheon of Hindu gods and goddesses, and that the number sixty-four simply represents a more vast number. With this interpretation in mind, one *sadhu* says that the *chowsat yogani* remind people that a *yagna* is "de time to invite all de deities".

10. Among the *mantras* collectively sung at occasions like *yagnas*, the following is almost invariably the first and last, a prayer which in effect frames all collective religious activity:

*Om Twameva Mata Chapita Twameva*
*Twameva Bandhusha Sakha Twameva*
*Twameva Vidya Dravinam Twameva*
*Twameva Sarvam mama Deva Deva*

(Thou art my mother, thou art my father,
Thou art my brother, thou art my my friend,
Thour art my learning, thour art my wealth,
O Lord, thou art all in all)

Each member of the congregation present puts his or her hands together in the manner of prayer or *pranam* (a gesture of respect), and sings this

with their eyes closed. Children, too, know this *mantra* well, and even
the otherwise nonchalant young men outside the door of *yagnas* usually
join in the same manner. The Vedic *Gayatri mantra* is another of the
most frequently used prayers at public functions.

11. Many young people become quite vexed if a *vyas* pundit carries on too
long in Hindi, for they understand little of it (especially with such
textual overtones). Often the technique of the *vyas* is rhetorical: he will
ask a certain question in English (for example, "How did Queen Kaikeyi
persuade King Dasaratha to banish Rama?" or "Why do we need a
banana tree in *puja*?"), for which he provides the answer in Hindi
through a sung verse or proverb. The young find this particularly
irritating, because they often never do eventually get the answer in
English.

12. *Yagnas* are one of the few occasions where young males and females
of the village have the condoned opportunity to meet and flirt. Many
marriages are still arranged on the basis of the couple's original meeting
in this context.

## Bibliography

Aberle, David, 1962: "A Note on Relative Deprivation Theory as Applied
to Millenarian and Other Cult Movements, in 'Millenial Dreams in
Action', Sylvia L. Thrupp (ed.)", *Comparative Studies in Society and
History* Supplement II, 209-214.

Angrosino, M.V., 1983: "Religion among Overseas Indian Communities", in:
Giri Raj Gupta, ed., *Religion in Modern India*, New Delhi, 357-398.

Braithwaite, Lloyd, 1953: *Social Stratification in Trinidad*, Kingston.

Crowley, Daniel, 1957: "Plural and Differential Acculturation", *American
Anthropologist* 59, 817-824.

Danielou, Alain, 1963: *Hindu Polytheism*, London.

Forbes, Richard, 1984: Arya Samaj in Trinidad: An Historical Study of
Hindu Organizational Process in Acculturative Conditions (unpub. Ph.D.
dissertation), University of Miami.

Forbes, Richard, 1987: "Hindu Organizational Process in Acculturative
Conditions: Significance of the Arya Samaj Experience in Trinidad", in:
I.J. Bahadur Singh, ed., *Indians in the Caribbean*, London, 193-216.

Hobsbawm, Eric, 1983: "Introduction: Inventing Traditions" in: Hobsbawn
& Ranger, 1983, 1-14

Hobsbawm, Eric & Terence Ranger, eds., 1983: *The Invention of Tradition*,
Cambridge.

Klass, Morton, 1961: *East Indians in Trinidad*, New York.

Linton, Ralph, 1943: "Nativistic Movements", *American Anthropologist* 45, 230-240.

Malik, Yogendra K., 1971: *East Indians in Trinidad*, London.

Niehoff, Arthur & Juanita Niehoff, 1960: *East Indians in the West Indies*, Milwaukee.

Ryan, Selwyn, 1972: *Race and Nationalism in Trinidad and Tobago*, University of the West Indies, Institute of Social and Economic Research.

Vertovec, Steven, 1987: Hinduism and Social Change in Village Trinidad. (unpublished D.Phil. thesis), University of Oxford.

Vertovec, Steven, 1989: "Hinduism in Diaspora: the Transformation of Tradition in Trinidad", in: G. Sontheimer & H. Kulke, eds., *Hinduism Reconsidered*, Delhi

Vertovec, Steven: "Oil Boom and Recession in Indian Villages", in: C. Clarke, C. Peach & S. Vertovec, eds., *South Asians Overseas: Migration and Ethnicity*, Cambridge, 89-111

Wallace, A.F.C., 1956: "Revitalization Movements", *American Anthropologist* 58, 264-281.

Weber, Max, 1963: *The Sociology of Religion*, Boston.

Weber, Max, 1968: *On Charisma and Institution Building* (Selected Papers edited by S.N. Eisenstadt), Chicago.

Worsley, Peter, 1968: *The Trumpet Shall Sound*, New York.

# The Near East:
# Change Over Time

# Diffusion of the Concept of Al-Qâ'im in the Middle East in Late Antiquity

## By Pieter F. Goedendorp

Tradition and renewal in religious systems as well as in the science of religion are the theme of this volume.[1] This paper will attempt to explain the spread of the so-called 'messianic' title 'the Standing One', appearing in Greek as *ho hestôs*, in Aramaean as *qâ'em*, and in Arabic as *al-qâ'im*. Scholars have supposed the transference of the title *al-Qâ'im al-Mahdî*, used by Shi'ite groups in times past as a designation for their expected saviour, the rightly guided *imâm al-Mahdî*, from a pre-islamic environment. Sources providing information on early Shi'ite factions in the Iraqi province are the primary evidence of this supposed transference. While these sources hardly permit a historic-genetic explanation, the theoretical approaches pass this problem by without further notice. It is the intention of this paper to investigate the theoretical problems of this historical issue.

It has been suggested that the origin of the title *ho hestôs* is to be found in the gnostic system of Simon the Magician in the first century A.D. But there seem to be other examples of its use outside of Simonian gnosticism: we find the title *ho hestôs* in philosophical treatises by Philo of Alexandria and in Samaritan liturgical texts used as an epithet for God. It seems to be an unspoken concensus that the homonyms involved do have synonym meanings in the various contexts where they appear. In other words, the meaning of the Shi'ite title would be dependent on the Simonian gnostic use of the title. This title in turn would be influenced by philosophical speech. The logic behind this conclusion seems to be problematical. I think that there is a better approach to this seemingly simple diffusion of the concept.

In the following, I will present a review of the data and then comment on the explanations which have been given until the present. Then I will introduce some of the theoretical aspects developed in symbolic anthropology, which can be fruitful for the science of religions as well.

## The Historical Phenomenon: The Proto-Shi'ite Title Al-Qâ'im

### The Historical Context

Some decades after the rise of Islam, a greater part of the kingdoms of Late Antiquity had been swept away by the Islamic-Arab forces. Thirty years after the death of Muhammad in 632, Islamic domination extended from the Arabic peninsula to Northern Africa and Egypt in the west and to Khorâsân in the east. The consolidation of the new order resulted in the foundation of new garrison-towns and settlements of Arabic Muslims among native populations. In many places, however, the original inhabitants continued to constitute the major part of the population, and, in this sense, one can speak of a cultural continuity despite the great political upheavals in the area.

Basra and Kûfa were two of the garrison-towns founded in the aftermath of the Arab campaigns. Kûfa was founded in 17 A.H./638 A.D. as a military encampment by units of the Arab army returning from the capture of al-Madâ'in (formerly Seleukia-Ktesiphon). The town's population originally consisted of the Arab warriors and their tribes, but also of *mawâlî*. In the years following the foundation of the town, the non-Arab converts to Islam increasingly determined the economical activities in the town. The *mawâlî*, with their Jewish, Christian, Zoroastrian, or Manichaean backgrounds, were probably bearers of gnostic ideas already circulating in the pre-Islamic period, examples of which we meet in some early Islamic ideas.[2]

In the introduction to his collection of early Islamic gnostic texts, Heinz Halm already noted the part Kûfa's countryside must have played in the spread of gnostic ideas. In the 3rd century A.H./9th century A.D., these 'black lands' (the *sawâd*, the agricultural land north and south of the town on the borders of the Euphrates where the nobles of Kûfa owned their estates) were the first fields of the Ismaili missionaries. Here, their preachers found a willing ear for the gnostic gospel, spread by them from Kûfa. It is important to note that in the communities of the *sawâd*, the Aramaean (Nabataean) language only slowly gave way to the Arabic tongue.[3]

### Ibn al-Hanafîja and the Kaisânites

The first sign of the proto-Shi'ite title of al-Qâ'im is found in al-Hasan ibn Mûsâ an-Naubakhtî in *Kitâb firaq ash-Shî'a* ("The book of the Shi'ite sects"). It is the oldest work preserved which provides description of the factions that existed in the early Shia. An-Naubakhtî was himself from an Imami-Shi'ite background, and he compiled the book sometime before 286 A.H./899 A.D. Hence, it is the earliest of the heresiographical works we now have at our disposal.[4]

Some decades after Muhammad's death, a division occurred among the followers of Islam concerning the legitimate authority. 'Alî, the fourth of the rightly guided caliphs, and Mu'âwija, commander of the Syrian army and a relative of the murdered third caliph 'Utman, were up against each other.[5] The successful assault on 'Alî's life by a Kharijite in a mosque at Kûfa in 40 A.H./661 A.D. brought the control of the entire empire to Mu'âwija. This assault marked the beginning of the Shia as the party of 'Alî in Islam. Within this party, the idea of resistance to Mu'âwija's caliphate was cherished. A number of groups in the party denied the fact of 'Alî's death and expected his return and reinstatement, while others tried to encourage 'Alî's sons to try to seize the caliphate. After Mu'âwija's death that same year, his son Yazid took his place. Inhabitants of Kûfa invited Husain, son of 'Alî, to react and to proclaim his caliphate in their town. Nevertheless, it became apparent that they could not guarantee him their support: on his way to Kûfa, he and most of his company were attacked and killed by Yazid's soldiers in the famous battle of Kerbalâ on the 10th of Muharram 680.

Some years after this unfortunate event, after the death of Yazid in 684, a movement originated, called the *Tawwabun* ("penitents"). During riots against Umajjad authority, the mourning for Husain gave way to the call for revenge and the demand for loyalty. In a number of paragraphs, our heresiograph an-Naubakhtî describes this faction. Mukhtâr ibn Abî 'Ubaid al-Taqafî is held to be the founder of the faction, known as the Kaisânîja.[6] In the words of an-Naubakhtî, Mukhtâr who was "the one who demanded revenge for Husain, son of 'Alî, eventually killed some of his murderers and others, and claimed that Muhammad ibn al-Hanafîja had ordered him to do so".

Mukhtâr claimed to be the representative of 'Alî's son Muhammad ibn al-Hanafîja. He taught his adherents that ibn al-Hanafîja was the proxy (*wasî*) of 'Alî, that he was *imâm*, and finally that he himself was the representative of ibn al-Hanafîja.[7] According to Mukhtâr, this ibn al-Hanafîja was the true *imâm* leading the Shia of 'Alî after Husain's death. Ibn al-Hanafîja seems not to have been involved actively with these political ambitions on his behalf, and he is even said to cautiously have held back from the claims of this Kûfian *shiat 'Alî*.

In 686, Mukhtâr's revolt was suppressed, and following the death of ibn al-Hanafîja in 700, several groups developed in this Kaisânîja, each of them with different opinions with respect to the succession in the position of the imamate. Some assert that ibn al-Hanafîja did not die, but was hiding in the mountains between Mecca and Medina and at some time would rise as the expected *imâm*. Some assert that ibn al-Hanafîja did not assign a successor to his position: after his death there would be no *imâm* until his return as Qâ'im al-Mahdî. Others assert that the imamate was incumbent on his progeny: the Qâ'im al-Mahdî would arise from his kinsmen. Abû Hâshim, in particular, is named as Imâm Qâ'im Mahdî.[8] While according to some groups, the Qâ'im al-Mahdî would originate from the progeny of Muhammad ibn al-Hanafîja. There are others who hold that after the death of al-Hasan ibn 'Alî, there will be no *imâm* until the return of ibn al-Hanafîja, himself being the Qâ'im al-Mahdî.

Information such as this, provided by an-Naubakhtî, concerning ibn al-Hanafîja or one of his progeny as being the Qâ'im al-Mahdî, are among the earliest reports on his adherents. These terms are not accompanied by any explanation regarding their meaning. It seems that a standard expression is introduced here, a set expression about the *imâm* who in the end will distribute justice and equity among his suppressed adherents. The impression of a standard form of speech is confirmed in other places in Naubakhtî's work by the diverging interpretations of the term al-Qâ'im which the author mentions when discussing various proto-shiite sects.[9]

It appears that many different aspects may be connected to being al-Qâ'im. There seems to be an implicit link between being Qâ'im, being Mahdî, and holding the imamate, for the last *imâm* is called *mahdî* ("rightly guided") as well as *Qâ'im*. The imamate is a hereditary function, transferred from father to son through a specific lineage. In the succession to this function, al-Qâ'im is the final one. Opinions diverge in early Shia on the meaning of the word *qâ'im* (see note 9). Both resurrection and insurrection are mentioned, but as an "explanation", the circumscription "that he will revive the earth" is also given. For the rest, the tasks of al-Qâ'im, the bringing of justice and equity, are in the centre of interest.

One final remark should be made concerning the phenomenology of the Qâ'im in this early Islamic context. First, as to his place in the succession of imâms, al-Qâ'im seems to be the last one in their function, at least the last of the "this-worldly" heirs of the Prophet. Naubakhtî mentions the adherents of 'Abd-Allâh ibn Mu'âwîja, confessing that the last *imâm* is al-Qâ'im, who will hand over the authority to a descendant of 'Alî before his death (§73-74). As to the institutional side of the doctrine of al-Qâ'im, the role of the representative must be stressed: the *imâm*, not being there to emphasize his claims, is represented by a *wasî*. The claim to being Qâ'im is laid by his agent, that is, by someone who steps forward out of a group of followers.[10]

The exact meaning of the term al-Qâ'im was not at all clear to the participants in the various groups of the proto-shiite movement. An-Naubakhtî's information does not provide any clues to the origins or introduction of the notions in Islam. It seems that al-Mahdî and al-Qâ'im entered Islamic history as a fixed duo.

## Explaining the Occurrence of the Title Al-Qâ'im in the Early Islamic Context

Now, how is it possible that the title al-Qâ'im ended up being a technical term with so many connotations? Scholars have thought about this, and two lines of argument can be said to be distinguished.

Wladimir Ivanow has to be reckoned among the most prominent authorities on the history of Islam, particularly of the history of the shiite Ismaili-movement. He did not spend much effort on the question we're working on, but he had a clear-cut idea concerning the meaning of the term *al-qâ'im* in Ismailian early shiite contexts. In his "Ismaili Tradition Concerning the Rise of the Fatimids", he interprets the term Qâ'im in the *hadîths* quoted by him as the one of the 'Alîd progeny who *successfully rises in revolt against the present order*.[11] Without going into detail, it can be said that the origin of the figure of al-Qâ'im lies in the linguistic usage of the early shiites. The participle *qâ'im* indicated the imam who would rise against the regime. The role of the Qâ'im towards the end of time is a later development.

Among students of post-war science of religion, one of the most influential has been Geo Widengren. Widengren places the question of the provenance of the title al-Qâ'im in the broader framework of his investigations into the relations between, and the influences on, the religions in the Middle East in antiquity. In his book on Muhammad's prophethood and traditions relating this mission with the ascension of the apostle, he went further into the resemblances of the term *Qâ'im* in early islamic context and the Samaritan Aramaean *Q'ym*. Being a messenger of God, the heavenly journey and insight in esoteric wisdom are the central issues in the traditions collected by Widengren. Some early Islamic groups, such as the Ismailites, confessed their *imâm* to share in the same heavenly wisdom as Muhammad experienced. The title al-Qâ'im is closely related, according to

Widengren, to the idea of being sent as a prophet and the introduction of a new religious law. In this respect, he called attention to the resemblance of the shiite *Qâ'im*, Samaritan *Q'ym* and the gnostic *hestôs*: the shiite notion of *al-qâ'im*:

is the same expression as the Aramaic *qâ'em*, found in Samaritan texts and translated in Greek as *hestôs*. We remember that the Samaritan Gnostic leader Simon Magus claimed to be *ho hestôs*. In the Mandaean texts with their clear Jewish-Gnostic background we met the idea of a Custodian of every epoch. In Shî'ah we thus meet with these two ideas, joined together in the person of al-Qâ'im.[12]

The remarks of Widengren have been influential. Scholars in the field of early Islamic gnosticism cite him with approval and tend to clarify the meaning of the technical term by reference to the Simonian gnosis, as well as to the doctrine of God's durability and the exalted place of the Prophet like Moses as expressed in Samaritan writings.[13]

### The Title Ho Hestôs in Philosophical and Gnostic Material

Matters seem to get complicated with the invocation of materials from antiquity. But since Widengren, and many scholars influenced by him, refer to the simonian gnosis and Samaritanism, we will have to mention the reports on this heresiarch.

Various reports exist on the appearance of Simon the Magician. In most of them his name is linked with that of Dositheos.[14] However, not all sources mention the claim of both sectarian leaders on the title or status of being *ho hestôs*. Only the Pseudo-Clementine *Homilies and Recognitions*, and some short references in Clement of Alexandria's *Stromateis*, and Hippolytus' *Refutatio* contain indications.[15]

The tradition on Dositheos and the Dositheans in the Samaritan chronicle of Abu'l Fath offers some valuable material on the connotations linked with Dositheos' function as Prophet like Moses. Abu'l Fath compiled his chronicle in the 14th century, but he included earlier Samaritan material. The Dositheos material belonged to this earlier stratum. In the chronicle it is suggested that Dositheos wrote his own version of the Pentateuch. This version was accepted by his followers as autoritative. Dositheos himself, after he had written these holy books, disappeared. Polemically it is told that he went up to a mountain, hid in a cave, and eventually died of hunger (Isser 1976, 74-87).

Stanley J. Isser suggested that the title "Standing One" assumed by Dositheos and Simon, as well as the practice of magic, may be part of the theme of the eschatological prophet: "The Clementina understand the use of this title as signifying messiahship and divinity; he will always endure; he is incorruptible". According to him, the question is not in what sense Simon was the Standing One; but, assuming the title itself is older than Simon, what its implications were when used by Dositheos or earlier claimants (Isser 1976, 138). Like Widengren, he is trying to link the notion of the "Standing One" to that of the Prophet like Moses. In his effort, he refers to the occurence of *hestôs* in Philo of Alexandria's works, where it is used about God himself in the first place, but in a derived sense for anyone who wants to approach God. The *sofoi*, Abraham and Moses in particular, do share in God's immutable nature. Philo is eager to cite Biblical texts, for instance Deuteronomy 5,31 (= Masoretic Text 5,28: "stand by me", said by God to Moses) in this connection.

The philosophical genre in which this use of *ho hestôs* appears has led to another view on the meaning of the term in gnostic systems. Some scholars have noted the philosophical influences in gnostic systems, sometimes defending this link with Philo of Alexandria's work viewing the term *ho hestôs* as a part of a philosophical system. H. Leisegang is one of the most prominent among them.[16]

Others stressed the place of the term in the philosophical discourse on the nature of the worldly and the divine things. The role of the Platonic schools in the transference of such ideas is stressed in this context. Antonie Wlosok, with her study "Laktanz und die philosophische Gnosis", is among those who vindicate this explanation for the diffusion of terms centering on the theme of stability: the term *ho hestôs* was part of a common discourse in late antiquity. In more recent times, this perspective has been adopted in the field of gnosticism: Michael A. Williams being one of the authors in this line (1985).

## Evaluating the Approaches

So far, we have met different approaches by which scholars have tried to account for the seemingly parallel usage of the term. The first line holds *ho hestôs* to be a term connected with the notion of the 'Prophet like Moses', or the 'Apostle of God'. The diffusion of the terms are not explained but are taken as a phenomenological fact. This approach, as promoted by Widengren, tends to look at the distinct terms under the shadow of the study of syncretism.

The hypothesis Widengren proposes to account for the spread of the term 'the Standing One' has its strength in explaining the appearance of the term, and related notions, in various - qua time and place distinct - religions in the Middle East. From his effort to link the diffusion of the *Qâ'im/Q'ym* concept with other implicit and explicit notions, a very important point comes out, namely, diffusionist explanations can work when a concept is obscured by the connotations attached to it, when an endogeneous explanation can not work *per se*.[17]

The other way to look at the materials has been sketched very roughly as the philosophical perspective. It offers a solution that tends to see the occurrence of "the Standing One" and other terms connected with stability as a consequence of the late antique "spirit of the age". In the philosophical jargon of Philo, surely *hestôs* entails "standing firm". But recalling the many aspects of the early shiite use of the term *al-qâ'im*, can we make sure that there is a primary meaning as Ivanow did when declaring that the primary meaning of *al-qâ'im* is "rising in revolt"?[18]

It is not an easy task to extract ourselves from these conflicting explanations. Before we can succeed in realizing a method of investigation, we have to realize why it is that the explanation of the term is so difficult. At this point, I am sure the inscrutability is a consequence of the opaqueness of the term in the midst of the many connotations it carries. One can consider whether the way out is to stress one particular meaning of the connotations.

## Symbolic Theory and an Analysis of "The Standing One"

The diffusionism of Geo Widengren offers an explanation of the spread of "the Standing One". Nevertheless, it passes the contexts and the institutionalization of concepts without further notice. A diffusionist approach which makes allowance for this aspect offers a more adequate method for investigating highly connotated concepts. Heuristic categories from the study of symbolism can provide adequate criteria.[19]

### Presentational Symbolism

The creation of symbols is a unique human ability. Susanne Langer took this as a point of departure for her book *Philosophy in a New Key*. She demonstrated how people convert experience into symbols by means of their language. Symbols adapt reality as experienced into conceptions of it by means of the instruments that language supplies. These "symbolic transformations of experience", as Langer called these concepts, are of discursive nature, in spite of their invisibility, and therefore their validity can be tested.

Symbols adopt their meaning either from their denotation or from their connotation, in which case the possibility exists for a symbol to accept meanings that deviate from the denotation of the word.[20] If this is the case, i.e., that the meaning of a concept is no longer self-evident, then one can wonder how the survival of such a complex symbol is guaranteed.

Clifford Geertz has offered a solution worth introducing: symbols only are viable by the grace of the actors who make use of them. In other words, such symbols which are rich in connotations and not dependent on the denotation can survive and function only in an institutionalized form. Geertz' essay "Religion as a Cultural System" goes into this matter. In this famous article, the author delineates two distinct aspects in symbols set apart from other sorts of significative forms: the "model of" and "model for" functions. Geertz summarizes the activities of a religion within a culture in this double aspect. When religion is said to offer a model of the world, then it is meant that the "model of" supplied by religion enables men to cope with the problems of evil, the theodicy. That is, to deal with the threat that pain, suffering, and injustice entail for man, which bring him to the limits of his power of endurance, to the limits of his morality, and to the limits of his intellectual capacities. Religion represents the processes taking place in the world, and men can interpret their experiences with the help of this "model of" aspect of religion. On the other hand, religion offers an orientation, a blueprint in accordance to which people can act in order to make the surrounding world coincide with the image they have of it. Thus, religion not only describes the social order, but also contributes to the making of it.

Geertz supposes that the abstract "models of" reality, which help men to interpret their experiences, will not survive unless they are invested with an "aura of factuality" that in a way realizes the model. Here rituals have an important part. In religious "performances" the abstract "models of" are objectified. Performances of this kind present a certain perspective, but along with it also realize it: "the performance makes the model for and the model of aspects of religious belief mere transpositions of one another" (Geertz 1973, 118).

*Key symbols*

Discoursive symbols find their expression and definition in language. Herewith the possibility arises to draw these symbols into the reality, which has a non-symbolic character. Sherry Ortner pointed to the fact that cultures have certain key elements which are crucial to its organization. It is possible to indicate key symbols for a culture: symbols in the centre of attention that appeal more than other symbols to the people, or in terms of which other symbols can be understood. Among these key symbols, Ortner distinguishes two categories: summarizing and elaborating symbols. Summarizing symbols sum up fundamental experiences, represent what the system means for the participants in an emotionally powerful and relatively undifferentiated way. They appeal to the participant's bonds with society. These symbols mostly represent implicit notions. Elaborating symbols, on the other hand, provide the possibility to make complex and undifferentiated feelings comprehensible, communicable, and translatable into orderly action. Symbols can have elaborating power in two distinctive modes. In the conceptual field, they can work as root metaphors, sorting out experience, placing it in cultural categories and helping us think how everything hangs together (Ortner 1973, 1341). In the second mode as key scenarios, they imply modes of action appropriate to successful living in the culture. Ortner mentioned the criteria which mark off key symbols: participants in a culture may value a concept; they further may not be indifferent about it; it may come up in many different contexts; there may be a greater cultural elaboration around it; and, finally there may be greater cultural restrictions surrounding the concept.[21]

The role key symbols play in a society is not necessarily confined to the religious sphere. This may seem a superfluous point. Nevertheless, it should be kept in mind that their function does contribute to the very survival of society. Recently, Professor Hans G. Kippenberg pointed this out in an article in which he tried to make the general theory of symbols a fertile framework for the sociology of religion based on the ideas of É. Durkheim and M. Weber (Kippenberg 1985, 177-193). It is important to hold that social order cannot exist without key symbols, but symbols do need a way to reinforce them as well. This reinforcement is provided in collective rituals as group pressure as well as public presentation.[22]

*Diffusionism and Symbolic Theory*

There is an important point in all this concerning the investigation of a highly connotated concept such as "the Standing One". A diffusionist approach might well gain support by considerations of this sort, because the peculiarities of the various terms are taken into account. The philosophical notions involved in Philo's use of the term *ho hestôs* are detached from the denotative meanings of the verb *histêmi*, although the denotation "standing firm" certainly remains clear. The title *al-Qâ'im* enters into so many representations that one can only speak of a cluster of representations wherein no special part is reserved for denotative meanings. However, when a denotation and meaning of a symbol come apart from one another, as in the cited examples, the question arises in which way the secondary meanings are guaranteed. Here the collective representations as accepted by society, reinforced in public rituals or performances, and play their important part. Attention should be paid to the way in which secondary meanings are institutionalized by means of "performances" or "scenarios".

The symbolist approach, as represented by Geertz among others, has an important advantage over the pure diffusionist explanations of a concept. In my opinion, looking for an explanation in terms of diffusionism in itself requires an investigation into a massive amount of data, all of potential importance. However, when one is prepared to accept the insights from the general theory of symbols, one can renounce this weight, and focus on the institutionalization of a concept, which can be recovered via collective representations and collective rituals. It is necessary to find among the data the fitting interpretative criteria. It might be that previously current gnostic ideas are involved but, besides the existing tradition, one should be aware of the active process of interpreting ideas. The circumstances that go with the actual promotion of a person claiming to be a Qâ'im al-Mahdî and the connotations that go with the use of this claim can provide more insight into the backgrounds of the early shiite usage of the term.

An inventory of source texts, however, places the usages with respect to the heresiarchs Simon Magus and Dositheos half-way between a type of philosophical speech and soteriological expectation. When a clear philosophical notion on divine *stasis* gets surrounded by many connotations, the institutionalization in a social context, in communities, becomes urgent. It appears that in the case of simonianism and dositheanism, an important step has been taken in the designation of religious leaders as *hestôs*. Especially in the case of Dositheos, a merging of the idea of stability and mosaic prophethood can be noticed. Connotations such as immortality, concealment, and limitation of religious authority make him a bridge to the early shiite Qâ'im al-Mahdî.

## A Point of View

The use of heuristic categories from symbolic anthropology in the field of the science of religion can be fruitful. The recurrent concept of "the Standing One" has in this discipline been understood as an example of some sort of syncretistic diffusion. In this way, one could speak of a renewing tradition. On the other hand, there is the scholarly debate on the nature and significance of the re-emergence of this title and the connotations that play a part in it. Here, the diffusionist tradition can profit from some of the results of symbolic theory as presented in anthropological discourse. The tradition of diffusionism renewing itself in a science of religion co-operating with symbolic anthropology was the second theme of this contribution.

A concluding remark should be made concerning the contribution to be expected from the symbolist approach to the study of syncretism. Carsten Colpe is among those who have tried to develop the notion of syncretism into an effective tool for historical studies. In his view, the notion of syncretism can help to discern the data required for a historical-genetical explanation. Step by step one is in need of supplementary information which together with general regularities make up explanations. In the science of religion, these hypotheses will never have the power of natural laws that are statistically verifiable. But, if we succeed in finding the substantial data to account for a phenomenon, then we will be able to clarify the internal structure of this phenomenon and the circumstances that have led to the syncretistic process. Colpe states that the explanation of religious syncretisms may involve a great amount of social, historical, political, and psychological data. I suggest it is on this terrain that the study of religious symbolism may well play an important part.

The analysis of religious syncretisms involves complex antecedent data: because of the heterogeneous character of religion there must be taken stock of the non-religious, in particular the social and the economical, data in order to produce real explanations, not only indications of parallels or affiliations, of religious motives (Colpe 1980, 183ff.). For Colpe, this is the very reason why a methodologically aware science of religion can be more penetrating than in the other social sciences.

## Notes

1. These investigations were supported by the Foundation for Research in the Field of Theology and the Science of Religions in the Netherlands, which is subsidized by the Netherlands Organization for Scientific Research (N.W.O.).
2. The plan of Kûfa is strictly divided into tribal quarters, each having its own mosque, in which the daily religious duties and other activities could be performed, and its own cemetery. At night, the main streets connecting the various quarters were closed off. Cf. "al-Kûfa" (H. Djäit), in: *Encyclopaedia of Islam* 2; Massignon 1963, 35-60; Halm 1982, 19-23; Morony 1984, 239-245.
3. Morony 1984, 176; Halm 1982, 22-23.
4. On an-Naubakhtî see Halm 1984, 28. Following Hodgson 1955, 1-13, the term 'Proto-Shia' is reserved for the period in Shi'ite history in which the element of personal loyalty and direct, charismatic leadership are most prominent in the political action of the imams. Persons introducing themselves as the leader of the family of the Prophet could from this position claim political authority and legitimate these claims by referring to their Hashimite descent. The Shia proved to be in this period more a temporary movement than an institutionalized religion.
5. As is known, the controversial issue was 'Alî's alleged relaxed attitude concerning the prosecution of 'Utman's murderers. He could not bring himself to punish the responsible persons. The "Battle of the Camel" (656 A.D.), the battle at Siffîn (657 A.D.), and the decision of the arbiters from both camps in this matter meant a threat to the unity that had grown between the different Arab groups: between the adherents of both leaders as well as internally in 'Alî's camp. The secessions of the Kharijites and 'Alî's violent action in reincorporating these groups in the massacre of Nahrawan in the month of July, 658 A.D., were the direct consequences.
6. The party's name, "Kaisânites", is said to have been derived from Mukhtâr's commander who was named Kaisân. The name "Kaisânites" is generally used by heresiographs to designate those sects that hold to the imamate of 'Alî ibn Abî Tâlib's third son, Muhammad ibn al-Hanafîja, who, after his disappearance, was expected to return, or one of his sons was to accomplish his task.
7. Ibn al-Hanafîja was the son of 'Alî by a woman of the central-arabian clan of the Banû Hanîfa, Hasan and Husain being descendents of the Prophet's daughter Fatîma. In contrast with the sons of 'Alî by Fatîma, this Muhammad did not directly spring from the Prophet, but nevertheless was a member of the Hâshimite clan.

8. Naubakhtî: Firaq §71.
9. Some elucidating examples: Naubakhtî: Firaq §73-74: 'Abd-Allâh ibn Mu'âwija is the Qâ'im al-Mahdî whose advent was already predicted by the Prophet. He will reign over the earth with righteousness and equality. Then he will die after transferring authority to one of 'Alî's descendants. §77: Abû Mansûr claimed to be in the succession to the imamate, being a prophet and a messenger of God, that six of his progeny as well would be prophets: "the last among them is al-Qâ'im". §113: The Qarmats, coming from the *Sawâd*, claim that Muhammad ibn Ismâ'îl did not die, but is still alive in Byzantium: "Al-Qâ'im to them means that he will be sent with a new message and religion, abolishing the law of Muhammad". Among them there are some wishing to confine the number of imâms to seven. The last *imâm*, al-Qâ'im al-Mahdî, is also a messenger of God (*rasûl*). §118-120: An early-shiite group claims that Mûsâ ibn Ja'far did not die and will not die before he will reign over the entire world, replenishing it with justice and equality. They have a tradition saying "Al-Qâ'im is named Qâ'im because after his death he will rise again", just as Isâ ibn Marjam (Jesus). §123: One faction, the Mamtûra, confesses not to know whether Mûsâ ibn Ja'far did die or not, "according to many sources of information, he would be Qâ'im al-Mahdî". §124:
10. From other sources, such as the work of al-Qummi, one can add the ideas of *taqîja, raja* and *tanasukh* as phenomenological elements of the Qâ'im-doctrine.Followers of Muhammad ibn Bâsir, *mawla* of the Banû Asad from Kûfa, confess that Mûsa ibn Ja'far is alive but in concealment and that he is Qâ'im al-Mahdî. §79-80: After Hasan ibn 'Alî died, the opinions among his adherents became divided. One group maintains that Hasan did die, but that he has been raised from death and that he is the Qâ'im al-Mahdî: "Al-Qâ'im is the one who rises after his death and who does not leave a son", being the last in the succession to the imamate. Another group, on the other hand, holds that there was a son, named Muhammad, appointed as successor. This Muhammad is "Imâm Qâ'im, the one who will rise in revolt, and he was born some years before his father died". §87-88 mentions a faction holding the following tradition: "On this moment the earth is without *hujja* [i.e., God's witness to creation] until Allah will send to us the Qâ'im from the progeny of Muhammad. He will revive the earth after its death".
11. Ivanow 1942, 101, footnote: "In all these prophecies the term qâ'im has none of the implications which it has acquired in later Ismaili literature, where it means the initiator of a new era in religion, the Qâ'im of the *qiyâmat*. Here obviously the sentence *idhâ qâm qâ'im min-nâ* means simply: when one of our progeny (successfully) rises in a revolt (to uphold the purity of religion)".
12. Widengren 1955, 40-41. In 1950, in his study of the Heavenly Book, he already had pointed to a series of technical terms, one of them being

the title "the Standing One", alluding to a connection between Samaritan, Jewish-gnostic, and Mandaean circles.

13. For instance, Tijdens 1977, 241-526, 268; Halm 1978, 124-125. However, Halm is prudent. He dismisses the idea that the so-called 'simonian heritage' could be pointed to as a direct paradigm or forerunner to the early Islamic (in his case: Ismailitic) doctrine. In case of a pure transfer of a complete gnostic system, there would have remained more original terms. However, simonian gnosis may have provided the pattern for a new creation in an Islamic milieu (98-99, 125 ff.).

14. All reports have been compiled by S.J. Isser (1976). His investigations led to a differing evaluation of the traditions, although several principal streams of traditions exist. The earliest ones among them seem to be the reports ascribed to Hegesippus, an early form of the Clementina, Origen, a lost work probably by Hippolytus and unknown Samaritan sources, op.cit., 110.

15. Clement of Alexandria, *Stromateis* II, 11.53, 1-2; Pseudo-Clementine, *Homilies* 2.22-24; 2.24, 5-7; *Recognitions* 2, 7-12 (// *Hom* 2.22-25); Hippolytus, *Refutatio* 6.12, 3; 13; *Homilies* 2.24:

When Simon was away in Egypt to (acquire) practice in magic, and John was killed, a certain Dositheos, who desired the leadership, falsely gave out that Simon was dead, and succeeded to the leadership of the sect. But Simon returned not long after and strenuously claimed the place as his own. Nevertheless, when he met with Dositheos he did not demand the place, for he knew that a man who has attained power beyond his expectations cannot be removed from it. Therefore, with pretended friendship, he put himself temporarily in the second place, under Dositheos. But having been placed after a few days among the thirty fellow-disciples, he began to malign Dositheos as not delivering the instructions correctly. And he said that (Dositheos) did this not through unwillingness to deliver them correctly, but through ignorance. And on one occasion, Dositheos somehow sensing that Simon's artful accusation was dissipating the common people's notion of himself, so that they did not think he was the Standing One, came in a rage to the usual meeting place, found Simon, and struck him with a staff. But it seemed to pass through Simon's body as if he had been smoke. Thereupon Dositheos was astounded and said to him, "If you are the Standing One, I will also worship you." When Simon said, "I am" [Mk. 13.6 and parallels]. Dositheos, knowing that he himself was not the Standing One, fell down and worshipped; and associating himself with the twenty-nine chiefs, he raised Simon to his own place of repute. Then, not many days after, while he (Simon) stood, Dositheos himself fell down and died.

16. Leisegang 1924, 62-63:

Der Ausdruck Hestos ist besonders aus Philon bekannt. Unter ihm versteht Philon Gott selbst, den ewig Stillstehenden. Er hat diesem Motiv eine besondere Schrift mit dem Titel "Über die Unveränderlichkeit Gottes" gewidmet. Jeder, der sich dem ewig stillstehenden Gott nahern will, muss nach Philons Lehre selbst ein Stillstehender, ein Hestos, werden. Das liest er aus seinem Septuagintatext heraus. So heisst es von Abraham: "Er war ein Hestos, ein Stillstehender, gegenüber dem Herrn", und von Moses: "Du aber stehe neben mir selbst". Wir dürfen wohl annehmen, dass die Bezeichnung des Dositheos als Hestos nichts anderes bedeuten sollte.

17. A drawback might be the underexposure of the endogene aspects in the evolution of a concept, the lack of attention to its literary denotations. The institutionalization of the concepts is a point that calls for attention, but which the diffusionist approach did not care for.

18. The literalist approach has an important drawback in the lack of interest for external influences.

19. Gellner 1970, 22,38 ff., went into the interpretation by western scholars of concepts and beliefs held by non-western societies. Gellner indicated that concepts and beliefs do not exist in isolation in the minds or psyches of individuals or in texts but that they are a part of the lives of people and societies. This Durkheimian view on the nature of concepts stresses the primarily social nature of concepts. Religious concepts do provide the individual with notions or beliefs that enable him to represent his society and the ties that link him with his society to himself. Society only exists when these notions are reinforced by collective actions. Thus, before we can really understand a concept or a belief, we must know the activities and institutions which provide the contexts of a word or a sentence (Durkheim 1975, 99 ff.).

20. Langer 1942. In her words, symbols are "vehicles for the conception of objects". In language, men convert experience into symbols. Langer distinguished several aspects in the symbol function. While "signs" involve three things (a subject, a sign, and an object being indicated), symbols involve besides subject, symbol, and object the aspects of denotation and connotation of the conceptions that the symbols convey. The relationship which a name (a symbol) has to an object which bears it is called denotation, while the relation to connected concepts is called connotation. One could summarize this position as: a signal has its meaning in its reference, symbols can derive their meaning either from their denotation or from their connotation. When a symbol (a word) refers to an object, then the direct contents of the object are known. This defined extension is also called the object's denotation. When a symbol, besides it direct meaning, also represents other meanings, then we can say there is a connotative content. This connotation consists of meanings that may well be derived from the denotation but in andy case raise the symbol above its denotation. Possibly in this way the application of the symbol exceeds or deviates from its denotative meaning.

Schematically has its meaning in:

21. Symbol as a focus of interest: p. 1339. Distinction between types of key symbols: p. 1339-1343. In scheme:

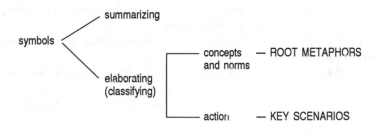

22. Kippenberg 1985, 189. The peculiar quality of "key symbols" in the religious area is that they can equally have a social (every day life) function: For instance, as has been argued by Kippenberg, by demanding a certain behaviour in respect to religious principles or loyalty to a person.

## Bibliography

*Sources*

Clemens of Alexandria: M. Mondésert, ed., *Les Stromates: II,* (Sources Chrétiennes 38), Paris 1951.

Pseudo-Clemens of Rome: B. Rehm, ed., *Die Pseudo Klementinen I: Homilien*, Berlin, Leipzig 1953

Pseudo-Clemens of Rome: B. Rehm, ed., *Die Pseudo Klementinen II: Rekognitionen in Rufinus Übersetzung*, Berlin 1965

Hippolytus: M. Marcovich, ed., *Refutatio omnium haeresium*, (Patristische Texte und Studien 25) Berlin, New York 1986.

an-Naubakhtî, Al-Hasan ibn Mûsâ: H. Ritter, ed., *Kitâb firaq ash-Shî'a,* (Bibliotheca Islamica 4), Istanbul 1932.

*General*

Colpe, C., 1980: "Die Vereinbarkeit historischer und struktureller Bestimmungen des Synkretismus", in: idem, *Theologie, Ideologie, Reli-*

*gionswissenschaft: Demonstrationen ihrer Unterscheidung*, München, 162-185.

Durkheim, Émile, 1975: *Textes II: Religion, Morale, Anomie*, V. Karady (ed.), Paris.

Geertz, C., 1973: "Religion as a Cultural System", in: C. Geertz, *The Interpretation of Cultures*, New York, 87-125.

Gellner, E., 1970: "Concepts and Society", in: R. Wilson, ed., *Rationality*, Oxford 1970, rpr. 1981, 18-49.

Halm, H., 1978: *Kosmologie und Heilslehre der frühen Ismâ'îlîyya: eine Studie zur islamischen Gnosis*, Wiesbaden.

Halm, H., 1982: *Die islamische Gnosis. Die extreme Schia und die 'Alawiten*, Zürich/München.

Hodgson, M.G.S., 1955: "How Did the Early Shi'a become Sectarian?", *Journal of the American Oriental Society* 75, 1-13.

Isser, S.J., 1976: *The Dositheans. A Samaritan Sect in Late Antiquity*, Leiden.

Ivanow, W.A., 1942: *Ismaili Tradition Concerning the Rise of the Fatimids*, London/Bombay.

Kippenberg, H.G., 1985: "Religionssoziologie ohne Säkularisierungsthese: É. Durkheim und M. Weber aus der Sicht der Symboltheorie", *Neue Zeitschrift für Systematische Theologie und Religionsphilosophie* 27, 177-193.

Langer, S.K., 1942: *Philosophy in a New Key. A Study in the Symbolism of Reason, Rite, and Art*, New York, 1942, 1955.

Leisegang, H., 1924: *Die Gnosis*, Stuttgart, 1924, 1955.

Massignon, L., 1963: "Explication du plan de Kufa (Iraq)" in: L. Massignon & Y. Moubarac, eds., *Opera Minora*, Vol. III, 35-60, Beirut.

Morony, M.G., 1984: *Iraq after the Muslim Conquest*, Princeton.

Ortner, S., 1973: "On Key Symbols", *American Anthropologist* 75, 1338-1346.

Tijdens, W.F., 1977: "Der mythologisch-gnostische Hintergrund des 'Umm al-Kitab'", *Acta Iranica* 7, 241-526.

Widengren, G., 1955: *Muhammad, the Apostle of God, and His Ascension*, Uppsala/Wiesbaden.

Williams, M.A., 1985: *The Immovable Race. A Gnostic Designation and the Theme of Stability in Late Antiquity*, Leiden.

Wlosok, Antonie, 1960: *Laktanz und die Philosophische Gnosis. Untersuchungen zu Geschichte und Terminologie der gnostischen Erlösungsvorstellungen*, Heidelberg.

# The Transformation of the Israelite Religion

*By Niels Peter Lemche*

It was with great pleasure that I received the invitation to read a paper at this conference, since it is always a privilege to unfold to an audience of non-theologians, though professional historians of religion, a few recent developments in O(ld) T(estament) studies. My theme may also be of some general importance because the modern direction of OT research is likely to change our general understanding of the development of the ancient Israelite religion in a way which was unthinkable just a few years ago. I can only regret that the space allows no more than a sketchy outline of this development.[1]

By way of introduction, I shall present an outline of what may be called the classical concensus among scholars of the Israelite religion, a topic which has more or less been the resort of professional theologians, whether of Christian or Jewish observance. A by-product of this is that the study of Israelite religion has never been totally free of theological concerns. It has always to some degree been confessional, formerly in a very direct way: the scholar might jeopardize his position in his church and his society - in any case his academic position - if he published results or views unacceptable to the tradition of his church (the same applied to Jewish scholars, of course, although the means of sanction may have been slightly different).[2] It is, however, even possible today to speak of a certain degree of church control over the results of scholars, though direct sanctions against the too radical or too different scholar may be indirect rather than direct. The psychological factor which binds the individual scholar to his church tradition, on the other hand, is still important. Of course, it is more difficult to approach one's subject when the scholar himself believes in the fundamental truth of what is written in the book which is his main source of knowledge.

Therefore, most history books describing the development of the Israelite religion may in reality be regarded as a kind of *rationalistic paraphrase* of the OT narrative, which has always been considered the

most important source for the study of the Israelite religion.[3] By using
the expression "rationalistic paraphrase", I allow for the fact that
modern histories of Israelite religion are not just resumés of the
biblical account of the development of Israelite religion, but the
general lines of this biblical account have been retained, although the
modern scholar has removed - maybe even "liberated" the biblical text
from - the elements of legendary character most offensive to our
understanding of the development of a living religion. Thus the
general outline of the biblical version of this history of the religion
of Israel has been made historically acceptable to modern Western
investigators.[4]

Accordingly, the starting point for almost every modern description
of the Israelite religion is the biblical idea that it was a Yahwistic
religion, the roots of which are to be sought outside Israel's hereditary
land, Palestine. The Yahweh religion is, according to these scholars,
clearly coloured by its non-Palestinian origin. Its main characteristics
are, so to speak, nomadic, not agrarian, whereas its counterpart, the
Canaanite religion, is a Palestinian peasant and urban religion originating in Palestine. Historical Israel is generally believed to be the
creation of a specific people or nation who settled in Palestine at the
end of the 2nd millennium B.C. as foreigners, and the Yahweh religion was introduced in Palestine by these newcomers from the desert.[5]

After the transplantation of the originally nomadic Yahwistic religion, we observe a transformation of some of its less important traits,
a transformation which was triggered by the encounter with the Canaanite religion, which until then had been the sole religious force
in the Palestinian society in the Bronze Age, that is, for at least 2,000
years. In general, OT scholars describe the Israelite religion after the
settlement in Palestine as a syncretistic religion in order to obscure the
real impact of the encounter between Israel and Canaan. The fact is
that, in reality, the true Israelite religion was contaminated by the
Canaanite religion.

This "pure" Israelite religion, which is the essence of the OT
account of the Yahwistic religion, was first and foremost characterized
by the subdued role allotted to the elements of fertility religion. The
true Yahwistic religion is thus supposed to have been a monotheistic
law-religion, the substance of which may be reduced to the content of
the so-called Decalogue in Exodus 20 (a reissue of this Decalogue is
to be found in Deuteronomy 5), a collection, or a corpus, of ten commandments, which, according to the OT, were promulgated by
Yahweh personally without human interference, as told in Exodus 20.[6]

At the centre of this religion we find the notion that Yahweh is a zealous god who does not accept other gods before him. Thus, the Israelite religion was "originally" a monotheistic religion, or at least a monolatrous one, which only allowed the worship of Yahweh.

Secondly, the Yahwistic religion was characterized by its high ethical standards - it was under no circumstances to be compared to the types of religion prevalent elsewhere in the ancient Near Eastern world. Many passages in the OT may be quoted in support of this notion; thus Amos 5,21-25:

> I hate, I spurn your pilgrim-feasts;
> I will not delight in your sacred ceremonies.
> When you present your sacrifices and offerings
> I will not accept them,
> nor look on the buffaloes of your shared-offerings.
> Spare me the sound of your songs;
> I cannot endure the music of your lutes.
> Let justice roll like a river
> and righteousness like an ever-flowing stream.
> Did you bring me sacrifices and gifts,
> you people of Israel, those forty years in the wilderness?[7]

Or Isaiah 1,10-17:

> Hear the word of the Lord, you rulers of Sodom:
> attend, you people of Gomorrah, to the instruction of your God:
> Your countless sacrifices, what are they to me?
> says the Lord.
> I am sated with whole-offerings of rams
> at the fat of buffaloes;
> I have no desire for the blood of bulls,
> of sheep and he-goats.
> Whenever you come to enter my presence-
> who asked you for this?
> No more shall you trample my courts.
> The offer of your gifts is useless,
> the reek of sacrifices is abhorrent to me.
> New moons and sabbaths and assemblies,
> sacred seasons and ceremonies, I cannot endure,
> I cannot tolerate your new moons and your festivals;
> they have become a burden to me,
> and I can put up with them no longer.
> When you lift your hands outspread in prayer,

> I will hide my eyes from you.
> Though you offer countless prayers,
> I will not listen.
> There is blood on your hands;
> wash yourselves and be clean.
> Put away the evil of your deeds,
> away out of my sight.
> Cease to do evil and learn to do right,
> pursue justice and champion the opressed;
> give the orphan his rights, plead the widow's cause.

In my short outline of Israelite history and culture, *Ancient Israel*, I have tried to describe the essence of this "official" Israelite religion, which the OT itself propagates as follows: "The Israelites worshipped one God, and only one God, Yahweh, who was the guarantee that one nation, the Israelite-Jewish people, owned one chosen country, the Land of Israel, if only this nation kept the covenant by which it was bound to its god, Yahweh, and which consisted in a long series of laws, which Israel was expected to follow" (Lemche 1988a, 219-221).

Of course, this law religion also left room for other considerations, such as the question of the fertility of Israel's land. We may be entitled to say that no Near Eastern religion can allow itself the luxury of totally disregarding the nature of its environment, an environment which has often been hostile to mankind. Until recently, it has always been a problem of vital importance whether there would be enough bread to feed the inhabitants of the area even for the coming year. Such vital matters are of course not the concern of man alone, but necessitate a divine guarantee. In such environments, man has always asked for a divine promise of personal survival. Accordingly, the OT also contains several passages describing how Yahweh is the provider of fertility to land and people. But only when Israel is bound to him, and to him alone, will he act as the truly merciful God providing for the needs of his people, thereby excluding other gods which may have been specially entrusted with the fertility of the country. Since Yahweh alone is the god of Israel, he must by necessity take upon himself functions fulfilled by specialized deities in the neighbouring cultures. But his function as the provider of fertility is always of secondary importance compared to his role as the guarantee of the ethical standard of his people.

The syncretistic traits of the Yahwistic religion owe their existence to the fact that after the Israelite settlement, elements of the previous fertility cult of the country were able to penetrate this pure ethical

Yahwistic religion, supported by the intrusion of a number of Canaanite deities and religious beliefs, which were clearly considered to be foreign to the Yahwistic religion. Let us quote another passage, e.g., Hosea 4,11-14:

> New wine and old steals my people's wits:
> they ask advice from a block of wood
> and take their orders from a fetish;
> for a spirit of wantonness has led them astray
> and in their lusts they are unfaithful to their God.
> Your men sacrifice on mountain-tops
> and burn offerings on the hills,
> under oak and poplar
> and the terebinth's pleasant shade.
> Therefore your daughters play the wanton
> and your sons' brides commit adultery.
> I will not punish your daughters for playing the wanton
> nor your sons' brides for their adultery,
> because your men resort to wanton women
> and sacrifices with temple prostitutes.

The same general attitude is also found in the historical literature of the OT. One quotation should be sufficient. In 2 Kings 17, the account of the fall of the Northern Kingdom (Samaria) in 722 B.C. is concluded by the following sermon (vv 7ff.):

All this happened to the Israelites because they had sinned against the Lord their God who brought them up from Egypt, from the rule of Pharaoh king of Egypt; they paid homage to other gods and observed the laws and customs of the nations whom the Lord has dispossessed before them and uttered blasphemies against the Lord their God; they built hill-shrines for themselves in all their settlements, from watch-tower to fortified city, and set up sacred pillars and sacred poles on every high hill and under every spreading tree, and burnt sacrifices at all the hill-shrines there, as the nations did, whom the Lord had displaced before them. By this wickedness of theirs they provoked the Lord's anger.

This version is thus the official OT version, and, in reality, it is the same which, in a slightly modified form, has been reproduced by theological scholars. The coherence of the account is, in fact, apparent due to a close connection between the secular history of Israel and her religious history. Both the secular and the religious history are totally in harmony. Just as Israel was "originally" a foreign nation which settled in Palestine, the Israelite religion was a foreign religion which was introduced by the Israelite newcomers in Palestine; and, just as Israel mingled with the previous Canaanite population in Palestine, the Israelite religion absorbed the most important features of the religion of these Canaanites.

Let us suppose that the OT account of the secular history of Israel turns out to be a result of human invention, a piece of fictive literature. What consequences would a totally new scientific reconstruction of the early and formative history of Israel have on our interpretation of the religious history of Israel?

By necessity I must be brief in my comments. This much should be emphasized, however: it is not wrong to say that the study of Israelite religion is approaching a point of no return. To us OT scholars, it becomes increasingly obvious that the OT account of the history of Israel, at least before her polity, is an ideological reconstruction (or, even better, a construction) of the prehistory of the Israelite society; and that this construction derives from a late period in the history of Israel around the middle of the 1st millennium B.C., or between 500 to 1000 years after the "events" narrated by the OT historical books. It is also now evident that this construction bears little resemblance to what may have been the historical reality.[8]

Accordingly, the OT model of the emergence of Israel, understood as a foreign nation or ethnos which transgressed the borders of Palestine from the outside to settle in the area as newcomers "from the desert", is outmoded. At present, we are attempting to develop an alternative model, according to which Israel was the outcome of a social development of the Palestinian population in the second half of the 2nd millennium B.C. In this connection, it is rather difficult - if not impossible - to find room for a foreign populace of newcomers of nomadic origin. If such an element existed, it must have been fairly small and politically unimportant.

This revised concept of the history of early Israel naturally induces us to question the long accepted description of the Israelite religion and its development.[9] We are certainly in the position to question whether this religion was originally as exclusive and idiosyncratic as expressed by the OT and the older histories of Israelite religion. Perhaps the idea of a monotheistic Yahwistic religion was the outcome or the result of a long religious development in Palestine in the 2nd and 1st millennia B.C. rather than the starting point of such an evolution.

In the OT itself, we find several important texts which provide us with a picture of a Yahwistic religion which can only be brought into accordance with the official version of Israel's Yahwistic religion with difficulty. These texts have until now been more or less explained away as exponents of the syncretism which prevailed in Israel after her polity around 1000 B.C. I shall quote a few examples of these texts:

Ps 82,1ff. 6f:

> God takes his stand in the court of heaven
> to deliver judgment among the gods themselves.
> How long will you judge unjustly
> and show favour to the wicked?
> You ought to give judgement for the weak and the orphan,
> and see right done to the destitute and downtrodden...
> This is my sentence: Gods you may be,
> sons all of you of a high god,
> yet you shall die as men die;
> princes fall, every one of them, and so shall you.

This text is to be compared to Deuteronomy 32,8-9:

> When the Most High parcelled out the nations
> when he dispersed all mankind,
> he laid down the boundaries of every people
> according to the number of the sons of God;
> but the Lord's share was Jacob,
> Israel his allotted portion.

The second quotation clearly shows that Yahweh was not necessarily to be identified with the High God himself, El Eljon, the god of creation, although other passages in the OT make it clear that such an identification was quite common. In Deuteronomy 32, Yahweh is only one of the sons of the High God, from whom he received Israel as a fief. In Ps 82, however, the pantheon, or the assembly of the gods, is clearly mentioned; and, in this assembly, all the lesser gods are evidently considered to be the sons of El Eljon.

These two passages have more to tell us, however. These psalms are first and foremost testimonies of a polytheistic religion which prevailed in Israel before the Babylonian exile. Secondly, they inform us that this polytheistic religion was not devoid of the ethical elements considered, for the most part, to be peculiar to the true Yahwistic religion.

On the other hand, this pre-exilic religion was not devoid of other religious elements and symbols. We can easily cite psalms which speak about Yahweh as the god of fertility. Perhaps the best known text in this connection is Ps 65 (vv 10ff.):

> Thou dost visit the earth and give it abundance,
> as often as thou dost enrich it
> with the waters of heaven, brimming in their channels,
> providing rain for men.
> For this is thy provision for it,
> watering its furrows, levelling its ridges,
> softening it with showers and blessing its growth.
> Thou dost crown the year with thy good gifts
> and the palm-trees drip with sweet juice;
> the pastures in the wild are rich with blessing
> and the hills wreathed in happiness,
> the meadows are clothed with sheep
> and the valleys mantled in corn,
> so that they shout, they break into song.

The same psalm informs us that Yahweh also played the part of the young god known elsewhere in Western Asia in antiquity. He is thus described as the hero of the battle against the forces of chaos. The preceding verses in Ps 65 demonstrate how Yahweh actually fulfills exactly the same tasks as the young god in the Ugaritic epic texts, that is, the tasks of Ba'al, since it is the duty of Ba'al as well as Yahweh both to provide fertility for the fields and to combat the forces of chaos.[10] Another psalm (Ps 89,6ff.) expresses this second theme of the battle against chaos in an impressive manner:

> In the skies who is like the Lord,
> who like the Lord in the court of heaven,
> like God who is dreaded among the assembled holy ones,
> great and terrible above all who stand about him?
> O Lord God of hosts, who is like thee?
> Thy strength and faithfulness, O Lord, surround thee.
> Thou rulest the surging sea,
> calming the turmoil of its waves.
> Thou didst crush the monster Rahab with a mortal blow
> and scatter your enemies with thy strong arm.

Characteristic of the Israelite psalms is that they describe Yahweh both as the hero of the battle against chaos and as the god of creation, just like Marduk, the Babylonian city god. But they differ from the West Asiatic texts from Ugarit in that the Ugaritic texts only reckon Ba'al as the hero of the battle, whereas the god of creation is the high god El. And for an Israelite text like Psalm 89, it is typical that the passage just quoted ends with a description of the righteousness of Yahweh (v 15):

> thy throne is built upon rithteousness and justice,
> true love and faithfulness herald thy coming.

It must be admitted that this combination of motives may not be exclusive for the Israelite religion since the Ugaritic epic texts also inform us that Ba'al was made king of the gods after his victory over chaos.

We may, however, be entitled to maintain that before her Babylonian exile, Israel was dominated by a polytheistic religion endowed with the religious symbols and beliefs normally attributed to the deities El and Ba'al.

The OT evidence may be compared to the results of modern archaeological investigations in Palestine. In Israel, Yahweh was depicted as a young bull, perhaps not in Jerusalem itself, but evidently in the Northern Kingdom (compare 1 Kings 12). Here, the bull was the official cult symbol at the royal shrine of Bethel for more than 200 years. The OT presents the erection of this statue as a transgression of the rules laid down by the Ten Commandments and as being foreign to the true Yahwistic religion. But in the last few years, depictions of bulls turn up regularly at nearly every archaeological site over most of the Israelite countryside.

Thus, Israeli archaeologists dug out a few years ago an early Israelite sanctuary situated in the mountains to the north of Jerusalem (Mazar 1982). This sanctuary seems to have been in use at the end of the 2nd millennium B.C., that is, in the so-called Period of the Judges,[11] and the most important cult symbol worshipped here was evidently a statue of a bull. Therefore we may be entitled to say that if the Yahwistic religion had old roots in Israelite society - and this is still the general opinion - then the usual iconographical expression of this Yahweh was the bull. Elsewhere in the West Asiatic world in antiquity, however, the bull is understood as the expression of the god El, whereas the young bull actually represented the young god Ba'al.

The identity between El and Yahweh is evident. I have already

quoted some OT texts in favour of this identification, and many more
may be found. Outside the OT, but belonging to the period of the
Hebrew kings (that is the period between c. 1000 and 587 B.C.),
other texts have turned up as a result of the intensive archaeological
activity in this small country. A couple of very important short texts
inform us that the goddess *Asherah* was considered to be the consort
of Yahweh.[12] This goddess is well-known in the West Semitic world,
but also in the OT itself. In the OT, Asherah is generally used as the
name of a cult object or symbol which, according to the OT,
belonged to the Canaanite religion and therefore must be abolished in
connection with the purification of the Israelite religion. The name
Asherah, however, designates much more than just a cult object or
symbol since this goddess was actually the queen of the gods as
testified by the Ugaritic religious literature.

The Palestinian Israelite inscriptions actually speak about a divine
couple, Yahweh and Asherah, whom we may consider to have been
the ruling gods of the pantheon.

The inscriptions in question are found in the Judaean countryside
outside Jerusalem. They do not, however, stand alone, for Asherah
was obviously worshipped as the consort of Yahweh even in the
temple of Jerusalem, although this is not expressly mentioned by the
OT. The OT nevertheless provides information which indicates that it
must have been so. A comparison with the description of the extent
of the religious reformation in 2 Kings 23 presenting the details of
the purification of the cult in Jerusalem under king Josiah in 622 B.C.
gives this result:

Next, the king ordered the high priest Hilkiah, the deputy high priest, and
those on duty at the entrance, to remove from the house of the Lord all the
objects made for Baal and Asherah and all the host of heaven; he burnt
these outside Jerusalem, in the open country by the Kidron, and carried the
ashes to Bethel. He suppressed the heathen priests whom the kings of Judah
had appointed to burn sacrifices at the hill-shrines in the cities of Judah and
in the neighbourhood of Jerusalem, as well as those who burnt sacrifices to
Baal, to the sun and moon and planets and all the host of heaven. He took
the symbol of Asherah from the house of the Lord to the gorge of the
Kidron outside Jerusalem, burnt it there and pounded it to dust, which was
than scattered over the common burial-ground. He also pulled down the
house of the male prostitutes attached to the house of the Lord, where the
women wove vestments in honour of Asherah.

After this follows a list of other deities who were worshipped in Israelite Jerusalem: Astarte, Kemosh, Milkom, etc.

## Summing Up

For me, there can be no doubt that the Israelite religion before the Babylonian exile in the 6th century B.C. was a polytheistic religion, and that its content was almost identical to the content of the neighbouring religions in the West Asiatic world. It is, of course, possible to trace local variations everywhere; but, generally, it was the same kind of religion whether one visited the temple of Jerusalem or those of Damascus or Aleppo. This Yahwistic religion of Jerusalem was neither monotheistic nor devoid of religious iconography, even statues of the deities.[13]

On the other hand, it would be wrong to consider this religion to have been a licentious fertility religion, which is obviously the impression which OT writers want to convey to their readers far too successfully, perhaps, even among modern OT scholars and theologians.[14] The elements of fertility cult were highly conspicuous, but the same applies also to the other elements of this religion, especially to its ethical content. These last ethical elements were not peculiar to the Israelite religion, but they were the common heritage of all ancient Near Eastern religions.[15]

The official religion of the OT is, however, purified of any other god than Yahweh himself, and the elements of fertility are very much played down. The result was a non-pictorial, monotheistic religion with a strong emphasis on its ethical contents. The question is now: how and why did this official religion arise? Why did it not allow pictures of the god, and how did it conquer the old religious beliefs?

The question about the iconography is, perhaps, most easily answered. I believe the main reason why religious pictures were abolished was that Yahweh was not endowed with a religious iconography of his own. In Palestine, with its many-coloured religious beliefs, Yahweh was identified with at least two other gods. It is, accordingly, very likely that his attributes were the same as those attached to El and Ba'al, and it was thus impossible to retain these pictorial representations without retaining other characteristic traits of these deities. The reformers of the Israelite religion wisely chose to abolish any image of their god. As I have expressed elsewhere, it would have been improper to depict Yahweh with a pair of horns on his head since these very symbols were later reserved for his counterpart the devil.

How did the change from a polytheistic, West Semitic religion to a Jewish monotheistic religion come about? First of all, we should not imagine that this religious transformation was peculiar to Israelite culture alone. The same tendency towards a reduction in the number of deities worshipped, or, to be brief, towards a religion with strong monotheistic traits, may be found elsewhere in the ancient Near Eastern world in the same period, that is, between 800 and 500 B.C. In Israel, this changing religious attitude of a general scepticism towards the old religious beliefs and practices resulted in the appearance of a religious reform movement which the German OT scholar, Bernhard Lang, has aptly termed the *Yahweh-Alone-Movement* (Lang 1983a). Thus it was a religious reform movement which demanded the worship of only one god, of Yahweh.

The spokesmen of this movement were the classical Hebrew prophets so well-known to us because of the biblical books bearing their names, from Amos around 750 B.C. to Ezekiel, who lived in the 6th century B.C. I shall quote a few passages as illustrations of their message (cf. the quotation above from Hosea 4). I shall start with another quotation from the book of Hosea:

Hosea 11,1ff.:

> When Israel was a boy, I loved him;
> I called my son out of Egypt;
> but the more I called, the further they went from me;
> they must needs sacrifice to the Baalim
> and burnt offerings before carved images.
> It was I who taught Ephraim to walk,
> I who had taken them in my arms;
> but they did not know that I harnessed them in leading-strings
> and led them with bonds of love...
> Back they shall go to Egypt,
> the Assyrians shall be their king,
> for they have refused to return to me.
> The sword shall be swung over their blood-spattered altars
> and put an end to their prattling priests
> and devour my people in return for all their schemings,
> etc.

Or let us read the Judaean prophet Micah from the turn of the 8th century B.C. (Chapter 1,3ff.):

> For look, the Lord is leaving his dwelling-place;
> down he comes and walks on the heights of the earth.
> Beneath him mountains dissolve
> like wax before the fire,
> valleys are torn open,
> as when torrents pour down the hill-side-
> and all for the crime of Jacob and the sin of Israel.
> What is the crime of Jacob? Is it not Samaria?
> What is the hill-shrine of Judah? Is it not Jerusalem?
> So I will make Samaria
> a heap of ruins in open country,
> a place for planting wines;
> I will pour her stones down into the valley
> and lay her foundations bare.
> All her carved figures shall be shattered,
> her images burnt one and all;
> I will make a waste heap of all her idols.
> She amassed them out of fees for harlotry,
> and a harlot's fee shall they become once more.
> etc.

The description of this transformation must necessarily be brief. The social and political crises in Israel during the monarchy led to a crisis of the official and long-established religion as well; and the outcome of this crisis was a religious reform movement, or reformation even, which demanded the worship of Yahweh alone and which placed its religious message in a historical frame, according to which the history of Israel was identical with one long-lasting desertion from Yahweh. The message of the reform movement must therefore be a message of the impending doom, including the loss of national independence and the deportation of the people to foreign countries. This prophetic sermon was then attached to an outspoken social message, demanding the abolition of the unrighteousness which had accumulated during the last centuries - or so the prophets argued.

Later, this prophetic sermon was adopted or supplemented by a specific school of thought which arose in Judah after the fall of the Northern Kingdom after the Assyrian destruction of Samaria. Normally, we call this school deuteronomistic after the 5th book of Moses, Deuteronomy.[16] This school of thought places the prophetic sermon in a specific theological system or framework, which may be identified as the OT covenant theology, created by this very school. According to this covenant theology, Israel's connection with Yahweh was understood as a covenant relationship. Here, Yahweh is the sovereign who guarantees his vassal Israel possession of her land as long as Israel remains faithful to Yahweh alone. The origin of this reformed religion is then placed back in Israel's history, at the beginning of it, so that covenant theology became the point of departure of historical Israel and not a consequence or result of her historical and religious experiences.

However, something must have happened before this renewed Yahwistic religion became generally accepted. We can find traces of reformation activities at the end of the period of the Monarchy which aimed at instituting this new religion as the official one, as in 2 Kings 23 quoted above. The writers of the books of Kings, on the other hand, leave no doubt that the activities of the deuteronomistic school were futile since the deuteronomistic and prophetic message was not immediately accepted by either the official representatives of the state of Judah or by the commoners. After the death of king Josiah in 609 B.C., the OT tells us that the people of Judah returned to its old religious practices.

It was the Babylonian exile which changed the religious milieu in a dramatic way. Central to the Yahweh-Alone-Movement was the prediction of the destruction of the Israelite and Judaean states, and it had now come true. Both Israelite states were obliterated by foreign powers, and a considerable section of the Israelite people were deported to Mesopotamia. We are thus entitled to say that the experience of this national catastrophe, as well as that of the exile, contributed to the endorsement of the new religious message as the only true one, and the exile thus acted in favour of the substitution of the formerly polytheistic religion with the new monotheistic faith.

It would, however, be wrong to suppose that the old religious beliefs just disappeared once and for all. Naturally, the experience of the exile was only the experience of a minor part of the total Judaean population.[17] This group of deportees was, on the other hand, leading members of their community, and, therefore, able to express its religious message in writing. As time went by, this reformed group was able to dominate the general picture of the Israelite religion and to impress its own opinions on religious developments. Later on, their writings created a new religious standard for the entire post-exilic Jewish community in Palestine and thus became the official Jewish religion. The old religion lived on, but now as an unofficial religion. Several of its features did, nevertheless, manage to survive, and some of its beliefs were even able to penetrate into Christianity.

## Notes

1. A longer, but certainly not exhaustive, presentation of my views on the Israelite religion and its historical development is included in Lemche 1988a, 197-257.
2. I believe scholars from many countries will be well acquainted with examples of this. The introduction of critical biblical scholarship even in the Scandinavian countries was never a matter of course, but always involved struggles with conservatives not only to defend freedom of research but also to obtain academic positions for its adherents. The conservative influence in USA of the so-called "Albright-school" is most conspicuous, and the reaction after the demise of its master, W.F. Albright, in 1971, as expressed above all in Thompson 1974, provoked bitter responses from members of the school.
3. This expression was coined by the Italian assyriologist Mario Liverani in his discussion of early Hettite historiography (Liverani 1977), where he demonstrates that this procedure is in no way confined to the study of Israelite history. A discussion of the means and manners of the study of Israelite history is to be found in Lemche 1984 & 1988b, 53-65.
4. There are a number of histories of the religion of Israel more or less along such lines. Most explicitly in two German studies: Schmidt 1968 and Fohrer 1969. Similar in outline is Ringgren 1963.
5. Standard representations of this classical view on the history of Israel are Noth 1950 and, the most recent, Donner 1984-86. The American "histories" have generally been more conservative (closer to paraphrase of the biblical account). See, however, Miller & Hayes 1986.
6. A history of research (until 1967) may be found in Stamm & Andrew 1967.
7. Biblical quotations have been taken from *The New English Bible*, 1970.
8. Examples of the reevaluation of the early history of Israel and of her history writing as found in the OT are Lemche 1985 and van Seters 1983.
9. The fact that N.K. Gottwald fails to recognize the obvious connection between Israel's profane or secular history and her religious history has had severe consequences for his imaginative work, *The Tribes of Yahweh* (Gottwald 1979), which might otherwise have been *the* book about the origin of Israel. As it now appears, it represents more or less a fanciful and disparate endeavour to reconcile the standard opinion of the religion and its origin with a necessary reevaluation of the secular history. The endeavour is not successful in my opinion.
10. I shall not present here a long list of books on Ugaritic religion. Of special interest is the epos of Ba'al. Recent studies of this are de Moor 1971 and Margalith 1980. The most important texts have been translated in J.B. Pritchard 1950, 129-155.

134                                                    *Niels Peter Lemche*

11. "So-called" because this period is no more historical than, say, the heroic age in Greek legendary literature.
12. A handy edition of the two most important texts, from *Hirbet el-Qôm* and *Kuntillat Ajrud* in southern Palestine, is Jaroš 1982, nos. 30 and 32.
13. An imposing collection of pictorial representations of female deities, all deriving from Palestine in the Iron Age, has been presented by Winter 1983. Less satisfying is his evaluation of this material (Winter 1983, 479 ff.), because, in this case again, it seems as if the author was hindered from drawing obvious conclusions because of his adherence to the still prevailing view on the historical development of Israel and her religion. Winter's book must, however, be counted as one of the most important studies on the religious role of the female half of mankind and gods, which has ever appeared in the field of OT studies.
14. An (in)famous example of this attitude is that of Albright 1942, 338.
15. To mention only one fine example of the importance of the ethical aspects of the religion in the ancient Near East, cf., Schmid 1968.
16. The school most likely originated among refugees from the north after 722 B.C. See on this Alt 1953. The literature on the subject is enormous. Most histories of Israel, including the examples mentioned in the notes in this article, will include sections on this phenomenon. My own opinion is expressed in Lemche 1988a, 164-172.
17. The number of deportees may not have exceeded more than 5-10 percent of the total population of Judah at the time. Perhaps some 5,000 to 10,000 Judaeans were forced to leave their country for Babylonia. On the other hand, the number of Judaean refugees in Egypt who more or less deliberately left the country after 587 B.C. is incalculable.

**Bibliography**

Albright, W.F., 1942: "The Role of the Canaanites in the History of Civilization", in: G.E. Wright 1961, 328-362.
Alt, A., 1953: "Die Heimat des Deuteronomiums", *Kleine Schriften zur Geschichte Israels* II, München, 250-275.
Donner, H., 1984-86: *Geschichte des Volkes Israel und seiner Nachbarn in Grundzügen* I-II, Göttingen.
Fohrer, G., 1969: *Geschichte der israelitischen Religion*, Berlin.
Gottwald, N.K., 1979: *The Tribes of Yahweh*, New York.
Jaroš, K., 1982: *Hundert Inschriften aus Kanaan und Israel*, Fribourg.
Lang, B., 1983a: "The Yahweh-Alone Movement and the Making of Jewish Monotheism", in: B. Lang 1983b, 13-59.
Lang, B., 1983b: *Monotheism and the Prophetic Minority,* Sheffield.
Lemche, N.P., 1984: "On the Problem of Studying Early Israelite History", *Biblische Notizen* 24, 1984, 94-124.

Lemche, N.P., 1985: *Early Israel*, Leiden.

Lemche, N.P., 1988a: *Ancient Israel*, Sheffield.

Lemche, N.P., 1988b: "Rachel and Lea. Or: On the Survival of Outdated Paradigmas in the Study of the Origin of Israel-II", *Scandinavian Journal of the Old Testament*, 1988/1, 39-45.

Liverani, M., 1977: "Storiografia politica hittita-II: Telipino, ovvero: della solidarietà", *Oriens Antiquus* 16, 1977, 105-131.

Margalith, B., 1980: *A Matter of "Life" and "Death"*, Neukirchen-Vluyn.

Mazar, A., 1962: "The 'Bull Site' - An Iron Age I Open Cult Place", *Bulletin of the American Schools of Oriental Research* 253, 1982, 27-42.

Miller, J.M. & J. Hayes, 1986: *A History of Ancient Israel and Judah*, Philadelphia.

Moor, J. de, 1971: *The Seasonal Pattern in the Ugaritic Myth of Ba'lu*, Kevelaer-Neukirchen-Vluyn.

Noth, M., 1950: *Geschichte Israels*, Göttingen.

Pritchard, J.B., 1950: *Ancient Near Eastern Texts Relating to the Old Testament*, Princeton 1950.

Ringgren, H., 1963: *Israelitische Religion*, Stuttgart.

Schmid, H.H., 1968: *Gerechtigkeit als Weltordnung*, Tübingen.

Schmidt, W.H., 1968: *Alttestamentlicher Glaube und seine Umwelt*, Neukirchen-Vluyn.

Seters, J van, 1983: *In Search of History*, New Haven.

Stamm, J.J. & M.E. Andrew, 1967: *The Ten Commandments in Recent Research*, London.

Thompson, T.L., 1974: *The Historicity of the Patriarchal Narratives*, Berlin/New York.

Winter, U., 1983: *Frau und Göttin*, Fribourg/Göttingen.

Wright, G.E., 1961: *The Bible and the Ancient Near East*, New York.

*Australia and Africa:*
*Change by Contact*

# Renewal as Tradition:
# New Cults in Aboriginal Australia

*By Monica Engelhart*

Tradition, it has been pointed out, is no static phenomenon. It includes the transmitting of cultural items as well as the cultural items themselves, and we know that every cultural item transferred to new generations or other groups of people changes during the process of transmission according to the giving and the receiving part. The term "re-creating" has been suggested to me for this process, but, in my opinion, "re-shaping" would be more to the point in describing the changes automatically made by the receiver's understanding ability and the modifications made by the transmitter due to his/her own experiences and ability to transmit an idea. We have to expect such changes also in a society where no changes are officially acknowledged, as among the Australian Aborigines, where it was dogmatically assumed that the world and the culture were unchanged since the mythical beginnings of time.

Yet various cultural items, also sacred ones, were traded far and wide. It follows, then, that the word "tradition" in its meaning of something stable and unalterable is out of place here. As Kolig (1971, 99) rightly points out: "there exists no generally applicable concept of 'traditional Aboriginal religion'". He also shows that a stability in religious ideas was impossible in this culture where no central religious authority controlled aberrations, if any (1971, 101).

On the other hand, "traditional" is still a rather handy concept in its sense of defining the receiving culture in an acculturation situation, notwithstanding the fact that the transmitting culture is as traditional in *its* own way... In this essay, "traditional" has been used to denote those ideas, actions, and objects that were current among the Aborigines at the time of European contact. It will be shown that the idea of renewal was well integrated in this "tradition", due to the continuous communication with the mythical, creative aspects of life, the Dreaming.

There are two main strands in the religious web of the Australian Aborigines, the one mythical, the other ritual. The mythical strand is what is usually called the Dreaming, that is, myths about the primeval ancestors, the great culture-heroes and creators, who fashioned the land according to their wishes and prepared it for men to live in, laying down all valid rules for social and political life, for economic business and material items, and for all kinds of spiritual culture - language, stories, songs, art, and so on. They were also responsible for the very existence of man in depositing their own spiritual and creative power as a kind of life-giving essence to vivify all beings in the world. The religious life of the Aborigines was entirely built on a belief in these ancestors and on the stories and songs of their creative deeds and wanderings on the earth, which were recalled and re-enacted in ritual.

Ritually, the principal issue in Aboriginal religious life is the idea of initiation. Initiation for the Aborigines was not just a matter of introducing a young man or girl to tribal knowledge and adult be-haviour, duties, and rights. Initiation was (and seems to be still) a process of still further learning; for some people, it is an endless journey into new lands of knowledge and action.

The initiation of the youth was in most parts of Australia a ritual in several stages, spanning over a period of some years. And in some regions, it never did actually end - there was always some new know-ledge of some other kind or in some deeper grade, to get initiated into, like particularly sacred/dangerous places and the mythology concerning them, or simply some secret meaning of a song-line already learned. And there were, particularly in the Western Desert, foreign ritual constellations that were introduced by visitors.

These beliefs, stories, and rules for living and for ritual behaviour, the Aborigines call the Law, with an implicit meaning of something firm and unalterable. But the Aborigines were never rigid about this binding firmness in details. In their system of rules and notions, a buffer was built-in that safe-guarded their acculturative adaptability (cf., Kolig 1971, 104).

The crucial point is that the ancestors are supposed to never have left this world and that the expression "Dreaming" refers to an on-going dimension of time which makes possible a continuous contact with their creative properties, which actually may take place in a nocturnal dream, but not necessarily so. And what is important here is that the mythic beings seem to take a vivid interest in contem-porary affairs as well, with all that it brings to the Aborigines of European ideas and things.

This is the case with Wuirangu, the mythical founder of the Djuluru cult, the performances of which are held among other places in Fitzroy Crossing, a small city in the northwestern part of Australia (Kolig 1979). The myth underlying the cult acts relates how Wuirangu as a spirit child watched the Japanese attack on the city of Broome on the west coast, a centre for the pearl-fishing industry. Wuirangu saw bombing and gun-fire, and he told the person he had chosen to organize the cult of this event afterwards. It is not known exactly where or when or by whom the Djuluru cult first originated. Kolig reports that it has been tracked with some certainty westwards, to the coast at Eighty Mile Beach and maybe further south to Port Hedland or maybe even Jigalong, where there lived, at least in the early seventies, an Aboriginal community strongly aware of their cultural heritage and resisting intensely the influence of the Christian mission (Tonkinson 1974). It is, however, uncertain whether Djuluru has really travelled that far. The mythic content seems to be related to the experiences of the living aborigines in the northwest, which does not imply, however, that the cult has remained unchanged during its expansion.

In the cultic performance at Fitzroy Crossing, there were several allusions to European items. At the dancing place, there should be a pot filled with clean water, if the season had been dry, for Wuirangu's horse to drink. Wuirangu himself was sometimes said to be a black man, sometimes a half-cast, and sometimes a white man; and it was even said that he could arrive at the performance as a car, an aeroplane, or a bell (Kolig 1979, 423).

On the other hand, most of the ritual paraphernalia used was of an Aboriginal kind, for example, thread-crosses which, particularly among the Western Desert groups, symbolized the mythic ancestors and played an important ritual role.

Anyway, whoever introduced the Djuluru and wherever it was first performed, the basic idea is that Wuirangu, the mythical hero, contacted an Aborigine and told him (it was probably a man, although it cannot be excluded that it might have been a woman) that the cult had to be performed and told him how to do it. Every detail in the cult was said to have been invented by Wuirangu and transmitted by him to the aboriginal agent. This is clearly in accordance with traditional beliefs about the mythical ancestors as being the sole inventors of every cultural trait - whatever the content of the cult may be (Kolig 1979, 424).

Kolig reports that Djuluru was immensely popular at Fitzroy Crossing, a place where a lot of Aboriginal people from various tribes and language units had come together for different reasons (Kolig 1979, 421). The Djuluru was arranged in the same way as in traditional cults: there were owners of the cult who acted as the spiritual experts, singing the song-lines and knowing the right ways to perform the cult, and there were managers or helpers who were responsible for collecting food and fuel, keeping people in order, preparing meals, and so on. The ritual place was arranged in traditional ways with a section open to the audience and a closed section for the initiated.

The division in owners and managers corresponds to ordinary ritual arrangements, where, according to moiety principles, people of the same moiety were the owners of some cults and people from the other moiety acted as managers and helpers. This ritual principle of cooperation between owners and managers operated also in the Djuluru, not because the performers were still related in specific ways to one another, but because the traditional ritual setting demanded that arrangement (Kolig 1979, 430f; cf., also Meggitt 1984, 221f and Bell 1983, 20).

*The Djuluru Performance*

The performance started one afternoon with a short introductory phase where everybody seemed to have come just to have a nice time together. Some men and women started singing, and a number of men stepped forward from the bushes dressed up in their ritual gear: loincloth, head-band, and other decorations. They approached the audience in short advances, throwing a board on the ground in front of them. Each time they reached the board, they stopped and waited for the singers to finish one more stanza of the opening song. When the dancers had arrived close to the audience, they stayed for a while as the singers sang yet a couple of stanzas, and then they all withdrew back into the bush, and the introductory part was over (Kolig 1979, 429).

In this way, everybody, active and passive participants alike, moved gradually from their everyday existence into the realm of ritual. Kolig calls it a "slow, spiritual preparation" (Kolig 1979, 429). The powerful parts of the ceremony could not be staged in the beginning, since that would be too dangerous. This evaluation of different levels of danger within the ritual was characteristic for the Aborigines' way of handling their supernatural environment: a sacred site had to be approached slowly, reverentially, and by roundabout ways; sacred boards or other items were to always be carefully hidden, songlines belonging to ritual could never be sung by unauthorized persons and so on. And since the ritual realm in every case was so carefully guarded, it is easy to understand why every cult, also the new ones that contained European elements, demanded an initiation: there were

sacred elements in it that were simply too dangerous to approach un-
prepared. Initiation served as a way of making an individual fit to
handle these dangers.

After the introductory part, the ceremony continued in a more
secret and earnest manner. The sessions went on for five days, a
couple of hours at a time, starting after sunset on the evening of the
introductory day, the next session following immediately after sunrise
the next day before anyone had had breakfast (Kolig 1979, 429). They
were performed in a secluded spot in the bush, the *wuragu*, rather far
from the general camp. The atmosphere was now one of tension,
reverence, and strict rules of behaviour. The participants were
carefully supervised by so-called "policemen" already when
approaching the *wuragu*, particularly when the evening session started.
Only active participants were permitted to camp in the close vicinity
of the *wuragu*, everybody else had to stay at the general camp and
approach the *wuragu* at twilight without making noise and talking in
whispers only. Wuirangu, like so many other Australian mythical
heroes, did not like noise; it made him angry. Kolig does not report
what possible consequences this might have for the assembly or for
people nearby.

The cultic performance at the *wuragu* consisted of dances
performed by men dressed in loin-cloths and with small boards stuck
in their hair, while some of the women beat the rhythm by clapping
their thighs. Later on, some men and women performed a contra-
dance, in which the couples were paired according to traditional
marriage rules, even though they were not actually married to each
other. The people in this part of Australia were organised into eight
named sections with strictly determined rules for marriage between the
sections. And though so many social accidents have happened to the
Aborigines, they still strive to stick to this social arrangement, not
only among themselves, but extending it to white people as well. So,
in spite of the assembly at Fitzroy Crossing consisting of several
tribes or language groups, the eight-section structure organization
permeated the performance of the new Djuluru cult. The couples
danced carrying fire-sticks, which is another old feature of many
rituals. The contra-dance ended with each partner touching one another
with the burning fire-sticks.

Traditional thread-crosses had also found their way into the
Djuluru. Women and children were not allowed to look at them, but
had to throw themselves to the ground and hide under blankets when
the crosses were brought forward from behind a screen of twigs. The
thread-crosses played a part in the initiation of new cult members.

When the women and children had left the cult ground, the novices were allowed to have a closer look at them and touch them while one of the ritual experts explained their meanings (Kolig 1979, 434).

During the next night's session, some men danced with sticks about two meters long that were called "rifles". The dance was designed as a military drill with men marching up and down with the sticks until they suddenly threw them like spears against a pole in a corner of the ritual ground, which was called *warmala*, a common designation among the people of the desert southwest of Fitzroy Crossing. This was sometimes interpreted as referring to a war in the Dream-time between mythical heroes, watched by Wuirangu, and sometimes to a war between White people.

The ritual sequence ended in the so-called *devil-gura* that is, "belonging to the devil". Now, cult objects - in this case two pencil-drawings showing an Aboriginal man dressed as a cult dancer with loin-cloth and a small board in his hair - were sent around among the spectators who handled them with the utmost reverence, since they were assumed to picture Wuirangu himself (Kolig 1979, 436). Four large boards were also sent around among the men only, who pressed them against their stomachs which is considered to be the centre of life. To press a cult object which is assumed to contain a great creative and life-giving power against certain parts of the body was a common feature, particularly in initiation rituals (cf., Meggitt 1984, 302; Tonkinson 1978, 101; Spencer-Gillen 1899, 326).

Everybody now moved to the *wuragu* where a man was standing still in the fire-light. When he moved, everybody saw a meter-high pole decorated with a meandering design and with two anthropomorphous figures, named Barolgada and Budagada at the bottom. It was said that they were incarnations of Wuirarnations of Wuirangu who was burned to death in the war that he witnessed but who imparted his life-essence to these two creatures called Baralgada and Budagada. But still, Wuirangu continued to exist in his own identity so that in the end he became a tripartite being. This cult pole constituted the centre of Djuluru, the principal manifestation of Wuirangu, in his three aspects. The song-lines now sung referred to a boat accident outside Derby, not far from Broome, which is said to have happened around the turn of the century and which Wuirangu was said to have witnessed (Kolig 1979, 437).

The word "devil" in the name of this last cultic event refers to Wuirangu. The highlight of the event was a dance by three men who were called the "devil-men" and who represented the three aspects of Wuirangu. They carried big thread-crosses that were put down in the earth. In the morning, the novices were allowed to have a look at them, but they had to start looking at the ground immediately in front of where they were sitting first, and then with their eyes follow a line drawn in the sand leading to the crosses, thus allowing their eyes to slowly approach the powerful crosses. In this way, they were protected from the harm which these dangerous objects could cause (Kolig 1979, 439f).

As the very last part of the ceremony, the spectators, including women and children and white people, were taken behind the bush-screen and shown the bells that were used to call people to the dancing place and which represented Wuirangu's voice. It was pointed out that they had not come from any cattle station in the vicinity (apparently they were ordinary cow-bells), but that they belonged to the cult gear and were probably taken over with the cult poles when the Djuluru was brought to Fitzroy Crossing.

## Still Walking the Old Tracks

Kolig calls this a syncretistic cult because of the use of bells and other European elements. He also pointed out that the traumatic experiences of the contact period and, particularly for the northern and northwestern peoples, during the Second World War had driven the Aborigines out of their static views of the world and forced them to accept changes, departures, and the idea that other processes than those based on the Dreaming had a creative power. But his example here does not show anything created by forces other than the Dreaming power. Wuirangu clearly belongs to the Dreaming even though he is not connected with any locality or clan.

Of course, we cannot deny some obviously European elements here: the bells as Wuirangu's voice may be derived from church-bells as God's voice calling people to Sunday service. The word "devil" clearly originates from the White people's interpretation of the Aborigines' beliefs. It is a common word used for important indigenous supernatural beings.

The idea of trinity might also derive from Christianity, although the concept of being simultaneously one being and several other beings is not intirely foreign to Aboriginal philosophy. After all, there existed the idea of an identity between man, land, beast, or plant, and mythical ancestor as a characteristic feature of Aboriginal thought, as well as the idea of time passed and at the same time still going on, i.e., the Dreaming.

The term "syncretistic" might be applicable to the experiences of a foreign culture which have been moulded into a traditional frame-work. But the strategy of translating experiences into the language of mythology must certainly be labelled indigenous. Looking at the Ab-original features of the cult, we find that the focus, the Wuirangu figure, is a traditional mythical hero who lived like the Aborigines and had the same experiences as they had. There is nothing intrin-sically different between Wuirangu's experiences and those of all the other mythical ancestors who moved over the land, hunting, eating, sleeping, making love, quarreling, and so on, just like ordinary black people did. His level of existence is the Dreaming. The authorization of the cult lies in Wuirangu's having instructed some special Abori-ginal person who was obliged to carry out his instructions. In fact, what we meet here is a traditional culture hero.

The socio-ritual order of the cult arrangements have already been mentioned: the division between "owners" and managers which in ritual confirmed the co-operation between different social groups (moieties or sections).

Another feature that should be mentioned is the site of the per-formance: a secluded spot out in the bush, carefully separated from places of everyday activities. In aboriginal ritual life, it was out of the question to put "the church in the middle of the village". This is an outcome of the importance attached to the danger of all ritual items, which is also indicated by the slow and careful manner of approach-ing it: the gradual escalation of the performances, the importance of quietness, the initiates' way of moving their eyes slowly along a track to the thread-crosses.

Besides the Djuluru, there are also many local variants of greater cult-complexes, such as Kurangara (Petri 1950 and 1967), Gadjari (Meggit 1966), Dingari, Wogaia (Kolig 1981), and others that belong to the wandering cults, constellations of myths, ritual actions, and beliefs which are spreading over the northern and western parts of Australia, some nativistic in scope, others less so. The myths under-lying these cults are connected with Dreaming heroes and defined localities, i.e., the wandering tracks of the mythical heroes are well recognized, intergrating certain land areas in the cult.

The question is whether these recent cults are an outcome of the acculturation situation as an answer to the stress of sudden changes in circumstances, or if they were traditionally secured also in pre-contact times. Historic times of the Aborigines in northern Australia is not much more than a hundred years, that is, since Europeans ar-rived and started documenting Aboriginal societies and beliefs. In these descriptions of Aboriginal religion, it was understood as being static, unchanged, and without a history, partly because the diachronic perspective was impossible to adopt, but also because so-called primitive peoples were conceived of as being peoples without the ability of developing. And yet, during this short time of Aboriginal history, we have seen cults constantly spreading, particularly up in the north and northwest. This, in combination with the institution of initiation and the interest in extending one's own ritual and mythological knowledge, reduces the term "new cults" to a mere construct, a methodological tool used to designate ritual constellations that were not connected to the land areas of local groups, which is one of the main features of rituals described from early contact times.

What strikes the reader in Kolig's report on the Djuluru is the fact that, in spite of being driven from home-lands that meant so much to Aboriginal identity and in spite of social groups being forced asunder and mixed into new conglomerates with no working relations between them, not even linguistically, these people were none the less driven together into a religious ritual that resembled its models under the former conditions. Though it does not seem to be related to any specific land area, it has all the other features common to a traditional ritual performance.

And yet, the expression "new" might well be defended and used within the traditional setting. It could stand for the not yet experienced. The institution of initiation was an all-pervading notion that structured Aboriginal religious thought. It is very likely that the tendency to accept new religious messages as long as they are founded within the constituting framework of Dreaming mythology had been common also in pre-contact times. Petri (1966, 336) has pointed out that cults sometimes lived a rather short life, without having been wiped out by European contact. He even calls some of them ephemeral: they came to a certain group, became the focus of interest for a short while, and then went on to another group. Something in the eager acceptance of these spreading cults is similar to the interest in European culture for new books, new music, new pieces of art, as if cults for the Aborigines filled the same function as European elements of culture with the same social implications: high social status was in a high degree dependent on a man's amount of ritual knowledge.

C.P. Mountford (1951, 109f) makes a rather interesting point when commenting on the Red-Ochre party which he met at Ernabella in the late 1940's. He assumes that the gathering was more social than ceremonial, pointing out that men and women were living in the same camp, mixing freely, and dancing together at least in the free dances.

148

This corroborates the idea that the social life was intimately connected to the ceremonial. There was not much of a social life (except in the immediate group living together) outside the big ceremonial gatherings, e.g., the tribal initiations. And since the ceremonial life had this all-important social function, the social life had to be modelled upon the ceremonial one.

But obviously, this is not the only reason why Djuluru and other cults are held. The performances seem to have filled an emotional need as well as having reinforced Aboriginal identity and securing ties with the Dreaming. The renewal of the cult relies heavily on tradition. I would suggest that they are just old traditions from pre-contact times that are still carried on.

## Bibliography

Bell, D., 1983: *Daughters of the Dreaming*, Melbourne.

Kolig, E., 1971: "Quo Vadis, Australian Aboriginal Religion?", *International Committee on Urgent Anthropological and Ethnological Research, Bulletin* No. 13, 99-113.

Kolig, E., 1979: "Djuluru: ein synkretistischer Kult Nord-West-Australiens", *Baessler-Archiv*, n.F., 27, 419-448.

Kolig, E., 1981: *The Silent Revolution. The Effects of Modernization on Australian Aboriginal Religion*, Philadelphia.

Meggitt, M., 1962: *Desert People*, Sydney, rpr. 1984.

Meggitt, M., 1966: *Gadjari among the Walbiri Agorigines of Central Australia*, Sydney.

Mountford, C.P., 1951: *Brown Men in Red Sand*, Melbourne.

Petri, H., 1950: "Kurangara. Neue magische Kulte im Nordwesten Australien", *Zeitschrift für Ethnologie* 75.

Petri, H., 1954: *Sterbende Welt in Nordwest-Australien*, Braunschweig.

Petri, H., 1966: "Badur, ein Felsbilderzentrum Australiens", *Baessler-Archiv*, n.F., 14, 331-370.

Petri, H., 1967: "Wandji-Kurangara. Ein mythischer Traditionskomplex aus der westlichen Wüste Australiens", *Baessler-Archiv*, n.F., 15, 1-34.

Spencer, B. & F. Gillen, 1899: *The Native Tribes of Central Australia*, London.

Tonkinson, R., 1974: *The Jigalong Mob: Aboriginal Victors of the Desert Crusade*, Menlo Park.

Tonkinson, R., 1978: *The Mardjudjara Aborigines. Living the Dream in Australia's Desert*, New York.

# "Renewal" By Retrospection: the Asante Anokye Traditions[1]

*By J.G. Platvoet*

Novelty is no less novel for being able to dress up easily as antiquity (Hobsbawm 1983, 5).

The theme of the Second International Conference of the Danish Association for the History of Religions, "Religion: Tradition and Renewal", calls for a comment. The use of "renewal" instead of "change", and in opposition to "tradition", seems to suggest that "tradition" is taken as a thing of the past which is maladjusted to the present and that believers adapt their religion to "modern" times by doing away with tradition. A secular(ist) or liberal(-theological) bias seems to underlie this view. Examples abound in the history of religions of believers adapting their religion to new circumstances by returning to "tradition", or by inventing it. Adaptation to new circumstances by the reinterpretation, elaboration, or invention of tradition occurs also in preliterate religions. In this contribution, I discuss one example of adaptation to altered, and altering, circumstances by the "retrospective invention of tradition" (Hobsbawn 1983, 1-6; Trevor-Roper 1983, 15): the Asante traditions about the priest Anokye. I outline the use which the Asante as a nation made of them since 1874, and the special use to which they were put by the "Anokyeists", more usually known as the Domankoma (Wilks 1975, 519-521; McCaskie 1981, 129-138) or Abonsamkomfo (Rattray 1927, 28-30) - between 1874 and 1880. I will dwell especially on the political and socio-psychological circumstances under which this traditionalizing option was pursued.

## The 1874 Crisis

In the late afternoon of February 4, 1874, British troops entered Kumase, the capital of Asante, ransacked it for a day, and blew up the stone treasure house of the *Asantehene* ("ruler of Asante"). Having set fire to the town during the night, they hastily withdrew on the morning of February 6th. This sack marked the end of the rule for over a century of Asante over most of present-day Ghana and the beginning of the decline of Asante power. But it was not until 1902 that Britain proclaimed the status of colony over Asante itself.

Asante had incorporated the coastal Akan states as provinces into its empire between 1707 and 1765 (Baesjou 1979, 9 n. 13). Throughout the 19th century, the British had fanned disaffection with the central authority at Kumase in these states. It had resulted in ten military clashes with the Asante in that century and the gradual increase of British influence in many of the coastal states. In most of the military engagements, the Asante had been victorious. In two, however, the British because they happened to possess the newest weaponry. They had won the battle of Katamanso in 1826 by the use of Congreve rockets (Wilks 1975, 183; Baesjou 1979, 9). And in 1874, the British managed to break through the Asante defenses and take Kumase because they possessed the newest Gatling machine guns (Gundert 1875, 239).

The defeat at Katamanso had forced the Asante to accept a treaty in 1831, which implied a *de facto* acknowledgment of a British protectorate over several southern provinces of the Asante empire. In 1844, moreover, Britain had concluded a treaty with these coastal states in which they ceded authority to it in criminal matters. The British position had been further strengthened by the withdrawal of Denmark from the Eastern half of the Gold Coast in 1850. Frictions over the interpretation of the 1831 treaty had led to an Asante invasion into Akyem and Fante in 1863 by which it meant to reassert its claims over the states under British protection. The British had made preparations in 1864 to retaliate by an invasion into Asante. They assembled West Indian and local troops at Praso on the southern border of Asante. Disease, however, had so heavily decimated the British forces that the invasion had to be called off. It had caused Kwaku Dua, Asantehene from 1834-1867, to remark: "The whitemen bring many cannon into the bush, but the bush is stronger than the cannon" (quoted in Baesjou 1979, 11).

The British had, however, strengthened their position further by exchanging "possessions" (the trading castles as seats of proto-colonial administration) with the Dutch on January 1, 1868. The scene for the 1873-1874 confrontation had, however, been set when the Dutch left the Gold Coast in April 1872 and ceded all their "territory" to the British (cf. Baesjou 1979, 14, 28-46). The war-party in Asante[2] had not been ready to accept the loss of its loyal ally on the coast, the town and state of Elmina, over and above the loss of the southern provinces, and of its staunch European trading partner, the Dutch, who had maintained their headquarters at Elmina since 1637. The war-party had, moreover, insisted that the "right" of the British over at least some of the former provinces should be contested. It had hoped to reassert Asante sovereignty over the Twi-speaking peoples nearest to the Asante border: the Akyem, Assin, Denkyere, and Wassaw (Gundert 1875, 181), and over the coastal states to the west of Elmina (Wilks 1975, 236). Three Asante armies had, therefore, crossed the river Pra in early 1873. Though suffering heavy casualties, they were victorious at first (Wilks 1975, 236-237). The turn of events had come on June 13, 1873 when an Asante army assisted the towns-people of Elmina in their attempt to dislocate the British from the fort and throw off their newly imposed authority. Their combined forces were repulsed by the British (Baesjou 1979, 49-52). The decimated Asante armies withdrew into Asante by early December 1873.[3]

After the return of the army, many Asante soldiers had publicly stated that they would not go back and fight unless the Asantehene himself accompanied them. They justified this insubordination by pointing out that "the whites have bullets, one of which shoots down time and again five Asante", causing the slain to lie around "as maize scattered on the ground" (Gundert 1875, 184, 212; Wilks 1975, 505-506, 682). On January 2, 1874, two Asante messengers arrived at Praso on the Asante border where the British had again begun to assemble an invasion force. They had been commissioned to convey the readiness of the Asantehene to negotiate a peace. The British commander, Wolseley, chose to disregard that message and, instead, ordered that they be given a demonstration of the firepower of the Gatling machine-guns. They were horrified. One of them stated that Asante could not be defended against it. When his fellow messenger rebuked him for his lack faith in the military strength of Asante, he committed suicide the following night (Gundert 1875, 219-220, 239).

The mood of gloom in Kumase was further deepened by two other "untoward" events which were believed to spell doom for Asante. Asante's most famous general, Asamoa Nkwanta,[4] had lost his war charm which was reputed to be invincible, in the river Pra when his army recrossed it in late 1873 (McCaskie 1986, 317). And on January 6, 1874, the ancient *Kum* tree in Kumase's Great Market, which, it is believed, had been planted by Anokye and from which Kumase ("Under the *Kum*-(tree)") derived its name, had been uprooted (by a rainstorm?) (Gundert 1875, 223, 240). As the destinies of a town or nation were believed to be closely linked to that of its central *gyedua* ("tree of reception") (Platvoet 1985), the "death" of this tree was felt to forebode dire events for Asante and its ruler.

When a month later Kumase was sacked, this was widely felt to be due not only to a gap in military technology, but also to other, "religious" - though for the Asante hardly less mundane - causes. The search for those causes had already begun in 1873 when fear had begun to spread that Asante would suffer the ignominy of an invasion. It continued for several years, producing elements of an "answer". In its final shape, which had been codified into accepted tradition by early colonial time, that answer was given in protological terms in the form of myths about the role of Anokye in the foundation of Kumase and Asante.

## Post-1874 Events

The sack shook Asante severely. It set in motion a train of political events that seemed to forebode the collapse of the empire and the disintegration of the nation. The consequences of the sack were at least threefold.

The first consequence was that the southern part of the empire and, more importantly, the dependable trading outlets, Elmina and other former Dutch "possessions", were irretrievably lost. The British followed up their success with the proclamation of the Crown Colony Gold Coast on August 6, 1874. As it comprised the whole length of the coast from Keta in the East to Half-Assini in the West, Asante was forced to develop the more westerly trade routes to Assini and Grand-Bassam in "French" territory (now Ivory Coast), and the more easterly smugglers' route over the Keta Lagoon into Ouidah, also a "French possession" to the south of Dahomey. European entrepreneurs, British, French, and Danish, were taken into Asante service for that purpose on the advice of "Prince" (*oheneba*) John Owusu Ansa.[5] He returned to Kumase in late 1875 to become the foremost adviser of the new Asantehene, Mensa Bonsu (1874-1883), in matters of modernization. Between 1875 and 1880, he designed the reform of the civil service, the army, and the traditional penal code (Wilks 1975, 606-630).

The second consequence of the sack was that the northern half of the empire immediately prepared to shake off the Asante shackles. The Dagomba had already killed most of the members of an Asante party in August 1873 (Gundert 1875, 193-194; Wilks 1975, 239). In the northwestern provinces, with Gyaman as its centre, a period of uncertain loyalty ensued. A secessionist party, headed by the *Gyaman-hene* Agyeman, made shows of asking for British "protection". It was opposed by a strong loyalist party which favoured the continuation of ties to Asante. Mensa Bonsu refrained from military action. Instead, he sent diplomatic missions to Gyaman in 1875 and in 1878 and managed to keep the secessionist forces in check (Wilks 1975, 287-295).

However, the northeastern part of the empire was lost to the Asante. It had Krakye, the home of the famous Dente oracle, as its centre and included the biggest market in the Asante empire, Salaga (Wilks 1975, 244, 262, 279-282, 611; Maier 1981, 230-233, 242; 1983, 89ff.). Also here, Asante refrained from attempting to re-impose its power by military means. It responded by withholding the all-important trade in kola nuts from Salaga. It developed a new market for it at Kintampo in Nkoranza territory which had long been its most faithful ally in the northern parts and was much nearer to Asante itself than Salaga (Wilks 1975, 282-287). Some of the new regiments, equipped with the latest guns, were, moreover, posted along the Volta to prevent the development of a direct trade route from Salaga over Kete Krakye to the coast and in the northwest to deflect trade between Gyaman and Salaga to Kintampo (Wilks 1975, 284, 286).

The third and most serious consequence was the immediate danger of the disintegration of the Asante nation itself. Dwaben, one of the founding states of Asante, rebelled against the Asantehene in February 1874, persuaded the northeastern districts led by Krakye to rebel, and seceded from Asante in an attempt to become itself the leader of an eastern confederacy of states between Asante and the Volta.[6] When Kofi Kakari failed to take action against Dwaben, he was deposed in October 1874 and replaced by Mensa Bonsu (1874-1883). In August 1975, the new Asantehene tested the loyalty of the remaining confederates by convening an extraordinary *Asantemanhyiamu* ("meeting of (the heads of state of) the Asante nation"). All voted for war against Dwaben. After heavy fighting and serious losses on both sides, Dwaben was defeated in early November 1875. Most of the Dwaben fled southwards into the Colony and were settled in Akyem Abuakwa territory (Wilks 1975, 511-516).

## The Search for Explanation

The events of 1873-1875 plunged the Asante into a period of deep uncertainty with respect to their national identity. A nation-wide search was set in motion by these events. A whole gamut of answers was given, ranging from a "modernist", rational one at one extreme to a "mythical", religious one at the other with most a mixture of the two.

The "modernist" answer was a sober analysis of the relative political and military strengths of Asante and the British and of the gaps in Asante military technology and organization, bureaucratic organization, infrastructure, and penal code, which had caused the Asante setback in 1873-1874. Owusu Ansa embodied this type of analysis. His answer was to set political and other processes in motion by which the gaps could be narrowed as quickly as possible in order that the encroachment of British power could be resisted, the unity of the nation safeguarded, and the remnants of the empire retained. These attempts at redress proved fairly effective at first. The unity of the nation was maintained at the cost of the secession and migration of Dwaben. A measure of control was maintained over the northwestern and central northern parts of the empire, and the kola-trade was rerouted. The northeastern parts were lost, but the British were prevented from establishing a direct trade route along the Volta from the coast through Krakye to Salaga. The army and its weaponry were modernized, and, in 1881, the threat of another British invasion was averted (Wilks 1975, 284-286, 290-292, 525-527, 606-631).

The success of the "modernist" measures proved, however, to be a temporary remedy only, as is apparent from the events of 1883-1888, when Asante slipped into a civil war. The more fundamental issue of the balance of power between Kumase and the other federates had not been addressed. The constitutional supremacy in a confederate Asante of the *Asantemanhyiamu* (the "meeting of the Asante nation") over the "Kumase Council" had not been reasserted (Wilks 1975, 409-411). This *de facto* supremacy of the Kumase Council seems to have inspired the broad wave of explanation of the 1873-1874 "disasters" in terms of the Anokye traditions. These opted for positions ranging from federalist-conservative to extreme traditionalist.

The earliest explanation had not, however, been in terms of Anokye, but of the war party's refusal, in 1870-1873, to release without ransom the Whites who had been held captive since 1869.[7] In February 1873, one of them wrote: "It is certain that many believe that we are the cause of their misfortune" (Gundert 1875, 175). Asamoa Nkwanta and Owusu Ansa had both warned Kofi Kakari that he better release the White captives or risk losing the war (Gundert 1874, 175, 179). So had some religious authorities. The first had been an oracle obtained in early February 1873 "from the interior" (the northern parts of the empire) through a Muslim.[8] It read "The war will go against you as long as you hold captive the whites who pray constantly to God; free them and you will be victorious" (Gundert 1875, 175; Wilks 1975, 239, 317). The pressure to release them had increased since mid-July 1873 when warning had been received from Kwankyeabo, a southwestern ally, that the British were planning to march on Kumase by Christmas 1873. The urgent advice had been added to release the war captives, White as well as Fante, immediately (Gundert 1874, 194-195). In mid-October 1873, intelligence was sent to Kumase by its southeastern ally Akwamu that many troops, White and Hausa, were landing in the ports and that the British were planning an invasion. Akwamu also urged that the captives be sent to the coast. At the same time, exceptionally heavy rainfall for late October had caused considerable damage to the royal residence and the stone treasure house. When the Asantehene sent for a female *okomfo* to explain the cause of all this misfortune, her god replied through her that it was because of the strangers, White and Fante, who were being held captive. Only if they were released could the war be won. Kofi Kakari had her put in irons for it (Gundert 1875, 203-205). By mid-November, however, the *Asantehemaa* (Queen-Mother), Afua Kobi, sided with this opinion. She stated in council on November 20th that all Asante were in danger of being destroyed by this war because it was unjust. The British had offered ransom, but the captives had not been released. She moved that the Whites be sent off in order that God might again "be on our side" (Gundert 1875, 208; Wilks 1975, 507).

The intervention of the Afua Kobi had clinched the issue, and the armies were recalled. On January 9, 1874, Kühne was sent to Wolseley, who was assembling his forces at Praso, in the company of messengers sent to sue for peace. Wolseley had, however, sent them back with a letter in which he demanded that the other prisoners be released at once. He also wrote that "it is essential that Your Majesty and your people should learn that you can no more prevent an army of white men marching into your territory [...] than you can stop the sun from rising every morning" (quoted in Wilks 1975, 508). So, after the other prisoners were released during January 21st-23rd (Gundert 1875, 229-223, 229-236), Wolseley marched on Kumase, which he entered on February 4th after five days of fierce fighting. As Asante resistance under Asamoa Nkwanta had nearly disproved his boast, he withdrew from Kumase on the 6th. He retreated southwards so hastily that the Asante had to plead with him to stop and wait for them at Fomena for the conclusion of a peace treaty on February 13, 1874 on his terms (Wilks 1975, 510).

## The Anokye Explanation

On July 29, 1873, Owusu Ansa published an outline of Asante history in the *The Times* of London. He made no mention of *Okomfo Anokye* in it (McCaskie 1986, 332). The earliest dateable reference to Anokye, though not by name, is in Gros (1884, 257). Bonnat describes there how he had been taken prisoner at Attebubu in September 1875 at the time when Asante forces had made their first attacks on secessionist Dwaben (Wilks 1975, 515). Bonnat was captured at the orders of the rebellious *Dwabenhene* Asafo Agyei, saw his fifty Asante attendants massacred, and was himself taken to Dwaben for trial. There, many clamoured for Bonnat's beheading since, having entered Asante civil service (Wilks 1975, 606), he was a man of the Asantehene. It was objected, however, that the "religious law of the nation" had always unequivocally forbidden the violent death of a White man in Asante or in its dependent nations. No traditional priest would contradict that if it ever came to pass, "all the people of our vast territories would be destroyed at once". This argument was accepted by all. Bonnat was escorted into the British colony instead of being beheaded.

Anokye is not mentioned by name in the speech which saved Bonnat's life. Yet it seems certain that everyone present understood the counterargument to refer to Anokye by the combination of references to the law of the nation, religion, and priests, and to a prediction about the future of the Asante nation that served both as a sanction of the law and as an explanation of Asante's decline. From 1875 onwards, it became commonly held that virtually every law and binding custom had been instituted by Anokye. He came to be regarded not only as the Solon and Manu of Asante[9] but also as the foremost founder of the Asante nation (Rattray 1929, 73, 270). All the important political institutions of Asante were said to be the "laws of Anokye". Among them were *Sika Dwa Kofi*, the "Golden Stool Friday",[10] the shrine of the "soul" (*sunsum*) of the Asante nation, and the "law of Anokye" that no other state in the Asante nation or empire could possess a gold-embossed stool. Other "laws of Anokye" decreed that all lower Asante rulers (*ahemfo*, "chiefs") must swear fealty to the Asantehene and bravery until victory or death before a war; that they must attend the weeklong annual *Odwira* ("cleansing") rites at Kumase; and that they must attend the *Asantemanhyiamu*, "meeting of the Asante nation", which was held in conjunction with it. He is said to have instituted the Asante version of "indirect rule", by which a tributary nation is ruled by a cooperative ruler from its own ruling house under the supervision of a Kumase notable who acts as its *adamfo* ("friend/patron") in the court of the Asantehene; to have devised the Asante judicial system and the central position in it of the *okyeame*, "court speaker"; and to have decreed that an *okomfo* who utters a false prophecy be put to death, (Rattray 1929, 35 n.2, 40, 82, 273-280; Kyerematen 1969, 4-5, 8).

Anokye, the statesman, is only one aspect of the post-1874 Anokye traditions. They also tell about his birth and youth in the Kyerepon-Guan town of Awukugua, his training there as a priest, and how he and Osee Tutu met and became friends in Akwamu or Denkyera, the two most powerful states in the Akan area in the second half of the 17th century. They detail his military and political role in throwing off Denkyera overlordship and in the constitution of Asante, his prophecies about future political fortunes,[11] and how, at the end of his life, he retired in order to search for the medicine against death. Traditions say he found it, but could not pass it on to his fellow men because his injunctions had not been obeyed.

A number of elements in these traditions strike the eye as relevant for explanatory purposes in the post-1874 period. Anokye's political, military, and other roles in the decades around 1700 are cast in those of a traditional priest and not of an Akan military and political leader, even though traditions say that he was, or was made, *Agonahene*, "ruler of [the town and state of] Agona". He is depicted as being involved in the events in extraordinary ways. E.g., whenever the forces of nascent Asante were on the verge of being overwhelmed by the enemy, he saved them from defeat by some military miracle, or by defeating the traditional priest supporting the other side in spiritual combat. His feats of statemanship, e.g., the selection of Kumase as Asante's capital and of Osee Tutu as Asantehene, are described as events in which he involved the meta-empirical realm heavily. These traditions depict him as having founded Asante by his possession of powers which transcend the ordinary and which he used to create the secure foundation of Osee Tutu's Asante. He securely legitimated the confederation in the eyes of post-1874 Asante. They believed him to have provided full legitimation to the "Asante" of his own time.

Though he is stated to have performed miracles of all sorts,[12] one special power is often attributed to him: that of "vanishing" and "causing to vanish" (*ayera*). Traditional connotations of *yera* are to be lost in the forest (in a first possession, or as a hunter), to be off on long travels to faraway places, to change into the form of someone else or of some animal and fly (witches "vanish" from their bodies at night and fly to the meeting place of their coven), to practice witchcraft (witches cause their victims' blood to "vanish"), and to be killed (people who happened to be out on the streets at night when a ruler had died, were said to have "vanished") (Christaller 1933, 588). *Ayera* evokes dense associations with the meta-empirical, particularly in its "wild" (undomesticated), fearful forms.

The Anokye traditions constantly touch upon the theme of *ayera*. Anokye is said to have disappeared for days on end from infancy onwards; to have withdrawn to solitary places all through his life; to have travelled much, e.g., to "*Obi* (some [unknown]) country", from which he brought back a new god (as priests often do). Traditions say that he flew through the air as a child and caused a man to fly over the battlelines in the war against Denkyera in order to cause confusion there. He changed into the shape of a woman in order to steal literally the heart of the ruler of Denkyera, Ntim Gyakari. He caused an albino and seven pythons to "vanish" into the Golden Stool, and the *Kumawuhene* Tweneboa Kodua into the earth. He is said to have "vanished" from this life in a peculiar way:

At last Anotche informed Osai Tutu that he was about to set out in quest of a medicine against death. He asked Osai Tutu to call his nephew, Kwame Siaw, and all the Elders of Agona Akyempim to come to Kumasi. When they did so, he informed them that he would be absent seven years and seventy-seven days and nights, and that during all that time no one must weep or fire a gun, or mourn for him, although he appeared to be dead. He returned to Agona Akyempim, and entered his house [...], and there he "died". Before he did so he gave orders that he was not to be disturbed for seven years and seventy-seven days and nights. The town was placed in charge of his elders. For seven years and seventy days his orders were obeyed, when his nephew at length declared that his uncle was really dead, and that people should weep and that guns should be fired. The door of the room was opened; the chamber was found to be empty.

On that very day, a man from Mampong was passing Agona, when at the place called *Abetene* he was addressed by a man who inquired what was happening at Agona Akyempim, as guns were being fired and people wailing. He replied that they were holding the funeral custom of Komfo Anotche. The man then said that he was Komfo Anotche, that he had obtained the medicine against death, and was returning with it, but as his kinsfolk had disobeyed his orders, he would go away for ever, and the Ashanti would never find the medicine against death, whose great taboo[13] was the holding of a funeral custom (Rattray 1929, 279).

The point of this myth is that the Asante were made to suffer for the disobedience of a ruler. Anokye's successor declared his uncle dead and himself ruler of Agona a week too early. Because he disobeyed an injunction of Anokye, the Asante continue to die. Life without death as men had enjoyed "long ago" before God withdrew up on high was not restored to men.

In the post-1874 traditions, disobedience of the laws of Anokye by rulers is given as a major cause of the "ruin of the nation" (*amansee*). It was held that Anokye had prophesied at the time of the constitution of *Sika Dwa Kofi* itself that Asante would be ruled by seven powerful kings, after which its strength would wane. These seven kings were all the pre-1867 rulers of Asante who had achieved full ancestral status.[14] In the Anokye prophecy which saved the life of Bonnat in Dwaben in September 1876, the destruction of Asante was linked to the violence towards the White captives. It continues the tradition of the prophecies in 1872-1873 which put the blame of defeat on Kofi Kakari because he had not released the captives. The Anokye prophecy which most explicitly links royal disobedience to the laws of Anokye, to British military ascendancy, and to Asante becoming a British colony was registered in 1925 by Rattray. That was on the occasion of his visit to Agona when he witnessed a rite performed by the *Agonahene* and heard him address his predecessor in office in the following words:

| | |
|---|---|
| Kwame Boakye, Boakye Tenten | Kwame Boakye, Boakye the Tall One, |
| Boakye Yiadom | Boakye, Vanquisher of armies, |
| wo nsa ni o | here is wine for you. |
| wo ne Englis abrofo | You and the English White men |
| namteye | have walked together well. |
| wo nana Komfo Anokye | Your grandfather, Komfo Anokye, |
| na obeye Asanteman | he made the Asante nation! |
| na okyekye mara horow | He made many laws |
| a ese se ye fa so ye bu man | by which we might rule the nation! |
| Ohyee nkom | He was possessed [and foretold] that, |
| se Asantehene ato mera a | if the Asantehene broke the laws, |
| onipa koko obeba | the red [i.e., White] man would come |
| obefa Asanteman | and take the Asante nation. |
| na nso aba m' | Which is what happened. |

(Twi text in Rattray 1929, 283 n.2; my translation.)

The Anokye traditions are a post-1874 retrospective "renewal" of

Asante religion. The Asante developed after 1874 a political "proto-
logy", with Anokye as their political charter, at the expense of the
primacy of Osee̱ Tutu, who was a ruler, though one of the seven
wise and powerful ones. By that body of traditions, the past glory of
the Asante nation and empire was given (religious) legitimation, and
the present decline was explained. By protologizing Asante identity at
a time when it was severely shaken, they considerably strengthened
it. They glorified and "sacralized" a past which was slipping away by
inventing traditions about it which enabled them to face an uncertain
future and, after 1902, to fit into the British colonial empire.

## Anokye Traditions and History

What proof can be adduced that the Anokye traditions, as we now
know them, date after the sack of Kumase? There are three different
types of proof. There is some evidence in the Anokye traditions
themselves. Some fail to fit into the political geography of the late
17th century when Asante emerged. Others fit closely to some of the
post-1874 political facts. Then there is Anokye's "publicity gap".
Finally, we happen to possess a lost tradition about Anokye from the
early eighteenth century which shows little continuity with the modern
ones.

The modern Anokye traditions contain at least two anachronistic
elements. One is that Osee̱ Tutu is said to have crossed the river
Volta when he was called home to assume leadership after the death
of his uncle Obiri Yeboa, ruler of Kwaaman (Rattray 1929, 272; Anti
1971, 55). This is very unlikely since the bulk and the capital of
Akwamu lay west of the Volta, above Accra, in Osee̱ Tutu's lifetime.
There was no need for Osee̱ Tutu to cross the Volta. The crossing
reflects, however, the political situation from 1731 onwards, when the
Akyem and Akuapim had destroyed Akwamu power west of the Volta
and had chased it across the Volta. By 1874, the Asante seem to have
associated Akwamu exclusively with a position to the east of the
Volta. Therefore, the modern traditions have Osee̱ Tutu cross it. The
same goes for the tradition which credits Anokye with the foundation
of the Akwapim town Akropon (Anti 1971, 36). It came into being
only after 1731, i.e., after the life-time of Anokye (Kwamena-Poh
1972, 41).

I have already pointed out that Anokye's prophecy about the seven
powerful kings matches the ancestral statuses of previous Asante kings
in the reigns of Kofi Kakari (1867-1875) and Mensa Bonsu
(1875-1883). As mentioned, the disobdience of these two rulers was

believed by many Asante to have caused the change of fortune for Asante. The Anokye traditions also describe the emerging Asante confederacy as time and again on the verge of defeat in battles with local groups, which were reluctant to join (Domaa, Amakom, and Tafo), and with the Denkyera - sometimes because a "ruler" failed to observe a rule of respect which Anokye had instituted[15] - and that it was saved from destruction only by the military miracles of Anokye.[16] The Anokye traditions also emphasize that Asante victories over Denkyera were won because three of the confederate rulers had volunteered before the battle to sacrifice their lives for the sake of victory.[17]

The second argument for the assumption that the Anokye traditions were produced after 1874 is the publicity gap of Anokye between 1704 and 1876. Anokye is not mentioned in any of the pre-1876 archival or published sources on Asante society and history. David van Nyendael was in Kumase from October 1701 to October 1702, but was terminally ill when he came back to Elmina, and his letters and reports were lost (van Dantzig 1974, 104, 108 n.7; 1976, 99; 1978, 83, 86, 101, 106). He may have been the only European to visit Asante in the 18th century. Much information about developments in Asante at that time was obtained, however, by Europeans from Asante traders and ambassadors who came down to the coast and from coastal negroes and mulattoes who had visited Asante as traders or were sent there on missions by the Europeans. In the 19th century, however, Kumase was regularly visited by Europeans. Some of them, like Bowdich and Dupuis,[18] had a great interest in Asante society and history and discussed these with many knowledgeable informants. They never even allude to a role of Anokye in the foundation of Asante in their extensive reports on Asante history.

The last argument is derived from a comparison of an early 18th century tradition about Anokye and the modern traditions about him. Bosman[19] reported that traders from the interior told "exceptional stories about a great traditional priest living in their parts in a big house" who had "command over the weather". He was able to cause the rain

to come down heavily or softly, and to stop again, as he pleases. His house is without roof and open but is always free from rain. The past is no problem at all for him, for he predicts the future as if it were present. He cures all the sick and diseases. [...] All his countrymen must appear before him after death and be examined by him. If they are found to have lived well, then he allows them to go in peace into bliss; however, if not, then he beats them to death for the second time with a piece of wood which has

been expressly made for that purpose and placed in front of his residence
to have it always ready at hand (Bosman 1704, 147-148).

Though the name of this "prodigious priest" is not given, it seems
certain that this is a report about *Okomfo* Anokye (McCaskie 1986,
321). If this is so, it corroborates Anokye as a historical person and
that his fame had already spread far and wide during his lifetime. It
was the fame of a traditional priest who was very successful in his
two most important trades: divination and healing. The two other
elements, the management of the weather and the examination of the
deceased, pose problems however. Rain being abundant and the
weather fairly steady in the Akan area, weather management has never
been prominent in the trade of Akan traditional priests. It may either
have been attributed to him by believers from non-Akan areas, who
were used to associate priesthood and weather management, or by
Akan believers in order to mark Anokye off in a special way from
other priests, which is less likely.

The element of beating some deceased to death for the second
time with a wooden club has probably been garbled in the transmission or has more likely been misunderstood by Bosman. He concluded
from it that the priest [Anokye] was taken for a demi-god in his
lifetime already (Bosman 1704, 1 148). However, in Akan terms,
Anokye seems to have acted as the *okyeame* ("court-speaker")[20] of
Osee Tutu in order to be able to pronounce the verdict of guilty or
not guilty in *post mortem* trials for the purpose of assessing what
death duties (*awunyadie*) were due. If the deceased were found not
guilty, the relatives would receive permission to send him or her off
to *asaman* (the realm of the ancestors) in the proper way (cf. Platvoet
1982b) and to inherit a sizable part of his or her liquid assets.
However, if the deceased were found guilty, the corpse was condemned to capital punishment, decapitated, and thrown into the
"thicket of the ghosts" (*asamanpow*). The relatives were then forbidden to celebrate that person's funerary rites, and his or her property
was confiscated by the ruler.[21]

There seems to be no historical continuity between this early
tradition about Anokye and the post-1874 ones. None of the elements
of the early tradition have a prominent place in the modern traditions,
and those typical for the modern traditions are not found in the early
tradition. The divinatory ability attributed to Anokye around 1700 is
the general one which is attributed to any traditional priest. It also fits
into the traditional pattern of being used mainly in relation to ilness.

In the modern traditions, Anokye exercises the very specific power of predicting political fortunes and sanctions correct political behaviour by them. In the early tradition, Anokye cured the sick of all diseases. In the modern ones, he is not portrayed as a healer at all, except in two very special ways. By curing the barrenness of women who happened to occupy crucial matrilineal positions in Akan political history, he caused them to produce key political figures, e.g., the *Denkyera-hene* Ntim Gyakari (Reindorf: 1895/1966, 52) and the *Mamponhene* Amaniampon (Rattray 1929, 277; Anti 1971, 39). And by preparing war medicine, he assured the victory of the Asante forces (Reindorf 1895/1966, 56; Rattray 1929, 279, 282; Anti 1971, 38, 41). Weather management is not completely absent from the post-1874 traditions, but it has only a small part in them (e.g., Anti 1971, 35, 37). Lastly, the modern traditions hold that the pivotal position of the *okyeame*, court speaker, in the court and in public political procedures was instituted by Anokye, but never attribute that function to him. It may therefore be concluded that the modern traditions about Anokye have lost touch with this early tradition about him in the intervening 170 years. McCaskie suggests that this was so because there was no need to mention Anokye's name before 1874: "a secure, expansionist political order does not rehearse publicly its ideological validation" (McCaskie 1986, 332).

## The "Anokyeist" Version of the Domankoma Movement

The modern Anokye traditions have not, however, only lost touch with an early tradition about him. An unacceptable tradition about him has also been suppressed. That was the more extreme, even "extremist", version propagated by the "Anokeyist" or *Domankoma* or *Abonsamkomfo* movement in 1879-1880.[22] It represents a striking case of Asante politically inspired amnesia. Those who were unsuccessful in their bid for power must not be remembered, the more so as they were associated with *bayi*, "witchcraft" (Wilks 1975, 520 n.222; McLeod 1975, 109-110; McCaskie 1981, 130).

The leader of that movement was one *Okomfo* Kwaku of Adwumakaase Wadie, a small town eight miles to the North of Kumase. He claimed that he was "the risen Komfo Anokye". Anokye had returned to earth by way of a shooting star and had taken abode in him. The movement claimed that the return of Anokye to earth had been confirmed by a message from *efoo* for *Okomfo* Kwaku, which had been received through a hunter. The hunter had met *efoo*, the white-bearded

black monkey (*Colobus caudatus*), in the forest. It sat there on a royal
stool and wore gold-studded royal sandals. The message was taken not
only as an affirmation of a royal commission for Anokye Redivivus,
but also as a confirmation of the belief, held firmly by the movement
and many others, that Anokye, like the Colobus monkey, had been
present at the creation of the world and, therefore, had power over the
destinies of single persons as well as whole nations. It was also
believed that the historical Anokye had been the incarnation of the
god (*obosom*) Anokye. Another important belief was that the traditional companions of (the historical) *Okomfo* Anokye, the priests
Odomankama, Dabe, Owu, and Kyerekye, had also returned in some
of the other leaders of the movement, as had some of the "wise rulers" of Asante, Osee Tutu and Kwaku Dua Panin (Ramseyer 1880a;
1880b, 4; McCaskie 1981, 130-131).

The witchfinding element of this movement has only become apparent to later investigators.[23] Cleansing the nation from witchcraft is
not an organic part of the accepted Anokye traditions. Yet, witch
hunting is a perfect complement to the Domankoma version of the
Anokye tradition. It enabled the movement to develop a power base
at the grass roots of the Asante towns and matrilineages before
bringing its political claims to bear at the national level. For, in
Asante tradition, witchcraft (*bayi*) is believed to operate within the
matrilineages.[24] It is perceived as a virtually insoluble moral problem:
death operating in what should be the stronghold of life by the greed
for life of one's closest relatives. Witchcraft involves the stealing of
the lifeblood (*mogya*) and lifeforce-soul (*okra*) of especially the young
and weak in a matrilineage by those in that same matrilineage who
should otherwise be producing, transmitting, feeding, and protecting
life. It is the very inversion of the moral and social order. Asante
witchcraft beliefs are full of images expressing that inversion. Witchcraft is a nocturnal, vampiristic, and cannibalistic activity. At night,
witches slough out of their sleeping bodies and fly, head backwards
or feet upwards, emitting fire from their anuses and armpits, to the
meeting place of their coven in a big tree in the marginal area around
their town. There they are believed to cook and eat those whose life-
force-souls (*akra*) they have stolen. Witches also represent the wild,
fearful world of the "forest" (i.e., of the undomesticated gods, ghosts,
and imps) within the cultured, orderly world of men in towns. The
forest is epitomized in the god of the deep, dense forest, Kwaku
Sasabonsam. He is the sole god in Asante religion who is represented
in anthropo-theriomorphic form. He is believed to have a huge ape-
like body, covered with long reddish hair, to have fierce red eyes, and

to live in the tops of the huge trees in the most dense part of the forest. His long, snakelike legs, with feet pointing both ways, dangle down from the tree tops in order to catch and devour those who venture into his domain. Witches are believed to be in league with him.[25] However, witches resemble Akan society in one respect. Their covens are said to be organized on the pattern of Akan political organization. Each coven has its *ohene* (ruler), *ohemmaa* (queen-mother), *okyeame* (court speaker), and other traditional functionaries (Rattray 1927, 29; Ringwald 1952, 96-105).

Compared to other Akan *abayiyi* ("witchcraft removal") cults,[26] the Domankoma/Abonsamkomfo movement was, or was perceived as, special in several ways. First, by organizing its core of over 1,000 *abonsamkomfo*, witchfinding priests, and devoted followers into a tight system of local cells. These operated with the secrecy of witch covens. Nation-wide, they were organized on the political model of the Asante nation, but with Adwumakaase Wadie as its capital instead of Kumase, and *Okomfo* Kwaku as its ruler instead of the Asantehene (Wilks 1975, 519-520). Secondly, the movement had Sasabonsam, the patron of the witches, for its god. It was held that he enabled the Domankoma *abonsamkomfo* to "see" who were witches when he took possession of them (Rattray 1927, 29-30). Thirdly, witches were traditionally seen as "destroying the nation" (*amansee*) and might, therefore, be handed over to the ruler for execution.[27] In the Domankoma/Abonsamkomfo movement, however, they were arraigned before the court of *Okomfo* Kwaku at Adwumakaase Wadie, even when the accused appealed to the court of the Asantehene, for it saw the Asantehene himself as guilty of "ruining the nation" by his failure to obey the laws of Anokye. Fourthly, *Okomfo* Kwaku, upon finding someone guilty of witchcraft, followed the set practice of Asante rulers of using the court of law as an instrument for extracting wealth from the *sikafo*, the well-to-do, mostly by imposing heavy fines on them. If he imposed the death penalty, he usually allowed them to "buy their heads" at a heavy price. However, if the death penalty was executed, the *abonsamkomfo*, like the traditional rulers, seized all the property of the victims (McCaskie 1981, 113).

As a result of these practices and of the many gifts which they received, Owusu Ansa wrote to Ramseyer that by 1879 the *abonsamkomfo* had become quite rich. This not only made them very proud in Owusu Ansa's eyes, but it also made them attractive prey for an Asantehene in dire need of money (Wilks 1975, 438, 681-683, 699-705). However, the king seems to have been well disposed towards the movement in 1879, probably because of its attractive ideology (the restoration of Asante's power), its prominent position in the upsurge of Anokye traditions, its broad following, and because the full implications of their ideology for his position as Asantehene had not yet become clear to Mensa Bonsu and his advisers. But they evidently had to Owusu Ansa. He had warned the King not to encourage "these impostors". Events in late 1879 and in early 1880, however, further clarified their position towards Asante rulers in general and Mensa Bonsu in particular.

In November 1879, messengers sent by *Okomfo* Kwaku from Agogo (the town which Anokye had ruled) arrived in Abene, the capital of Kwawu. The core of their message was that "the tree which Komfo Anokye had felled" had been "set upright for them" and been given life again by Anokye (Ramseyer 1880a, 1880b). As the tree of reception, the state, and the ruler are intimately linked in Akan political thinking (Platvoet 1985), the message elliptically referred to the "death" of the Kumase central *gyedua* on January 6, 1874, the sack of Kumase a month later, and the role of the Asantehene in these events. It implied that Anokye, ordainer of the destinies of nations, had allowed the British to defeat Asante in 1874 because the Asantehene had disobeyed his laws (especially by not releasing the White captives). Like the witches, the rulers of Asante were guilty of wrecking the nation (*amansee*). Anokye Redivivus, however, had also "set upright" that "tree" again and given life to it. That is, that he was rebuilding the Asante nation and was restoring its power. Therefore, the vassal state Kwawu was invited to reaffirm its allegiance to Asante. By sending out these messengers, *Okomfo* Kwaku was arrogating another of the political privileges of the Asantehene, that of testing the loyalty of parts of the Asante empire and of attempting to bring them back into the Asante fold.

By these actions, the movement fundamentally questioned Mensa Bonsu's title to his position, which was dynastically weak (Wilks 1975, 368-373) and politically weakening (Wilks 1975, 518-519, 674-683; McCaskie 1981, 131). He was perceived to have contravened, as Asantehene, the laws of Anokye by his programme of modernization. In their eyes, he was as guilty as Kofi Kakari, because he failed to restore the "ancient" order of Asante as established by Anokye. Now Anokye himself had returned to restore that order and the power and glory of Asante.

By early 1880, the movement had become a force on the Kumase political scene by aligning with the conservative party against Mensa Bonsu whose rule was becoming increasingly oppressive and autocratic. This shift from a liberal, presidential monarchy towards an autocratic one (Wilks 1975, 527-530) was in itself already seen as a violation of the proper political order (cf. Platvoet 1985) as laid down in "the laws of *Okomfo* Anokye". Enjoying the active political support of some "royals" and court officials (Wilks 1975, 521; McCaskie 1981, 132-133), the movement began to manifest an active presence in Kumase in early 1880 through a display of musketry in the great market (*Adwaberem*) in which the *Kum* tree had stood. Owusu Ansa reported to Ramseyer that they then gradually became so impudent that one morning they forced their way into the palace, allowed themselves all sorts of liberties, then - suddenly - one of them fired a shot at the king, but failed to hit him (BMA D-1,32.159). In the fracas that ensued, some *Abonsamkomfo* were killed, and the others were captured and put in irons. This attempt on his life caused Mensa Bonsu and his advisers to reverse their tolerant position towards the movement, and a purge was ordered. *Okomfo* Kwaku and some two hundred *Abonsamkomfo* were arrested, tried, and executed in 1880 at *Diakomfoase*, "under [the tree which] eats priests". All their wealth was confiscated.

## Conclusion

Three groups of Anokye traditions have been surveyed in this article: one that is forgotten, another one that has been supressed, and a third one that has been codified into the charter of Asante political organization. In colonial times, the third group was represented as having been handed down since the foundation of the Asante nation around 1700 and as having guided its political affairs ever since. In effect, it was developed only after 1874, at the tail-end of Asante's history as a sovereign nation, when it had suffered a devastating blow.

   In this third group of Anokye traditions, an idealized reconstruction of Asante precolonial political organization was undertaken in the face of the disintegration of the nation and its empire. It took the form of a body of political myths with protological overtones and a religious basis. It served several purposes: that of explaining the decline, that of restoring a modicum of the former cohesion and strength, that of explaining the final demise, and that of articulating and supporting Asante identity in times of adversity and in colonial times when sovereignty had been lost. These Anokye myths, therefore, represent an important chapter and process of change in Asante religious and political history. That change, however, was a highly traditionalizing event that addressed the present through developing a past.

   That is even more true of the second, suppressed body of Anokye

myths, those propagated by the *Doma<u>n</u>koma/Abonsamk<u>o</u>mfo* movement. They represent an even more radical attempt at Asante identity
management in the face of the decline of the nation's fortunes. That
movement drew the radical political conclusion from the general thesis
of the post-1874 Anokye myths that the rulers were a primary cause
of the decline of the nation. In this respect, the use of the Anokye
myths by the Doma<u>n</u>koma appears as a normal event in Asante traditional political processes. These consisted of constant shifts in the
balance of power between the ruler and the ruled. By these processes,
rulers were both brought to power and removed (Platvoet 1985). The
*Doma<u>n</u>koma* leaders attempted to remove a nation-wrecking ruler, but
failed to bide their time. When they made the attempt upon the life
of the Asantehene, Mensa Bonsu still had enough political support and
the means to be able to deal speedily and fatally with them.

The post-1874 Anokye traditions may be seen as the product of
cognitive dissonance.[28] The Asante had developed an identity by
building a nation and an empire, but it had remained inarticulate as
long as the nation prospered and ruled its empire. It was articulated
in a body of myths when the political framework by which it had
been produced began to disintegrate. At that moment, the myths began
to "protologize" Asante identity, thereby enabling it to continue to
function as identifier even after Asante had disappeared as an independent polity. It enabled the Asante to live with the dissonance of
being Asante within colonial and post-colonial polities. It enabled
them to accept a position within a colonial system of Indirect Rule
under the British Crown as Imperial Monarchy.[29]

This articulation by means of protological myths, in Asante and
in other preliterate societies, seems a parallel to the articulation of
ethnic or regional identities in European societies in recent times.
When a region is absorbed into a larger polity, people often begin to
collect, preserve, and study typical past items and customs. In the
process, an unarticulated identity takes articulate shape. Such an
identity development is often supported by the invention of traditions
(cf. Trevor-Roper 1983; Morgan 1983).

However, also in religion proper, many such products of "cognitive dissonance" are found. It seems to me that new religious movements, new cults within religions, and reformulations of religions,
may be fruitfully studied as articulations, or re-articulations, of earlier
beliefs in the face of, and for the sake of, coping with crises in
orientation caused by drastic processes of change which transform the
context of a religion.

## Notes

*Concerning the spelling of Twi words:* o̱ is open, as in French "tonne"; o is full, as in French "mot"; e̱ is open, as in French "belle"; e is full, as in English "prey"; ṉ is nasalized, as in English "gang".

1. This article is a revision of an earlier version, entitled "The Return of Anokye: the Ideological Use of a Political Myth by the Domaṉkoma/A-bonsamko̱mfo Movement in Asante in 1879-1880". I am grateful to Dr. Paul Jenkins at Basle, Dr. W. van Beek and Prof. H.U.E. Thoden van Velzen at Utrecht, and Dr. T. McCaskie at Birmingham for suggestions and help. Dr. McCaskie's article on Anokye (McCaskie 1986) has greatly helped to develop the earlier version into the present one.
2. On the war-parties and peace-parties in Asante politics in the 19th century, cf. Wilks 1975.
3. Ramseyer states that about half the army (of 80,000) perished and some 200 "chiefs" (Gundert 1875, 214-215; cf. also Wilks 1875, 82-83).
4. *Anantahene* Asamoa Nkwanta was the most experienced, beloved, and famous of the Asante generals at that time. He supported the peace party because he was thoroughly aware of the superiority in military technology of the British at that time. (Gundert 1875, 175, 249-250; Berberich/Johnson 1975, 7-9; Wilks 1975, 498, 509, 682).
5. Owusu Ansa (1822-1884) was a son of the Asantehene O̱sce̱ Bo̱nsu (1800-1823) and was, as such, debarred from the throne according to the Asante matrilineal system. He had been entrusted to the British under the terms of the 1831 treaty for schooling in Cape Coast and in England from 1831 to 1841. He was baptized into the Anglican Church in England, but joined the Methodist Church after his return to the Gold Coast in 1841. He first went to Kumase with the Methodist missionary T.B. Freeman (1844/1968, 97, 125-126, 137-141, 146-150, 178) in 1841. He returned to Cape Coast in 1844 because opposition to Western and Christian influences had increased markedly in Kumase (Wilks 1975, 591-592, 597). He was back again during 1850 to 1854 as a diplomat in Asante service and during 1867 to 1872 as secretary and adviser to Kofi Kakari (1867-1874). He was sent to Cape Coast as agent of the Asantehene in May 1872. His house there was attacked by an angry mob on April 13, 1873, when the Asante armies were camping within an hour's distance from Cape Coast. The mob lynched seven of his Asante servants, and his life was saved by the militia taking him into custody in Cape Coast Castle. The British administration then sent him into exile to Sierra Leone. But he was allowed to return to the Gold Coast in 1874. He visited Kumase again in October 1875, shortly after the Kofi Kakari had been replaced by Mensa Bonsu (Wilks 1975, 596-605).
6. For the long term reasons for this defection, cf. Gundert 1875, 51; Wilks 1875, 115-119; Maier 1983, 83-89; Platvoet 1985, 185, 194-196.

7.  They were the Basle missionaries Friedrich August Ramseyer, his wife
    Rosa, their baby son Fritzchen (born on 17 September 1868), and
    Johannes Kühne, and the French trader Marie-Joseph Bonnat. They had
    been taken prisoner in Ewe territory east of the Volta in June 1869
    (Gundert 1875, iv, 6, 54; Wilks 1975, 225). Fritzchen did not survive
    the hardships of the long marches from the trans-Volta area into Asante.
    He died on August 1, 1869 in a village near Dwaben (Gundert 1875,
    43-47). The others arrived in a village close to Kumase on April 22,
    1870 (Gundert 1875, 63). On December 5, 1870, they were permitted
    to take up residence in Kumase itself in the Wesleyan mission house
    (Gundert 1875, 86). In Kumase, two children were born to the Ram-
    seyers, a daughter, Röschen, on September 2, 1871 (Gundert 1875, 115,
    117-118, 125-126, 145, 158) and a son, Louis Immanuel, on November
    21, 1873 (Gundert 1875, 208, 215).
8.  Two other oracular events on the fortunes of this war had already
    preceded this one. The Asantehene had sent messengers to Dente, the
    famous oracle at Krakye - even though Dente had a subsidiary at
    Kumase itself (Maier 1983, 117) - probably in late 1872. The god had
    strongly advised against the war (Wilks 1975, 279-281; Maier 1983, 38-
    39). On January 26, 1873, when the first news of heavy Asante losses
    were received, the king had some fifty *akomfo* assemble in the great
    marketplace. The gods taking possession of them had foretold that the
    Asante army would subject the Akyem, Assin, Fante, and Denkyera
    peoples. "The great god" (Tano?) is said to have stated: "if the white
    man (the British governor) interferes, I will kill him in his castle and
    put someone else (a Dutch governor) in his place" (Gundert 1875, 173-
    174).
9.  On Anokye as lawgiver, cf. Rattray 1929, 179-180, 271; Kyerematen
    1969, 4; Fynn 1971, 30; Wilks 1975, 484; Wilks 1979, 4; McCaskie
    1986, 319, 320, 329, 331.
10. Asante traditions say that it was brought from heaven by Anokye in a
    cloud of white dust and black smoke. It descended upon the knees of
    Osee Tutu in the assembly of the leaders of the "five single states"
    (*amantoonum*) confederating the Asante nation (Rattray 1923, 288-230;
    other versions in Rattray 1929, 276-277; Kyerematen 1969, 2-5; Anti
    1971, 39-40, 60-70).
11. E.g., the tradition that Anokye, on being asked to cause as a traditional
    priest the conception of Ntim Gyakari, predicted that he would ruin
    Denkyera (Reindorf 1895/1966, 52). For other such predictions, cf.
    Rattray 1923, 289-290; Rattray 1929, 133 n.3, 274, 277, 283; Anti 1971,
    18, 20, 53.
12. Tying a knot in an elephant's tusk; obtaining water from a rock; leaving
    his footprints on a rock; causing a cooked plantain to germinate into a
    tree and harvesting from it the same day; causing a tall oilpalm to
    spring from the dregs of palmwine, climbing it with his sandalled feet,

and leaving their prints on it for proof; etc. (Rattray 1929, 270-284 passim; Anti 1971, 15, 23, 35-36; Sarpon 1971, 30, 77 n.12).

13. In Twi *akyide*, "thing hated/abhorred" (Rattray 1929, 279, n. 6). It is better rendered as "a rule of respect", observed by a believer in order not to offend the sensibilities of a "meta-empirical" being, than as "taboo" (Platvoet 1982a, 230).

14. Two Asante rulers had not attained that status because they had not died in office. They were Kusi Obodom (1750-1764) who had abdicated (Wilks 1975, 332) and Osee Kwame (1777-1798) who was deposed for his leanings towards Islam and executed at his own request in 1803 (Fynn 1971, 131-139; Wilks 1975, 252-253, 256). Nor were Kofi Kakari (1867-1875) and Mensa Bonsu (1875-1883) to achieve that status, as both were deposed (Rattray 1927, 144-145).

15. E.g. the failure of *oheneba* ("ruler's son") Saben to observe the *akyide* (palmwine) of the miraculous shield during a battle with the Domaa. Anokye had assured them of victory as long as Saben presented it to the Domaa and did not drink palmwine (Rattray 1929, 273-274).

16. He is said to have directed swarms of bees against the Denkyera troops, to have caused night to descend upon them, a forest of oilpalms to spring up when they were pursuing the Asante troops, and a silkcotton tree to expand into a fence which absorbed all the Denkyera bullets (alternatively, to have directed the Denkyera bullets by the power of his flywhisk into a big tree far away). He even caused the body of a dead Asante ruler to rise and join his men in their flight when the murderous fire prevented them from dragging his corpse off the battlefield (Rattray 1929, 278; Anti 1971, 41-43).

17. Traditions say that they were *Kumawuhene* Kwabena Tweneboa Kodua, *Edwesohene* Duku Pim, and *Bonwirehene* Bobie. The *Kumawuhene* is said either to have volunteered to be the first one to die in battle (Rattray 1929, 219-220, 277) or to have been struck on his head by Anokye, after which he "immediately vanished" into the earth, the spot being known after that as Tweneboanna, "[where] Tweneboa rests" (Anti 1971, 40-41). The *Edwesohene* volunteered to be cut to pieces for the preparation of a war medicine. The *Bonwirehene* is said to have consented to die in battle as a representative of the Kumase Oyoko (Rattray 1929, 277), or to have been decapitated, after which "he was seated in the pit [of a big hole] and his body firmly fixed in it with a sharp instrument; the cut-off head was then re-adjusted on the trunk in such a way that the face turned backwards" (Anti 1971, 41). For another example, see Anti 1971, 41. As his collection is the youngest one, it contains the most recent elaboration.

18. Bowdich (1819/1966, 31-148) was in Kumase from May 17th to September 22nd, 1817; Dupuis (1824/1966, 68-180) from February 28th to March 24th, 1819.

19. Willem Bosman served as factor in the castles of the Dutch West Indies Company on the Gold Coast from 1680 to July 1702. The first edition of his book was published both in Amsterdam in 1703 and in Utrecht in 1704. I have used the Utrecht edition. An English translation was published in 1905. For a critical revision of it, cf. van Dantzig 1974, 1976, 1977.

20. The *okyeame* plays a central role in the Akan judicial system as the alter ego of the ruler (*ohene*) in all public proceedings (cf. Rattray 1927, 276-278). The wooden club, which Anokye is said to wield in the death penalty for the deceased in Bosman's report, is probably a distortion of the legal formula by which an *okyeame* pronounces someone guilty:

| | |
|---|---|
| nti wamfa mma ha | because you did not bring [your case] here, |
| amma yamfa asopa ntie | that we might listen to it well, |
| na wo fa aba de bo Akyeame | but took a club [to strike] the Speakers, |
| wu ku yen a | by [thus] killing us, |
| wu di yen aboa | you treat us as [if we were] beasts |
| wu di fo | you are guilty. |

(Twi text in Rattray 1929, 295, 300, 383; my translation.)

21. On post mortem trials, cf. Rattray 1929, 124-125, 299-301, 335-336, 375, 386; Wilks 1975, 695; 1979, 4; on the confiscation of property of those condemned to death, cf. Hagan 1968, 27-29; Fynn 1971, 137; Wilks 1975, 671, 702.

22. *Domankama* expresses the protological basis of the movement. *Domankoma* ("copious") is the traditional name of God as the "abundant" Creator. Anokye was present at creation, they believed, in a pre-human form. *Abonsamkomfo* refers to their being priests of Sasabonsam, the fearful forest god, and to their role as witchhunters. Owusu Ansa refers to them as "these Anokyeists" (quoted by Ramseyer in BMA D-1,32.159).

23. To Rattray in 1923, Wilks in 1959, and to Lewin and McCaskie in the 1960's and 1970's. They interviewed people with a personal knowledge of the movement and studied Kumase court records from the 1920's and 1930's in which witnesses referred to the Domankoma movement.

24. Cf. Christaller 1933, 11, 55; Rattray 1927, 28; Bleek 1975, 319, 335-336.

25. Cf. Bosman 1704, i, 150; 1705/1967, 159; van Dantzig 1977, 253; Rattray 1916, 47-49; 1927, 27-31; Christaller 1933, 429; Ringwald 1952, 87-105; McLeod 1981, 40; Ross 1983, 97 and fig. 116.

26. On these cults, cf. Platvoet 1973, McLeod 1975, McCaskie 1981.

27. In pre-colonial times, "witches" who had been exposed by a possessed priest or by "carrying the corpse" (*afunsoa*) were sometimes handed over for execution to the ruler. Since they had sucked the blood of others, their blood was not to be shed. Therefore, they were strangled, drowned, or clubbed to death. Witches could, and did, appeal to the poison oracle (*odomwe*) in order to clear themselves of the accusation. Cf. Bosman 1704, ii, 11; 1705/1966, 228; Bowdich 1819/1966, 260; Cruickshank 1853/1966, ii, 179; Rattray 1927, 29-31, 167-170; Ringwald 1952, 95-105.
28. Festinger 1957; Festinger, Riecken & Schachter 1956; cf. also Platvoet 1982a, 74-83.
29. Imperial Monarchy was invented at the same time as the Anokye traditions. It was mystified by ceremonial aggrandizement after the British Crown had been shorn of all real political power (Cannadine 1983, 120-138). From this mystique, a common sentiment developed in early colonial time that was shared by both British administrators and African traditional elite. Myths about African monarchies ruling "tribes" within the framework of the British Empire developed well in that context (Ranger 1983, 229-246). Rattray's enthusiasm for Anokye and his contributions to the elaboration and codification of the Anokye traditions seem to fit into that context.

## Bibliography

Anti, A.A., 1971: *Akwamu, Denkyera, Akuapem and Ashanti in the Lives of Osei Tutu and Okomfo Anokye*, Tema (Ghana).

Baesjou, R., 1979: *An Asante Embassy on the Gold Coast: the Mission of Akyempon Yaw to Elmina, 1869-1872*, Leiden.

Berberich, C., & G. Johnson, 1975: "Asante Collective Biography Project: ACBP/pcs/7, Asamoa Nkwanta", *Asante Seminar '75 (Asantesem)* 3, June 1975, 7-9.

Bleek, W., 1975: *Marriage, Inheritance and Witchcraft; a Case Study of a Rural Ghanaian Family*, Leiden.

Bosman, W., 1704: *Nauwkeurige beschrijving van de Guinese Goud-, Tand-, en Slave-kust*, 2 vols., Utrecht.

Bosman, W., 1705/1967: *A New and Accurate Description of the Coast of Guinea, Divided into the Gold, the Slave, and the Ivory Coasts*, London.

Bowdich, T.E., 1819/1966: *Mission from Cape Coast Castle to Ashantee*, London.

Brokensha, D., ed., 1972: *Akwapim Handbook*, Accra.

Cannadine, D., 1983: "The Context, Performance and Meaning of Ritual: the British Monarchy and the Invention of Tradition", in Hobsbawm & Ranger 1983, 101-164.

Christaller, J.G., 1881/1933: *Dictionary of the Asante and Fante Language Called Tshi (Twi)*, Basle.

Cruickshank, B., 1853/1966: *Eighteen Years on the Gold Coast of Africa*, London.

Dalton, G., ed., 1979: *Research in Economic Anthropology*, Volume two. London.

Dantzig, A. van, 1974: "Willem Bosman's New and Accurate Description of the Coast of Guinea: How Accurate Is It?", *History in Africa, a Journal of Method* 1, 101-108.

Dantzig, A. van, 1976: "English Bosman and Dutch Bosman: a Comparison of Texts, II", *History in Africa, a Journal of Method*, 3, 91-126.

Dantzig, A. van, 1978: *The Dutch and the Guinea Coast 1674-1742; a Collection of Documents from the General State Archive at the Hague; Compiled and Translated by A. van Dantzig*, Accra.

Dupuis, J., 1824/1966: *Journal of a Residence in Ashentee*, London.

Festinger, L., 1957: *A Theory of Cognitive Dissonance*, London.

Festinger, L., H.W. Riecken & S. Schachter, 1956: *When Prophecy Fails; a Social and Psychological Study of a Modern Group That Predicted the Destruction of the World*, New York.

Freeman, T.B., 1844/1968: *Journal of Various Visits to the Kingdoms of Ashanti, Aku, and Dahomi in Western Africa*, London.

Fynn, J.K., 1971: *Asante and Its Neighbours, 1700-1807*, London.

Goody, J., ed., 1975: *Changing Social Structure in Ghana: Essays in the Comparative Sociology of a New State and an Old Tradition*, London.

Gros, J., 1884: *Voyages, aventures et captivité de J. Bonnat chez les Achantis*, Paris.

Gundert, H., 1875: *Vier Jahre in Asante: Tagebücher der Missionare Ramseyer und Kühne aus der Zeit ihrer Gefangenschaft*, Basel.

Hagan, G.P., 1968: "The Golden Stool and the Oaths to the King of Ashanti", *Research Review* (Legon: Institute of African Studies) 4 (3), 1-33.

Hobsbawm, E., & T. Ranger, eds., 1983: *The Invention of Tradition*, Cambridge.

Kwamenah-Poh, M.A., 1972: "History", in: Brokensha 1972, 33-57.

Kyerematen, A., 1969: "The Royal Stools of Ashanti", *Africa* 39, 1-9.

Maier, D.J.E., 1981: "The Dente Oracle, the Bron Confederation and the Politics of Secession", *Journal of African History* 22, 229-243.

Maier, D.J.E., 1983: *Priests and Power; the Case of the Dente Shrine in Nineteenth-Century Ghana*, Bloomington.

McCaskie, T.C., 1981: "Anti-Witchcraft Cults in Asante: an Essay in the Social History of an African People", *History in Africa, a Journal of Method* 8, 125-154.

McCaskie, T.C., 1986: "Komfo Anokye of Asante: Meaning, History and Philosophy in an African Society", *Journal of African History* 27, 315-339.

McLeod, M., 1975: "On the Spread of Anti-Witchcraft Cults in Modern Ghana", in: Goody 1975, 107-117.

McLeod, M., 1981: *The Asante*, London.

Morgan, P., 1983: "From a Death to a View: the Hunt for the Welsh Past in the Romantic Period", in Hobsbawm & Ranger 1983, 43-100.

Platvoet, J.G., 1973: "Verschuivingen in een West-Afrikaanse godsdienst: hekserijbekentenissen en de opkomst van de 'beul'-goden in de godsdienst van de Ashanti", *Bijdragen, Tijdschrift voor Filosofie en Theologie* 34, 15-39.

Platvoet, J.G., 1982a: *Comparing Religions, a Limitative Approach: an Analysis of Akan, Para-Creole and IFO-Sananda Rites and Prayers*, The Hague.

Platvoet, J.G., 1982b: "Commemoration by Communication: Akan Funerary Terracottas", *Visible Religion, Annual for Religious Iconography* 1, 113-134.

Platvoet, J.G., 1985: "Cool Shade, Peace and Power: The *Gyedua* ('Tree of Reception') as an Ideological Instrument of Identity Management among the Akan peoples of Southern Ghana", *Journal of Religion in Africa* 15 (3), 174-200.

Ramseyer, A., 1880a: Letter by Friederich Ramseyer at Abetifi to Committee at Basel, dd. 19 June 1880, in Archives of the Basel Mission, D-1,32.159, 6 p.

Ramseyer, A., 1880b: "Au Comité des Missions de Neuchatel", *Bulletin de la Mission Achantie* 3 (1), 1-16.

Ranger, T., 1983: "The Invention of Tradition in Colonial Africa", in: Hobsbawm & Ranger 1983, 211-262.

Rattray, R.S., 1916: *Ashanti Proverbs; the Primitive Ethics of a Savage People*, Oxford.

Rattray, R.S., 1923: *Ashanti*, Oxford.

Rattray, R.S., 1927: *Religion and Art in Ashanti*, Oxford.

Reindorf, C.C., 1895/1966: *The History of the Gold Coast and Asante*, Accra.

Ringwald, W., 1952: *Die Religion der Akanstämme und das Problem ihrer Bekehrung: eine religionsgeschichtliche und missionsgeschichtliche Untersuchung*, Stuttgart.

Ross, D.H., 1983: "Catalogue", in: Ross & Garrard 1983, 97-102.

Ross, D.H., & T.F. Garrard, eds., 1983: *Akan Transformations: Problems in Ghanaian Art History*, Los Angeles.

Sarpon, P., 1971: *The Sacred Stools of the Akan*, Tema.

Trevor-Roper, H., 1983: "The Invention of Tradition: the Highland Tradition of Scotland", in: Hobsbawm & Ranger 1983, 15-42.

Wilks, I., 1975: *Asante in the Nineteenth Century; the Structure and Evolution of a Political Order*, London.

Wilks, I., 1979: "The Golden Stool and the Elephant Tail: an Essay on Wealth in Asante", in: Dalton 1979, 1-36.

# Tradition and Renewal in the West African Concept of Person

*By Hans Witte*

Right at the start of this contribution we have our first difficulty: if such a thing as a West African concept of the person exists, it can hardly be called, with Clifford Geertz, "local knowledge". Indeed, I indicate with West Africa an enormous area that stretches from Senegal to Cameroon, inhabited by a great number of different societies living in ecological situations that go from near dessert to tropical rainforest and linguistically divided over at least four language-families. The area also contains very different cultures: small isolated rural groups of farmers, well-organized kingdoms, and sophisticated city-states.

Yet, I hope to demonstrate that West African world views and West African concepts of the person show a certain unity, an internal logic and coherence, that are, of course, best seen when they are compared to Western views and notions. We have to bear in mind, first of all, that the coherence of a symbolic universe is always discovered as a second step, that of taking perspective after the necessary immersion in the dazzling variety of local reality; and, second of all, that the discovery of significance in local behaviour in foreign cultures arises from - implicit or explicit - comparison with our own culture. It arises from the astonishment that people can be so different.

What I intend to do here is to sketch a general outline of the West African notion of the person. Its general and sketchy character, enhanced by the affirmative presentation imposed by the limitations of this article, must be vastly irritating to the specialized africanists among my readers. Let me assure you that I share your love for local detail, but that should not prevent us from making useful and prudent generalizations and comparisons. Being fully aware of the dangers of comparisons and the limited use of generalizations, we should not deny the existence of common denominators in human cultures, on which cultural anthropology is finally based.

As a second preliminary remark: some may wonder whether I

refer to a traditional or a modern West African world view. I will take this issue up at the end of my paper, but I note already that such fundamental notions as that of the person change very slowly, and, if they do, the original culture has ceased to exist.

With regard to the question of the person, it is, I think, useful to remember Clifford Geertz' remark in his essay "From the Native's Point of View":

The Western conception of the person as a bounded, unique, more or less integrated motivational and cognitive universe, a dynamic center of awareness, emotion, judgement, and action organized into a distinctive whole and set contrastively both against other such wholes and against its social and natural background, is, however incorrigible it may seem to us, a rather peculiar idea within the context of the world's cultures (1983, 59).

A notion of the person implies a world view and a world view implies a notion of the person. We obtain a first glimpse of the notion of the person and of something that can be called a West African world view if we examine very briefly West African creation myths. These myths do not focus on the creation of men, of the human individual, but on the creation of the civilized world, of civilization. The Yoruba, for example, tell us that Olorun, the sky god, sends his eldest son or first minister, Obatala, from the sky to create on the primordial waters what is to become the sacred city of Ile Ife. Obatala, however, gets drunk before he sets out on his mission, and his younger brother, Odudua, takes his place and becomes the first king of Ife. When Obatala awakens from his drunken sleep and realizes that his brother has taken his place, he becomes furious and starts a fight in which he obliges all the divinities of the sky to take sides with him or his brother. The quarrel ends with an agreement: Odudua remains the rightful king of Ife, and Obatala obtains the right to model the body of every human being from earth or mud, before the sky god Olorum breathes his life force into it. The creation of the human individual is nothing more than an appendix to the creation of the civilized world.

In other West African creation myths, the emphasis lies on the origin of the ancestors, but not as a paradigm for the creation of every human individual, rather as culture heroes that make civilization and society possible. The priority given to the creation of the civilized world over that of the human individual indicates already that the latter is defined much more with regard to the place he or she takes in the relational network of society than with regard to the individual personality.

The human body, modelled out of clay or earth by the sky god or one of his ministers or deputies, is informed by a whole range of spiritual forces that are variously named and described in the different West African cultures. Nevertheless, the spiritual forces of the individual can in general be classified into two categories: those that are associated with the sky god, and those that have to do with the ancestors. The sky god gives the body its vital force which is primarily expressed in the breath, the blood, and sexuality.

In many cases, the vital force is seen as the part of the creator god which is lodged in each human being, as Nukunya (1981, 124) reports from the Anlo Ewe, Idowu (1962, 21) from the Yoruba, Busia (1970, 197) from the Ashanti, and Mercier (1970, 227) from the Fon. This "inhabitation" does not mean that it gives the human being an intimate personal relationship with the sky god. The latter is in most cases a "deus otiosus" who shows no concern with his creation and who plays no important role in the cult. A few West African cultures developed a pantheon with divinities which do receive a cult and which in a sense can be considered as ministers or even manifestations of the sky god. These divinities are not interested either in the well-being of the human individual or of society. They should be manipulated or avoided.

Apart from the vital force, there is, as I mentioned, another spiritual element that is proper to the human being and that is associated with the ancestors. The ancestors were once part of the community of the living, and their whole being is still oriented to that community. There is a continuous interaction across the boundaries of death between the ancestors and the living. Without this interaction, the community of the living, and the individual within that community, could not exist. In the religious world view of West Africans, ancestors are much more important than gods or divinities. The latter manifest themselves in nature and illness. They are cosmic forces which operate in a certain domain in a specific way according to their particular character. For these reasons, their behaviour is more or less predictable, and this makes it possible for specialized priests to manipulate these forces for the benefit of society. In contrast to gods and divinities, ancestors are very much interested in the prosperity of society, of which they never ceased to be a part. The existence of the ancestors is completely oriented to the community of the living to which they hope, in a way, to return. The ancestors do not live in some kind of heaven. The only reason why West Africans hope to become an ancestor after their death is that in this way they more or less survive within the ancestral orientation to the community of the living and thus the ultimate catastrophe of their final exclusion and extinction is avoided.

The meaning of life is not derived from representations of a happier life after death in which human aspirations are finally and definitely fulfilled (cf. Busia 1970, 207; Le Moal 1981, 196). The images and representations of the existence of the ancestors are extremely vague (Fortes 1965, 126-127). The Yoruba say that the ancestors exist as "ancestral material", which is represented as formless mud (Witte 1982, 125-133).

To become an ancestor, the individual must have proven during his lifetime that he or she has fully assumed his or her responsibilities in the community. This means, for instance, that one has strengthened society by founding a family and having legitimate children, that one has not placed oneself outside society by antisocial or ego-oriented behaviour, or that one has not died prematurely by stupid neglect of ancestral laws. The community confirms that a dead person has fulfilled his responsibilities by celebrating funeral rites that help the deceased to become separated from the living and reach the domain of the ancestors.

After death, the elements that compose a human being fall apart. The body rejoins the earth and the vital force returns to the sky god. The only element that in a way, remains in the individual, is the ancestral spirit, which returns to the ancestors, but which is hoped to return in future children. This cycle from deceased to ancestor to "reincarnation" means a passage from individuality to collectivity and on to new individualities. The deceased keep their individuality as long as their name is remembered by the living, but gradually he or she fades away into the collectivity of the ancestors. "Reincarnation" does not mean that the individual ancestor returns among the living, because a particular ancestor is sometimes said to have returned in several children, even of different sexes. The passage through death and reincarnation can not be seen as an individual life-cycle. It indicates the process of renewal of the collective community through the collectivity of the ancestors, a renewal expressed by the death and birth of the individuals that make up the community.

I would like to summarize at this point what we have gained in our search for the West African notion of the person and a West African world view in general. I hope to have indicated in both notions a fundamental orientation to the community of the living, whether we describe this community in its nucleus and paradigm as the extended family or, in a wider sense, as the lineage or as society in general.

The creation myths are centered on the creation of the civilized world. The meaning of life is not expressed in representations of life after death or in a change of consciousness, but is sought in the life within the community of the living in which the individual assumes his responsibilities. The community of the living is the very centre of the West African world view. From this fundamental starting-point it will be clear that the notion of the self has to do with the place that each individual occupies within the whole of his society. This means that we have to examine the responsibilities, the rights, and the duties he or she has with regard to the collectivity.

Space permits only a brief outline of the two most important stratifications: a vertical one, so to say, running through society, that of age; and a horizontal one, that of gender.

The place one occupies within one's family is by nature a dynamic one: it develops and it changes. Growing older means bearing new responsibilities which change one's relation with the rest of the group. The West African notion of the self, which is essentially linked to the relation with the family, the community, or, if you prefer, society, is for that reason a dynamic one: ego is very much aware of being a developing link in the dynamic chain of successive generations.

Real responsibility can only be born when the child has grown into an adult which fortifies and renews the community with children. In a later phase the adult grows into an elder. The advanced age of elders forms the living proof that they know how to handle cosmic forces, because nobody can ignore these and live. The ancestors and the elders have to maintain the ancestral laws that teach humans how to survive.

The preoccupation with fertility of young adults, which is enormously underlined by social pressure, leads to an ego-oriented mentality which widens in old age to a sense of responsibility for the whole of the community. After the children, the adults, and the elders, we have already mentioned a fourth category of humans: after death, ego-consciousness and the notion of the self slowly dim into the genderless collectivity of the ancestors which, however, loses nothing of its fundamental orientation to the society of the living. The ancestors know how cosmic forces operate, therefore, they can warn and protect the living and thus assure prosperity and fertility.

The notion of the self in West Africa is a dynamic, developing notion which changes in every phase of life in which the relation to society alter.

The other element which is fundamental for the position of ego in society is that of gender and sexuality. The society of the living, which is the very heart of the West African world view, finds its paradigm in the model of the extended family that is based on the complementarity of the sexes. Ivan Illich (1982, 99) remarks: "kinship primarily structures gender domains in their complementarity.... Kinship presupposes the two genders, which it relates to one another. Gender not only tells who is who, but it also defines who is when, where, and with which tools and words; it divides space, time and technique".

West African men and women live indeed in two different but closely related worlds, each with its own social space, vital rythm, and experience of time. There is a division in work and social function. Each gender has its own social behaviour, language, gestures, dances, and aesthetic ideals. West African cultures place the individual either in a male or in a female world, each with its own symbolic coherence. Identification with its own gender and opposition or rather differentiation from the other gender world "is part of a child's earliest empirical, but not yet verbal growth", as Illich (1982, 127) puts it.

Men and women symbolize, as such, complementary cosmic forces that are articulated differently in various West African cultures. In general, the phenomena of menstruation and pregnancy are taken as indications that women have a more intrinsic relationship to fertility than men. In view of the enormous importance of fertility for West African society, its association with women has repercussions for the ego-consciousness of men and women. The vital force of women is often considered to be greater than that of men. The Yoruba think that all women are, for that reason, potential witches who have to control their feelings in order to keep their life-force "cool" and prevent anti-social behaviour.

The element of gender strongly influences the notion of the person in the eyes of the individual and from the point of view of society, but it plays a different role in the various phases of life. Ancestors who are no longer individually remembered by the living have no gender. Children and elders belong to the male or the female world according to their sex, but sexuality and fertility are not yet - or no longer - a dominant preoccupation for their ego. For adults, on the other hand, the complementarity of gender is strongly coloured by sexual differentiation as the essential condition for fertility.

We are now, perhaps, in a position to examine briefly the question of a possible renewal in the notion of the person in the context of a West African world view. Being a poor prophet, I can only give some suggestions.

Renewal means change on the basis of continuity. We cannot, I am afraid, rule out the possibility that West Africa will lose altogether the essential values of its culture in the end. It has happened elsewhere in the past and in the present.

If we consider renewal, it is, I think, in our minds that such a renewal will be brought about by the massive exposure to Western civilization of African cultures that we witness in our days. The very real attraction of Western civilization for West Africans lies, however, in our technological and economic achievements, and not in the philosophical or social implications of our individualistic world view. The question is whether technological and economic progress can be achieved without adopting the analytic and mechanical world view that it seems to suppose. The economic and political changes in West African countries which we have seen during the last decades - recalling the phenomena of national armies, migrant labour, and the growth of cities - tend to promote a notion of community that is quite different from the traditional one. The community based on the image of the extended family, lineage ties, and local settlement tends to erode under the needs of national economies and the, perhaps superficial, attractions of foreign cultures presented by the media It seems unlikely that there will ever be a nation-wide sense of community, but the erosion of traditional conceptions of community may result in a widening gap between an indifferent society at large and the immediate family.

I have tried to show that the West African notion of the person is defined by a fundamental orientation of the individual towards the community of the living. A renewal of this notion that implies a certain continuity of traditional values seems only possible if the idea of the community to which the individual belongs is not entirely separated from that of the lineage as its original paradigm.

## Bibliography

Busia, K.A., 1970: "The Ashanti of the Gold Coast", in: Forde 1970, 190-209.

Dieterlen, G., ed., 1981: *La notion de personne en Afrique noire*, Paris

Forbes, M. & G. Dieterlen, eds., 1965: *African Systems of Thought*, London.

Forde, D., ed., 1970: *African Worlds. Studies in the Cosmological Ideas and Social Values of African Peoples*, London.

Fortes, M., 1965: "Some Reflections on Ancestor Worship in Africa", in: Forbes & Dieterlen 1965, 122-144.

Geertz, Clifford, 1983: "'From the Native's Point of View': On the Nature

184

of Anthropological Understanding", in: Clifford Geertz, *Local Knowledge. Further Essays in Interpretative Anthropology*, New York, 55-72.

Idowu, E.B., 1962: *Olodumare. God in Yoruba Belief*, London.

Illich, I., 1982: *Gender*, New York.

Moal, G. le, 1981: "Quelques aperçus sur la notion de personne chez les Bobo", in: Dieterlen 1981, 193-204.

Mercier, P., 1970: "The Fon of Dahomey", in: Forde 1970, 210-234.

Nukunya, G.K., 1981: "Some Underlying Beliefs in Ancestor Worship and Mortuary Rites among the Ewe", in: Dieterlen 1981, 119-130.

Witte, H.A., 1982: Symboliek van de aarde bij de Yoruba, Unpublished thesis, University Microfilms, Ann Arbor.

*European Contexts:*
*Revival and Mission*

# Economic Change and Religious Tradition in a Dutch Maritime Culture. The Case of Urk[1]

*By Durk Hak*

## Urk and Its Culture

In the decades before and after World War II, there was fear for the future of the inhabitants of the island of Urk. The question was whether they still would be able to earn their daily bread at sea despite the many changes that had occurred. In 1932, the ZuyderZee was closed by a dam (the *Afsluitdijk*) making direct access to their North Sea fishing grounds impossible. Some ten years later, Urk was not an island any longer. It had become part of the new reclaimed land, the Noordoostpolder.

The Urkers, as the residents of Urk are called, lived, for the most part, off the sea. They were either fishermen, or they earned their wages in the small businesses connected with fishing. The newly created IJselmeer could not accomodate all the fishermen of the former ZuyderZee. Moreover, because of the enclosing dam, it would take the Urkers many hours of extra sailing to reach their traditional fishing grounds in the northern part of the ZuyderZee and the North Sea. This would be an extra handicap for the Urkers, who set sail for home every Friday or Saturday in order to come home in time to celebrate their traditional Sabbath.

The Dutch government had appointed a special committee to soften the blow for the Urkers. The committee proposed all sorts of measures, such as schemes to establish small scale industrial and farming concerns in which the Urkers could find employment. These turned out to be failures since the newly created jobs did not "smell of fish". But more importantly, the ex-fishermen were not interested in fixed working hours nor in working in-doors. Most of the Urker men and women had not yet developed a modern labour ethos. Many Urkers, too, were concerned about whether they would be able to preserve their particular insular identity in the face of the arrival of new agricultural colonists of the reclaimed land. Moreover, the many visitors to the former island would be bringing the modern world to Urk as well. The Urker cultural identity, which has fundamental influence on the Urker personality, consisted of a strange mixture of the originally Calvinistic, Reformed religion and a lightheartedness and jauntiness ressembling that of Roman Catholicism. Maybe it was a remnant of Urk's earlier days as a Roman Catholic village, which lasted well into the seventeenth century before Protestantism had found a foothold.

On the basis of research in Urk in the late 1930's, a social scientist concluded: "Neither in the field of economic life, nor in the fields of social or intellectual life do the Urkers show signs of powerful and purposeful aspirations" (Plomp 1940, 118; my translation). The worst was feared at the time. And yet, by the early 1970's, the Urkers possessed the most modern and largest coastal fishing-fleet in Western Europe: about 170 cutters, manned by some nine hundred fishermen, with an average engine power of 900 bhp. (In 1955 the average engine power was "only" 140 bhp.) Some cutters were even equipped with engines of over 2,000 bhp. Urk had become a prosperous village. Never before had so many people been so well off there. Young fishing hands of twenty had luxurious houses built for themselves. Many fishermen bought themselves cutters and started their own fishing firms.

What had happened in the meantime? What had caused this "miracle of Urk"? An astonishing miracle, when you take into consideration that in nearly all former ZuyderZee fishing villages there is hardly any fishing left worth mentioning. Were these economic changes the result of Urk being incorporated into the greater Dutch society which had also experienced an increased economic growth? Had these changes been brought about by internal processes, which, in turn, had caused a new modern mentality? Or had it been a combination of internal and external developments which had caused them?

### The Maritime Personality

Before proceeding, I must comment a little on the personalities of the participants in the fishing variant of maritime cultures. The participants are very individualistic and egalitarian. They feel little need for privacy. A better characterization may be that private life is public to a degree unimaginable to outsiders. The participants are regarded as being very religious. The position of women is a very particular one. Though they are the pillars of these cultures, the male participants do not consider them as such. Finally, they have plenty of time. There is a time to work and a time to rest and sleep. Leisure and sleep are highly valued, as is play. In short, there is no *Wahlverwandtschaft* between the ethos- and eidos-systems of (early-modern) fishing cultures and modern, rational-economic behaviour.

Urk as a maritime culture displays some of these traits. The Urkers are also arch individualists. They dislike authority in general and the public authorities in particular. They are egalitarian to a degree. Private life at Urk is public and it is often ostentatious. People, especially the women, look intently into the windows of other people's homes in order to see what is going on in the living rooms. In maritime cultures, the male participants drink quite a lot. More often than not, they do it quite openly. Public drunkenness is quite common. In this respect, Urk is different: married men drink in the dark at home. Street scenes are not filled with drunkards, as is often the case in other fishing villages.

The (young) men boast of their bodily strength and the quantity of alcohol they can manage. People boast in an ill-concealed manner of their possessions, and they like to show off their big vessels, their big houses, their luxurious cars, and their clothes. They are also fond of debates. The "Letters to the Editor" section in the Urker local weekly bears witness to this trait. Taking issue appears to be more than it seems to be. They also have a playful attitude. Urkers, as all other fishermen, are big spenders. When there is money to be spent, they do it with much pleasure. The Urkers are also fond of their rest for which, because of the strong, large, and expensive vessels used in fishing nowadays, there is far less opportunity.

Urkers are very individualistic, as are other fishermen. As a rule, the fishermen are young men. Both skipper and crew are usually less than fifty years old. There are a number of reasons for this, some of which are quite practical. Modern fishing is a hard and tough job, the wear and tear on the men is severe, and not many men are physically able to continue fishing past a certain age. At the same time, this fact gives the young men the opportunity to distinguish themselves and to succeed their fathers or uncles as skippers. They can then run their own businesses. New skippers are either the sons of existing and retired skippers or are (able) deckhands who are selected as skippers or who have started their own fishing firm. The latter is (was) easily achieved. A skipper-to-be needed "only" fifty percent of the necessary investment, and the banks were only too willing to lend the rest.

Fishing is done in a so-called *maatschap*, a kind of production cooperative. The owner, very often the skipper himself or the skipper's father, supplies the *maatschap* with his vessel and nets, the rest of the crew supplies the labour. The fishermen do not receive fixed wages, but are paid in relation to the weekly catch and in relation to age and ability. After deducting costs for fuel, rent of electronic equipment, and insurance, the net proceeds are divided according to a fixed distribution key between the ship, nets, skipper, and crew. This *maatschap* may be looked upon as an aspect of the egalitarianism of fishing cultures. In turn, the *maatschap* also strengthens this feeling of equality. A skipper usually asks a crew-member-to-be if he is willing to fish with him the following year. If a fisherman is forced to ask a skipper for a job, it is slightly humiliating for the fisherman.

The Urkers have always been very willing to accept new technical equipment for fishing. In the years after the closing of the ZuyderZee, when fishing was endangered, there were, for instance, some Urkers who went to Denmark to learn fishing by means of seinenets. Their vessels also came to be equipped with the latest and most sophisticated instruments. This seems to be in sharp contrast to the otherwise so traditional Urkers. I think this is partly explained by the fact that the men want to pursue fishing in a modern way. At the same time, they are showing off their wealth and their "success" in fishing.

Despite all this, the Urkers have become the capitalists of the ZuyderZee. For example the stereotyped exchange I encountered when meeting young Urker fishermen on Saturday nights on "neutral grounds" (in cafes in the polder) during the 1960's was: "What have you been doing?" I would ask, and the Urkers would invariably reply, "Making money". Something must have changed in the ethos and eidos system of the Urkers because "making money" is not an inherent quality of the personalities and of the cultures of fishermen.

It would be interesting to know when and where these modernization processes had begun. For example, what aspects of these changes had caused the lust for money? Had everything started when Urk was not an island any longer? And had these processes been accelerated by internal developments, such as (the possibility of) going into debt, because of their ostentatious character? Had buying big cutters and big houses and furniture caused the men to work harder and more regularly so that they could pay the interest and instalments to the bank? Interesting as these questions may seem, they need not bother us here.

## The Fishermen's Wives in Urk

Most Urker fishermen come home every Saturday. In accordance with the commandment that the Sabbath shall be a day of rest and worship, the Urkers are never at sea on Sundays. Moreover, the Urkers do not like to be in foreign ports on Sundays. They would miss their traditional Sunday with sermons and songs of praise. Consequently, the women have an extra task. When the husbands are home, everything in the household must run smoothly. The whole house must shine. The food must be especially good, and the women also have to smarten themselves up: a special hairdo and nice clothes.

On coming home, the men like to find everything as they left it last Monday. It is the task of the women to keep it that way. One could say that the Urker women are the keepers of tradition. They sit on the many committees which take care of the "social" and "cultural" life. When the men are adventuring at sea with their sophisticated vessels, the women, together with the non-fishing men, see to it that everything runs smoothly and remains as it was. This holds in religious affairs as well. The wives bear the children. They bring them up. They keep their households and ultimately society going, while the men are away.

Before World War II, the Urker women were reported to be losing their social and economic roles in public life after marriage. Religious reasons were given for this loss. I seriously doubt whether this was an accurate observation of the position of women in "menless" societies. Anyhow, nowadays the women are active in all kinds of organizations and committees. They play a conspicuous part in the religious spheres, and they "man" many church functions. But they cannot become church or chapel elders because of the traditional role of women in many orthodox Protestant denominations. Mrs. Nooy-Palm, a Dutch anthropologist who studied a strictly orthodox Protestant peasant community in the Netherlands, came to the conclusion that, as in many other communities, the women were more intensely concerned with religious and church affairs than the men, even though they could not become church elders (Nooy-Palm 1971). She mentions "old wise women" with great authority and semi-hidden power. Her observations support my doubts about the above-mentioned report. The more so, since the author, Dr. Plomp, thought that "...the women displayed a deeper religious inclination that the men..." (Plomp 1940, 37; my translation). I think that women are active in socio-cultural affairs together with the non-fishing men as solicitors for their absent husbands, sons, and brothers in maritime cultures.

Dr. Plomp expected men to be more religious than women at Urk. He gave no reasons for this, and I could not find them myself, apart from the possibility that he did not quite understand the position of women in fishing cultures. Perhaps he is referring to the conclusion reached some years before by the great Dutch sociologist Dr. Kruijt. In his thesis on religious practice in the Netherlands, Dr. Kruijt came to the conclusion that there is a positive correlation between living off the sea and the intensity of religious practice. Fishermen were religious to a high degree, and religious in a magical way at that (Kruijt 1933). This seems to be in agreement with the conclusions reached by Max Weber, who thought pre-modern men (*traditionale Bauern*) to adhere to a magico-religious complex. I have my doubts on this point. Fishermen are not by definition religious - religious in the, alas, also among social scientists all too common sense of believing in a god (YHWH), etc. In a neighbouring ZuyderZee fishing-village, up to one third of the fishing families were atheistic socialists. Using Dr. Kruijt's definition, one could not label them as religious. This seems to refute the rule. Therefore, one should be careful in making such sweeping statements and especially when applying them to particular cases. The British historian Paul Thompson concludes from his research in fishing cultures that in these communities all kinds of "solutions" have been reached by the fishermen. They have turned to church, chapel, sect, or the pub (Thompson 1983).

I am of opinion that these socialist fishermen must be looked upon as religious. In their symbolic behaviour, their socialist ideology provided the hard core with a model of the world and, at the same time, a model for the world (cf. Geertz). To put it in a different way: it gave them acts and symbols pertaining to man's ultimate conditions (cf. Bellah). They knew why they had terribly bad social conditions. They knew that things would be all right in the end, and they knew how to advance and speed up the coming of this sunny future. They had got the answers both on a general level and on an individual, personal level. They had their rituals at the meetings. They also had their icons in the form of portraits of their leaders, which were often the only pictures these people had conspicuously hanging on the wall or standing on the mantelpiece.

## Religion in Urk

I already mentioned that the Urkers are traditional in religious matters, which seems to be in sharp contrast to the eagerness with which new technological inventions are accepted. There is nothing new about the co-existence of "traditional" religious ideas and the acceptance of progressive and modern technology in certain aspects of economic life. For example, anthropologists have demonstrated this for the Hutterites and other Anabaptist and Piestist Protestant sects. Mrs. Nooy-Palm also observed this trait in the above mentioned Dutch traditional peasant community which she studied. She found that the so-called experiential[2] Protestant peasants, who were very negative about such new things as insurance and vaccinations which are regarded as interference with the Lord's providence, were the first to re-allot their meadows in order to facilitate more rational and more profitable farming. An Urker informant gave the following explanation to an anthropologist:

It is the longing for certainty which causes this apparent contradiction. The things you've got, you want to keep. And the things you don't have in your grasp, you can only get by trying to be the best. Unfurl your sails in your business and take risks (Lips 1982; my translation).

It is evident that he neither sought an explanation in terms of religion nor in terms of the fishing culture. But this is exactly where I think the explanation is to be found.

## An Explosion of Churches

It is not only in the economic sphere that Urk has witnessed an explosive growth. The last decades have also brought a large increase in the number of religious denominations. Around 1930, the Urkers could choose for their Sunday sermons out of three orthodox Protestant denominations. To wit, the Nederlandse Hervormde Kerk, the oldest Urker parish, dating from the second half of the seventeenth century, is the oldest Dutch Calvinistic denomination. It can in a sense be seen as the successor of the Vereenigde Gereformeerde Kerken in Nederland, instituted in 1568 and 1573, which had 340 members in 1930. The second oldest, dating in Urk from 1836 and, since 1869, called Christelijk Gereformeerde Kerk, counted 140 members. Finally, the largest parish, one of the Gereformeerde Kerken in Nederland, constituted in 1892, had around 2,750 members.

In passing, I note that all Urkers were church menbers to some degree, and orthodox Protestants at that. As a lot of Urkers were "searching", they visited the sermons and readings of denominations other than the ones they were members of. Or, they did not go to church at all, reading "old writers" at home instead.

Some fifty years later there are nine denominations with fourteen parishes at Urk.[3] Nearly all denominations are of an orthodox Protestant type. Most of the newcomers are to be found on the right wing of the gamut of Dutch Protestantism: both neo-Calvinistic and experiential. Only a very small number of Urkers belong to Pentecostal groups.

All the groups can be labeled orthodox, but, from the participants' point of view, they are not. Apart from the general distinction between neo-Calvinistic and experientialistic, it is almost impossible for the outsider to see the theological distinctions between the denominations. For the observer there are, e.g., groups with and without television, groups which sing psalms and hymns, groups which sing only psalms in their services, groups using the "new translation" of the bible dating from 1951, and groups using the *Statenvertaling* (i.e., the Dutch Authorised Version of the Bible from 1637), and people who consider the organ as an instrument of the devil. But for the worshippers themselves, the differences are manifold. The main contrast is between the neo-Calvinistic and the experiential groups. One can probably illustrate this contrast best by examining the conceptions each group has of YHWH.

For the experiential groups - some of the Nederlands Hervormden, some of the Christelijk Gereformeerden, the Oud Gereformeerden, the Gereformeerde Gemeente, and the Vrije Gereformeerden - YHWH (Dutch: *HEERE*) is an awe-inspiring and jealous god, who visits the iniquities of the fathers upon the children. He punishes immediately and unsparingly. The number of those saved is very small: one out of every family and one out of every village. These people, both the chosen and the damned, are always wrestling with the question of whether or not they are saved. The chosen know the place and time that their salvation took place. But even they are only certain for short periods. Every now and then, they are assaulted by severe doubts about their own salvation. Life for those not (yet) chosen is often unbearable, as they are uncertain of their fates in the eternal life after death.

For the other neo-Calvinistic groups - part of the Nederlandse Hervormden, part of the Christelijk Gereformeerden, the Gereformeerden, the Gereformeerden Vrijgemaakt to a degree, and the Nederlands Gereformeerden - YHWH is a merciful and loving father. The number of those saved by the blood of his son Jesus Christ cannot be counted. At the end of the nineteenth century, Calvin's doctrine of (double) predestination had been revised by the (later) Dutch prime minister Abraham Kuyper. He replaced it with his doctrine of common grace. That is why the tones of these neo-Calvinists are more soteriological. Though a number of neo-Calvinists still differ on the issue of YHWH's offer of common or particularist grace.

This difference in conception deeply influences the ethos and eidos system of the different groups, which is to be expected.

The members of the "strict" groups especially those of the Oud Gereformeerde Gemeente and Gereformeerde Gemeente, consider themselves to be the elite. We may find among them men who wield real economic and political power, but most of the non-experiential Urkers are annoyed by the practices of the "worthy". The latter group distinguishes between the "broken world", in which they live because of Adam's fall, and the natural order. Consequently, sin unavoidably clings to everything they do. The curious thing is that they use this reasoning as a legitimation for the lying and stealing, offenses, and tresspasses often done on purpose in everyday life. Many of the other groups severely question the ease with which the "worthy" break the commandments of YHWH, as well as the laws and rules of the secular authorities. The non-experiential groups try to bring orthodoxis and orthopraxis into tune with each other. But they, too, are inclined not to observe the public laws. I think that here we are witnessing the inclination, inherent in fishing culture, to a dislike of authority. But it is interesting to note, that all the Urkers have more or less the same excuse for their disobedience. They distinguish between the king as appointed by the Lord, on the one hand, and the governmental authorities, on the other hand. Since the latter do not care for YHWH and are a tool in the hands of those who hate YHWH, one need not obey them. They "only" regret that the king (at present the queen) is far from being a heavenly instrument.

During the 1930's, Dr. Plomp wrote: "The religious differences have relatively little effect on mutual relations since tolerance prevails to a large extent in the field of religion" (Plomp 1940, 103; my translation). Perhaps Dr. Plomp was right at the time, although I have my doubts. Nowadays, personal and group conflicts are fought out and settled in terms of religious parlance. Put in another way, apart from being religion (!), religion in Urk is a way of taking issue. For that matter, taking issue is partly play which, it is true, may get out of control and take a turn for the worse. More often than not, personal conflicts are given a religious twist and are fought out in theological and biblical terms with a vengeance.

Religion is also the great appeaser. Church elders in particular sometimes have an appeasing influence on Urker matters. They do not allow their members to attend the regularly held communion until they have resolved their conflicts, be it only for a few weeks before and after communion. This mechanism is of minor importance for the experiential denominations. It is not that the elders are powerless, but, in these circles, there are few people worthy of sitting at the Lord's table. They are afraid of eating and drinking themselves to condemnation, in the words of St. Paul in the first epistle to the Corinthians: "Let a man test himself; then he can eat from the loaf and drink from the cup. For he who eats and drinks without a proper sense of the Body, eats and drinks to his own condemnation" (1 Cor. 12:28,29).

The other sanctions church elders impose are: refusing to perform wedding services or baptism until the involved resolve their conflicts.

## A Demographic Explanation

Now, there are a number of issues which call for explanation. Why this explosion of denominations in Urk? Why are nearly all the new-comers of the traditional, experiential type and not of the revivalistic type? Why are there only fissions and hardly any fusions?

In Urk, there are far less valued positions than there are aspiring men. In the past, with a population of, say, 3,000 people, there were three denominations. Only three or four dozen men could fill the prominent positions, other ways to prominence being non-existent. The far lesser ranked public sphere was no alternative either. The municipal council offered the opportunity of distinction to only a few men. Having quit the fishing trade, or having never been fishermen, this route of earning respect was closed to them. In a population nearly 4 times greater than it was in 1930, there must be at least 4 times as many men aspiring to prominence. With a tradition of confrontations clothed in theological and biblical terminology and with the religious sphere considered as the most important, these aspirations can only be resolved in the prominence and distinction offered by the hierarchy of the church. The established officers, however, have not the slightest intention of giving up their seats which they retain until old age. Thus the only solution for aspirants is to start a conflict which will place them in the centre of attention. Very often they end it by establishing a church of their own. A new parish will give quite a number of men positions of prominence. If the ringleader or leaders choose the right issues, he or they can be assured of a following.

Church members agree for the most part on the main issues. That is why they go to the same church every Sunday. Here they can only disagree on basic principles at the risk of being ostracized. Their contentions are restricted to "minor" issues, but they do resort to exaggerating the issues. The issues are such questions as which bible translation should be used, which translation of the Book of Psalms should be sung, should only psalms be sung in the Sunday sermons or hymns as well, should these psalms be sung rhythmically or non-rhythmically, should the singing be accompanied by organ music, should one have television sets in one's home, and so on.

Attractive as this argument may seem, there are a few catches. The participants themselves may only refer to the holy cause. They act because they see the honour of YHWH endangered. They act for the sake of faith. Of course, this is almost always the case. But the participants seem to be unaware of the fact that some men may distinguish themselves by putting the mechanism of holy indignation into motion and keeping it going. But what prevents us from going beyond the participant's view?[4]

What can't be explained by this argument is the problem of why almost all the new groups are to be found on the right wing of Dutch Protestantism. An attractive argument, still in keeping with the above explanation, would run as follows: one group in particular seems to wield power at Urk. Among the members of the Oud Gereformeerde Gemeente, there are quite a few who occupy high positions. We find members of this denomination on the boards of diverse companies and in public office. Also some of the most prominent and wealthiest fishermen are found in this church. The greater part of the Urker population is said to be in fear of these men. One might think that they choose a conservative and traditional religious life in order to be near the centre of power, but this argument doesn't hold for a number of reasons. For one thing, it is also possible to find Urkers in powerful positions who none the less belong to less experiential denominations. Why have new parishes not been created around them?

The above arguments do not convincingly explain religious and "traditional" fissions. I think it is possible to find a more satisfactory explanation based on the insights of the late Dutch scholar, Fokke Sierksma, on so-called prophetic movements. According to him, processes of neuroticization can be observed in rapidly modernizing cultures. Writing abourt acculturation processes under colonial conditions, what he meant by neurosis was *das mit sich selbst entzweit sein*. Both the participants and culture as a whole are struck by neuroses. The participants see the advantages of adopting the new, superior culture which superiority is especially evident in technological and economic spheres. Many people try to adopt (part of) this new culture as quickly as possible. They realize that there is no escape from modernization, and groups of progressive people come into existence. On the other hand, groups of people who wish to cling to traditional, ancestral norms and values also come into existence. But they have to face the reality of the new order as well, so they try to bridge the unbridgeable. They want to live in both worlds and have the best of the two. They try to sit on two stools, so to speak, at the same time. The result is that they fall in between them. To put it otherwise, they try to find a way out of their dilemma. But a "way out" does not exist. The participants realize this only too well. The result is neuroses, on two levels: on the personal as well as on the cultural. Subsequently, they opt for tradition. This is, of course, "tradition", which they perceive to be ancient and ancestral. This results more often than not in one or more persons "organizing" a revivalistic or a millennialistic (or whatever you would like to call it) movement, in which the "neurotics" can feel themselves connected with their ancestors.

I think that to a certain extent this is what is to be found in Urk as well. The Urker fishermen are aware of the fact that there is no escape from modernization and no return to former days. If they want to continue their strategy of fishing, they have to embrace the norms and laws of rational, modern economic behaviour. (Economic behaviour must be analytically distinguished from that other trait in their ethos-system and eidos-system, i.e., their readiness to embrace new technological developments.) But at the same time, they also realize that they have to pay a price. They have to give up considerable areas of their traditional way of life, and that is precisely what they do not want to do. So they try to find an outlet for their misgivings. Because religion is the steering mechanism of culture, it is the sphere which is hit hardest. Religion is also the participant's only outlet. The "neuroticized" Urkers thus return to the creed of their forefathers, and, since most of the Urker forms of protestantism have always had an emotional and experiential accent, that is where they try to find new "traditional" norms and values. Religious fusion and fission at Urk may be looked upon as a result of both nation-wide and local modernization which, at the same time, provide able and capable men with the opportunity to demonstrate their capacities and to distinguish themselves.

There are only minor problems in regard to the relationship between the new economic ethic and religion. The religious practices of the Urkers date back to an earlier phase of culture, but they can easily be brought into line with their new "materialistic" outlooks. Early-modern Protestant ethic and modern-capitalistic spirit can go hand in hand, as Max Weber has shown.

The modernization process changes the position of women in the culture, but it is especially the men who lose their traditional roles. Women become more prominent in westernizing cultures. This is different in fishing cultures. Women are the pillars of society. They account for both physical and economic reproduction. Moreover, they manage affairs during the absence of their fishing husbands and sons. Not much change is to be expected, then, in the position of Urker women. They then will continue acting as solicitors for their absent husbands and sons.

## Afterthought

Since the late 1970's, things have taken a turn for the worse at Urk. Many Urker fishermen have run into serious financial difficulties and quite a few have gone bankrupt. For the most part, these difficulties are the result of the fishing methods of the Urker and other fishermen. Biologists have warned against the extinction of many fish species in the North Sea, and EEC authorities have placed restrictions on fishing. The Urkers are among those hit hardest, especially since the control of the measures taken has grown more and more strict. Can we then expect a new (explosive) rise of religions at Urk and of Pentecostal variants in particular? I do not think so, because it is only the individual Urker fisherman and his family who is affected and not the economic sphere as such. Most of the Urker variants of Protestantism have always had an element of passiveness and patience in which the individual Urker may find his consolation.

## Notes
1. I would like to thank Jim Allen, Ale Dijkstra, and Ton Kee for their advice.
2. I use the term experiential in accordance with the name they themselves prefer. More often than not, they are called members of the "black stocking churches" because of the black clothes and especially the black stockings they wear, or members of "right wing" Protestant churches. It is especially the former name which they think very deprecating and which offends and hurts them.
3. Nederlandse Hervormde Kerk (1816): de Ark, Elim (Gereformeerde Evangelisatie), deelgemeente de Bron (Evangelical 1982). Gereformeerde Kerk (1836;1892): Bethelkerk, Petrakerk, kerkelijk centrum de Poort. Christelijk Gereformeerde Kerk (1834; 1894; 1976): Eben Haezerkerk, Maranathakerk, Kerkje aan de Zee. Oud Gereformeerde Gemeente in Nederland (1960): Jochin Boazkerk. Gereformeerde Gemeente in Nederland (1980): Sionkerk. Gereformeerde Kerk Vrijgemaakt (1944): Rehoboth. Nederlands Gereformeerde Kerk (1967): Jeruzalemkerk. Vrije Gereformeerde Gemeente: Kerkstraat. Volle Evangelie Gemeente: Gebouw Irene.

200

4. By this, we could also account for a fission process in 1976. Under the influence of modern theological developments in the Gereformeerde Kerk, three groups had come into existence. Apart from the mainstream, there were "dolerenden" and "reformerenden". The "reformerenden" eventually joined the Gereformeerde Kerk Vrijgemaakt. The "dolerenden" approached the Christelijk Gereformeerden for fusion talks and ended up as a separate parish of the Christelijk Gereformeerden.

## Bibliography

Bellah, Robert N., 1976: "Religious Evolution", in: Robert N. Bellah, *Beyond Belief*, New York 1976, 20-45.

'*t Christelijke Karkien*, Geschiedenis van de Christelijke Gereformeerde Kerk "Eben Haëzer" 1894-1984, Urk n.d.

*De Bethelkerk van Urk* Stichting urker Uitgaven, Urk 1982.

Hak, Durk H., 1981: "Lemmer forneamde haven oan 'e Sudersé", *Het Peperhuis*, Enkhuizen.

Hak, Durk H., 1988: "Early-Modern Hunting and Gathering Cultures. Fishing at de Lemmer 1870-1920", *Focaal* 7, 40-57.

Hak, Durk H., 1990: *Lemmer forneamde haven oan 'e Sudersé*, Alphen aan den Rijn.

Kruijt, J.P., 1933: *De onkerkelikheid in Nederland*, Groningen/Batavia.

Lips, M.E.M., 1982: *Eruit halen wat erin zit*, (ms) Utrecht 1982.

Moffat, James: *The New Testament. A New Translation*, London 1913, 1935.

Nooy-Palm, Hetty, 1971: *Staphorster Volk*, Meppel.

Plomp, Chr., 1940: *Urk sociography van een eilandbevolking*, Alphen aan den Rijn.

Sierksma, F., 1961: *Een nieuwe hemel en een nieuwe aarde*, The Hague.

Weber, Max, 1920: *Gesammelte Aufsatze zur Religionssoziologie*, Bd. 1, Tübingen 1978.

# The Circle, the Brotherhood, and the Ecclesiastical Body: Bahá'í in Denmark, 1925-1987

## By Margit Warburg

Research into contemporary religious groups is often made difficult by an insufficient access to data. The Danish Bahá'í Community, however, provides a fortunate exception in this respect, as the co-operation of the Bahá'ís has enabled me to analyze the historical development of the Danish Bahá'í Community over a period of sixty-two years.[1] From the perspective of the sociologist of religion, this has made it possible to point out some parallels in the historical development of the Danish Bahá'í Community and the development of the great founded religions as described by Joachim Wach in his classical work, *Sociology of Religion* (1971, 130-145). Here, he presents a three-phase model of the development of founded religions and illustrates it with many examples, including the Bábí and Bahá'í religions (132, 138). Wach draws heavily on empirical rather than on theoretical arguments, but his profound empirical knowledge means that his descriptive model generally complies well with the facts and is theoretically useful. In the present work, it shall be demonstrated that his description can be extended to the spreading of an existing religion into a new country.

Briefly, Wach's description of the development of the founded religions is as follows: in its initial phase, the religion is founded and advanced by an individual of great charisma, who soon becomes the centre of a "circle" of disciples. Wach makes use of Max Weber's concept of charisma (337-338)[2] and emphasizes charisma as a *personal quality* of crucial importance to the founders of new religions (342-343). According to Wach, personal charisma *explains* why a person could exercise such influence on his followers that he could become the founder of a new religion. In other passages, Wach seems to moderate this by pointing out that religious authority as such is also ascribed to a leader by his followers (338). Nevertheless, Wach maintains that personal charisma is indispensable to the founder.

To see charisma as a *cause*, as Wach does, has later been

criticized in the sociology of religion.[3] Charisma should be seen purely as a description of that particular form of leadership where the followers ascribe to the leader an extraordinary appeal and personal power. Without the followers, there is no charisma! Despite this theoretical objection, Wach was probably right, also from a modern sociological point of view, when he regarded the initial phase of the founded religion as being based on charismatic authority, because there is no doubt that the followers of, e.g., Buddha, Zoroaster, Jesus, Muhammad, Báb, and Bahá'u'lláh regarded these men as individuals with extraordinary personal qualities and powers.

The second phase begins with the death of the founder during which the religious community is turned into a new organization, which Wach coined the "brotherhood". Without the guidance of their leader, the disciples must now interpret, systematize, and promulgate what shall become the doctrines, rituals, and traditions of the new religion. Those disciples who have known the founder personally and those who have the capabilities of leadership will typically dominate the life of the brotherhood. Eventually, as Wach argues, charisma and seniority become insufficient as sources of authority, and duties and privileges become more formalized (141). The third phase is marked by a gradual reorganization of the religious community into an "ecclesiastical body". There is no sharp division between the second and the third phase, however, and no single event marks the transition in the same way as the death of the founder marks the beginning of the second phase.

The three phases mentioned above are recognizable in the history of Bahá'í which began in the middle of the last century when Ḥusayn 'Alí Nurí (1817-1892), called Bahá'u'lláh, was accepted as a prophet and a leader of the Iranian Bábí movement and proclaimed its transformation into a new religion, Bahá'í. Then followed the period of the writings and missionary efforts of Bahá'u'lláh's son, 'Abdu'l-Bahá 'Abbás (1844-1921) who called himself 'Abdul-Bahá, "the servant of Bahá". The third phase is the establishment of the Administrative Order by Shoghi Effendi (Rabbání) (1896-1957), eventually leading to the present Universal House of Justice. Today, leadership is no longer carried out by an individual religious leader but by the elected nine-member board of the Universal House of Justice supported by professionals running the administrative machinery in Haifa, where the Bahá'í World Centre is seated. Individually, none of these nine men is seen as having any extraordinary capabilities, but together during their meetings they are believed to be divinely inspired and infallible.

As will be shown in the following, the same three phases can be seen over a much shorter period of time in the history of the Danish Bahá'í Community: the first phase began in 1947 with the arrival of two American pioneers (Bahá'í missionaries), around whom a circle was built up. Their departure (the last left in 1951) marked the beginning of the second phase in which the Danish Bahá'í Community, despite initial difficulties in finding its own feet, functioned as a brotherhood. The third phase, the transformation into an ecclesiastical body, may be said to have its beginning in 1962, when the familial structure of the brotherhood was changed into a hierachical organization with a national spiritual assembly at the head of the local spiritual assemblies. This transformation is far from complete today, and the Danish Bahá'í Community still retains many traits from the period of the brotherhood.

There is evidently an important point to be clarified in the above discussion: does the introduction of a religion into a new area represent a situation so similar to the founding of a religion that it is meaningful to compare the missionary *vis-à-vis* the converts with the founder in relation to his disciples? It should be emphasized, however, that to the adherents of the religion the two situations are fundamentally different, which means that the proposed parallel is valid only from a sociological point of view.

In the initial phase, the founding of a religion and the introduction of a religion into a new area have at least the following characteristics in common:

1. The religion has been hitherto unknown to the public at large.
2. The founder and the first missionary/missionaries have a monopoly on the information about the new religion.
3. To the new converts, the founder and the first missionary/ missionaries are undisputed religious authorities.

This structural similarity between the two situations means that the missionary's position in the religious community is similar to that of the founder, both enjoying a special status among the believers. Both are sole mediators of religious knowledge directly from superior authority. The relation between the missionary(ies) and the first converts will be a structural parallel to the founder's relation to his first disciples, because both the founder and the missionary act as a centre of undisputed authority communicating with each convert directly. In Wach's terminology, this type of organization is called a "circle". This concept, therefore, will also be applicable to a situation where a missionizing religion is first introduced into a new area.

The application of Wach's model of founded religions to the development of the Danish Bahá'í Community needs, however, an additional comment, because Bahá'í existed in Denmark for many years *before* the arrival of the 'founding' missionaries from America in 1947. These early years of Bahá'í history in Denmark hold the story of one dedicated and stubborn woman, Johanne Sørensen. She was a hospital nurse and had converted to Bahá'í already in 1925 during a stay in Honolulu.[4] She returned to Denmark, and, since she was the only Bahá'í in the country, she started corresponding with the world leader of Bahá'í, Shoghi Effendi, in order to seek advice and support. After her marriage with a physician, Dr. Høeg, she moved to the provinces. In the coming years, much of her time, money, and efforts were spent on translating and publishing Bahá'í writings, so that other Danes could become acquainted with the religion.[5] These publications were stimulated by Shoghi Effendi's emphasis on translating Bahá'í literature.[6]

In the case of Bahá'í in Denmark, the general conditions for comparing Johanne Høeg's situation with that of the founder were present: the religion was unknown, and only Johanne Høeg herself had access to the supreme authority (Shoghi Effendi). Nevertheless, she failed to create the first circle of converts.

Johanne Høeg did not represent a unique case, however. Both in Norway (White 1981, 677-679) and Iceland (*Saga Bahá'í*...1985, 11) Bahá'í was introduced by women who translated Bahá'í writings but remained solitary Bahá'ís for many years. The position of all three women was in many respects like that of the religious founder - for example, they had the authority of doctrine and the monopoly of information *vis-à-vis* their compatriots. So, when they failed in attracting new converts to Bahá'í, it may be explained by their lack of resources compared to what the more succesful American post-war missionaries had. Thus, the ladies were all alone with almost no practical or financial assistance from the Bahá'í administration in Haifa or in the U.S. and they had no training in mission work. In addition, there were more personal reasons which probably played a negative role; for instance, Johanne Høeg was a very shy person who lived rather isolated in a small provincial town and detested publicity.

Johanne Høeg's work on translations brought her into contact with the Danish professor in Iranian philology, Arthur Christensen,[7] who had studied Bahá'í in Iran and published a number of minor articles on the subject.[8] He furthermore introduced her to his successor, Kaj

Barr, who assisted her in translating some of Bahá'u'lláh's writings from the Iranian and Arabic texts (Bahá'u'lláh 1947 and 1948). The contact between Johanne Høeg and the two university professors, whose interest in Bahá'í was purely academic, is an interesting example of the relationship between the researcher and the object of research. This relationship has in later years been debated regularly among sociologists and social anthropologists,[9] but within Oriental philology and similar fields, it has never been an issue of much concern, although the discussion has been opened with Edward Said's "Orientalism" criticism in 1978.

Nevertheless, the translations made by Christensen and Barr constitute a fine example of how the object of research, *in casu* Bahá'í, as represented by Johanne Sørensen/Høeg, uses the researchers to their own advantage. The consequence of the two professors' purely academic interest in Bahá'í was in fact an active contribution to the spreading of knowledge on the Bahá'í religion in Denmark.

### The Establishment of the Circle: the First Bahá'í Community (1947-1951)

The various "teaching plans" now issued from the Universal House of Justice constitute the basis for organizing the promulgation of and conversion to Bahá'í. The Second Seven Year Plan from 1946, however, was organized by Shoghi Effendi, and the American Bahá'í Community was given the responsibility of working for the establishment of Bahá'í communities in several European countries, including Denmark (Shoghi Effendi 1947, 87-89). The European Teaching Committee, a Bahá'í suborganisation resident in Wilmette near Chicago, therefore sent a number of missionaries to Denmark for periods varying from a couple of months up to a few years.[10] Apart from the missionaries, "travelling teachers" also came to Denmark quite early.[11]

Among the pioneers, Dagmar Dole and Eleanor Hollibaugh were to have the greatest influence on the first Danish Bahá'ís. From interviews with those Danish Bahá'ís who knew Dagmar Dole and Eleanor Hollibaugh, it appears that the two American missionaries were indeed strong extrovertive personalities who succeeded in gathering around them the group of newly converted Danish Bahá'ís. Johanne Høeg played no role in this, and the new Danish Bahá'ís felt themselves to be a closely knit unit, and organized themselves as a circle around Dagmar Dole and Eleanor Hollibaugh and not around the forerunner, Johanne Høeg.

To understand why the two American missionaries were success-ful, it is not enough, however, to refer to their personal qualities. They were not only the right persons to introduce Bahá'í in Denmark, but they appeared to be the right persons at the right time and place to form the circle of adherents. What, then, was so "right" about the situation in Copenhagen in 1947?

The few foreigners coming to Denmark just after World War II were admiringly welcomed. After five years without contact with the friendly world outside, all foreign artists were great artists and all foreign literature was great literature! Accordingly, when Dagmar Dole and Eleanor Hollibaugh arrived in Denmark in 1947, it was easy for them to establish contacts, and everybody was delighted with the op-portunity to speak English. Furthermore, the Bahá'í missionaries' message of world unity and world peace was well received by a people sick of war and anxious of the prospects of a new one.

The two ladies had quite different characters. Eleanor Hollibaugh has been described to me as "a stylish bird, red-haired, wearing nylons, and very enthusiastic".[12] She was an actress and had been married to an actor whom she had divorced. Although she was 58 years old, she dressed and used make-up exactly as Danes would ex-pect from a Hollywood actress. Dagmar Dole was quite different. She was an intellectual and is remembered as being "a calm, steady lady wearing a dress and low-heeled shoes".[13] She is remembered as being an unforgettable personality and meant so much that some of the early Bahá'ís still keep a picture of her tomb in their purse.

The two American missionaries and their cause appealed to a group of people who were oriented towards humanistic rather than religious ideals. Many were artists or well-educated individualists, and quite a few had been active in the resistance movement against the German occupation forces during World War II. Politically, many of them adhered to the "Radikale Venstre", a social-liberal and pacifist party with a strong basis in the Copenhagen middle class. They usually had an international outlook, and welcomed the many contacts with the American missionaries and the travelling teachers from different countries. The fact that the language of the Bahá'í meetings was usually English meant no barrier, it was rather an attraction. The many different accents together with the new persuasive ideas made the atmosphere of the meetings almost intoxicating to the participants, even in the eyes and ears of a young girl.[14]

Together, Dagmar Dole and Eleanor Hollibaugh embodied a new world with new ideals for society. It was significant, for example, that they were both middle-aged, single women. In the late 1940's it was unusual to see single women exhibit such a degree of independence as the two Bahá'í missionaries, but many Danes, in particular younger people, agreed that this was how it ought to be. Those working for women's rights and equality were often members of other idealistic organizations, such as the Save the Children Fund, One World, and the Women's International League for Peace and Freedom. The American missionaries gave talks at meetings in these organizations, and, here, many of the future Bahá'ís heard about the religion for the first time.[15]

From a comparative point of view, it is noteworthy that there are striking similarities between the way the first Danish Bahá'ís converted and the pattern of conversion to Christianity which can be seen in the Third World during the 19th and 20th centuries. From the growing literature on the subject, it generally appears that the potential converts were attracted by the *cultural style* which the missionaries represented (Peel 1977). The Danes were attracted by the style of the emancipated, independent, and idealistic American Bahá'í missionaries, in much the same way as Africans were attracted by the power of the Europeans, by their literacy, and by their culture of "modernity". It is also noticeable that the American missionaries, by giving talks for idealistic organizations, exploited already existing cultural traditions in Denmark in their missionary work. Christian missionaries used a similar method in Africa and South America when they adapted Christianity to local cultural traditions in the process of evangelization.[16]

During the *Riḍván*,[17] April 21, 1949, the Danish Bahá'ís elected the first administrative body, the Local Spiritual Assembly of Copenhagen. The election of the assembly meant that a formal Danish Bahá'í community now existed. The missionaries were of great significance in this period. They were able to answer questions and radiated the conviction that Bahá'í could be a serious religious alternative for many Danes. It actually did seem as if they were right. During the years 1948-1951, 38 persons converted to Bahá'í and none resigned membership. A Bahá'í children's class was established, and optimism among the Danish Bahá'ís was further nourished by their holding the Third European Bahá'í Teaching Conference from the 24th to the 27th of July, 1950, and the First European Teaching Summer School from the 28th to the 30th of July, 1950. The conference and the summer school were held in Elsinore and were attended by 177 Bahá'ís from 22 different countries.[18] Dagmar Dole and Eleanor Hollibaugh were described by many of the early Bahá'ís as the ever inspiring centre of the Danish Bahá'í Community. Thus it seemed that a circle of disciples was formed around these two women who, in Wach's words, embodied "final spiritual and disciplinary authority" (137).

All this took place in Copenhagen far away from Johanne Høeg, and the development more or less passed her by. In particular, it was difficult for Johanne Høeg to adapt to the new administration. She had formerly been the only Bahá'í in Denmark and had enjoyed the privilege of corresponding with Shoghi Effendi. Now all questions were to be directed to the new assembly which, in Johanne Høeg's opinion, consisted of young and inexperienced people. Before the establishment of the Local Spiritual Assembly, her particular position and special relationship with Shoghi Effendi had been acknowledged, but now it seemed to her as if the young Bahá'ís did not care about the elderly lady living in the provinces.[19] In Max Weber's terminology, the routinization (*Veralltäglichung*) (275) became a problem to Johanne Høeg, and most of her life in the Danish Bahá'í Community was virtually spent in isolation.

## The Second Phase: the Brotherhood of the First Danish Bahá'ís (1951-1961)

The summer of 1951 was "very decisive"[20] because Dagmar Dole left for mission work in Italy (Eleanor Hollibaugh had already left earlier). The "circle" lost its centre of gravity, and the Danish Bahá'ís now experienced a new and by no means easy time, "because unconciously we had leaned so much against her that the change was indeed pronounced".[21] These last words express, as well as Wach might have done it, the transformation of the circle into the brotherhood. The small, young Bahá'í community had to stand on its own feet, and the Bahá'ís spent most of their time together trying to consolidate the group. Being only 38 persons (apart from Johanne Høeg in the provinces) meant that a series of characteristic small group features emerged. The strongest personalities became informal spiritual leaders, and cliques, friendships, and enmities flourished. The consequence was that recruitment almost ceased. In the words of an early Bahá'í, "we felt that we were grinding to a halt,"[22] and there was a general feeling of stagnation. Many of those Bahá'ís who had converted in fascination of Dagmar Dole and Eleanor Hollibaugh experienced a hard time, and some of them eventually resigned membership. In fact, the majority of the early members have resigned or are totally inactive today. The remaining few, on the other hand, form the active nucleus of the Danish Bahá'í Community today.

It is interesting to note how closely the troubles of the Danish Bahá'í Community follow Wach's description of the crisis caused by the passing of the religious founder: "With his passing, new problems appear. What is to be the meaning of discipleship, now that there is no more master? Personal discipleship, originally a *sine qua non*, can no longer be a prerequisite although the remaining disciples gain considerably in prestige and authority" (137).

In the same period, i.e., the first half of the 1950's, the Danish Bahá'í Community was requested through the Bahá'í administration to comply with the municipal boundaries of the country, which meant that the Bahá'ís of Copenhagen were split into six different municipalities, each with its own Bahá'í locality.[23] This was difficult to adapt to for the small group of people who had been accustomed to working closely together for a good many years. When I interviewed some of the early Bahá'ís on these events, they clearly expressed that also at that time they knew that the community had reached an organizational turning point. By accepting the change to a higher degree of organization, they had to face the difficulty of leaving the warm, intimate community. This development can be characterized by Wach's words: "The brotherhood evidences also the development toward ecclesiastical organization in the steady growth of its doctrine, cult, and organization into an objective one" (139-140). With this reorganization, the Danish Bahá'í Community began the long process of becoming an ecclesiastical body.

It is not possible to conclude whether Bahá'í became better known to the public as a result of the reorganization. However, it can be stated that the community did not have much success in recruiting more members. There were 47 adult members in 1954, and, five years later, they had only grown to 50. The brotherhood had just entered a phase of transformation towards a more complex organization, but their prospects of success were not high. However, the necessary assistance came from outside with the arrival of a group of Iranian missionaries.

## The Iranian Pioneers and the Emergence of the Ecclesiastical Body (1961-1971)

Shoghi Effendi had several times requested Iranian Bahá'ís to move to those countries in greatest need of new blood, but only a few had gone to Denmark, and those who did soon left again.[24] However, the situation in the late 1950's was quite desperate for the Danish Bahá'í Community, and the arrival of 17 Iranian missionaries in 1961 had a tremendous effect. Not only did this boost the number of members considerably, but more importantly, the Iranians possessed knowledge, insight, and experience of the religion at a level hitherto unknown to the Danish Bahá'í Community.

Since 1961, the Iranians have constituted a significant contingent among the Bahá'ís of Denmark. After a slight decline in the mid-1960's, the number of Iranians has grown steadily through the immigration of missionaries, and later through the arrival of refugees from the Iranian revolution of 1979. The relationship between the Iranians and the native Danes is an important feature of everyday life in the community, but in the present context it is sufficient to note that the two groups have become Bahá'ís in two quite different ways. At the time of the Iranian arrival, almost all adult Danish Bahá'ís had converted through personal conviction in an often mature age. The Iranians, on the other hand, were born into families which had been Bahá'ís for several generations. They knew the religion from early childhood, and Bahá'í was an inseparable part of their entire cultural background. Among other things, this difference between the Danes and the Iranians is reflected demographically. For example, the Danish group has always been characterized by a considerable majority of women, whereas the Iranian group exhibits an even distribution of the sexes as would obviously be the case for any group where the members usually are not first-generation converts.[25]

It was evident that the arrival of the Iranian missionaries would influence the Danish Bahá'í Community profoundly. Iran has a particular position in the mind of every Bahá'í - it is the "Cradle of the Faith" - and Iranians are all endowed with a sprinkle of Báb's and Bahá'u'lláh's *mana*. An Iranian Bahá'í has an internalized Bahá'í way-of-life, knowledge of the holy scriptures, and an ability to read them in the original language. In addition, there is a certainty of ethnic and religious affiliation, not shared to the same extent by the Danish Bahá'ís, and the sense of belonging to a religious minority amid a hostile majority.

The level of expectation was high when the 17 Iranian missionaries arrived, indeed, to such an extent that it was only too natural that not all Iranians could live up to those expectations. On the other hand, the rate of recruitment of the new Danish born Bahá'ís began to increase in the following years, and it seems reasonable to ascribe at least part of this to the influence of the Iranians. Already in 1962, the Bahá'ís could form a national spiritual assembly, and in 1971, the total membership had grown to 95, of which 73 were native Danes, 14 Iranians, and the remaining 8 came from various other countries, mainly the U.S.

It seems clear that the Iranian arrival advanced the transformation from the simple organization of the brotherhood into the more complex and hierarchical organization, which Wach termed "ecclesiastical body". The transformation of the brotherhood into an ecclesiastical body is a process of long duration characterized by a multitude of changes in the organization rather than by one single, revolutionary event. One of the important organizational and sociological changes indicative of the transformation is the routinization of leadership (Wach 1971, 141-156, especially 151).

## Routinization of Leadership (1971-1979)

In the case of the Danish Bahá'í Community, the routinization of leadership was prevalent during the 1970's. In this period, the community experienced an extraordinary growth in membership. The number of members increased more than seventy per cent in just three years from *Naw Rúz*[26] 1971 to *Naw Rúz* 1974. The overwhelming majority of the new members were Danes who converted to Bahá'í, and it can most likely be related to the generally growing interest in religious renewal which came in the wake of the youth rebellion in 1968-69.[27] Within the Danish Bahá'í Community, it created a situation with two generations, the "old" one which was tied together by the informal, personal network and the "new" one which yet lacked strong personal relations to other Bahá'ís. The strengthening of the formal organization was a structural response to the weakening of the informal network caused by the increase in membership and the emerging generation gap.

The routinization was enhanced by a factor specific to Bahá'í, namely, that a formalized leadership is an important feature of the religion. The Administrative Order is a detailed set of religiously binding rules for the work of the various Bahá'í bodies, and these rules are thought to be applied to the governing of mankind in a future Bahá'í world (*Principles of Bahá'í Adminstration. A Compilation,* 1976). Therefore, there is an *urge* within Bahá'í more than within most other religious communities to enter the process of the routinization of leadership.

A well-documented example of this urge is the case of the recognition of Bahá'i marriages by the Danish authorities. The case is important in the discussion of the routinization of leadership, because it is evident that the recognized authority of a religious group to perform *legally* binding acts must imply that this group is considered by the state bureaucracy to be a reliable adminstrative counterpart.

The Danish constitution guarantees the freedom of conscience (Constitution of June 5, 1953, §§ 67, 68, and 70), which means that everyone is free to exercise his or her religion without infringements of his or her rights as a citizen. However, this principle of religious liberty does not imply equality between the different religions, because the Constitution also gives the national Evangelical Lutheran Church a preferential status (§4). The position of other religious communities is to be regulated by law according to the Constitution (§69), but this has in fact never been effectuated. Notwithstanding, a few traditionally established religious communities in Denmark have acquired the status of "recognized religious communities".[28] This means, among other things, that their marriage ritual has the same legal status as that of the National Church.

In 1972, the secretary of the National Spiritual Assembly wrote to the Ministry of Ecclesiastical Affairs in order to clarify the conditions under which the Danish Bahá'í Community could become a recognized community.[29] This letter sparked off a year-long correspondence between the two parties which ended in March 1979. The Ministry of Ecclesiastical Affairs did not formally deny the Danish Bahá'í Community the status of a recognized religious community in the sense described in a treatise on Danish canon law by the Permanent Under-Secretary of the Ministry.[30] Instead, the case was referred to the Bishop of Copenhagen, who suggested that the Danish Bahá'í Community should be allowed to perform legal marriages, provided a marriage ritual was formalized and a petition was delivered to the Ministry in each individual case.[31] This became the position of the Ministry in their final letter to the Bahá'ís, dated 16 March 1979.[32] The Danish Bahá'í Community thereby acquired the same legal status as, for example, the American Lutheran Church, Jehovah's Witnesses, and various Moslem communities. They are neither recognized religious communities nor non-recognized, "private" assemblies, but apparently enjoy a kind of "grade-B" status in terms of recognition.

## The Contemporary Situation (1979-87)

The year 1979, however, was not only the year of governmental recognition for the Danish Bahá'ís. In Iran the year also marked the beginning of new and abominable persecutions of Bahá'ís and many other groups condemned as enemies of the new Islamic Republic.

Thousands of refugees came to Europe in the following years, and many obtained the right of asylum in Denmark. The great majority of the Iranian refugees in Denmark are political opponents of the Khomeini regime or deserters from the service, but a considerable number of Bahá'ís have also arrived. The Iranian element in the Danish Bahá'í Community is therefore quite strong now, constituting about 25%.

The atrocities of the Iranian regime were a regular issue in the Danish mass media in the beginning of the 1980's, and, for the first time, the persecutions of the Iranian Bahá'ís were reported in wider circles.[33] Following the urge of the Universal House of Justice, the Danish Bahá'í Community played their role in this mainly through press releases and letters to the newspapers in order to inform about the Bahá'í religion and its suppression in Iran or to correct misunderstandings.

Apart from the effects of the Iranian revolution, there is little to say about recent years. The stagnation in the late 1970's has been superseded by a moderate, but steady, growth in total membership, so that by May 1987 the community consisted of 213 Bahá'ís above 15 years of age. 137, or 64%, were native Danish converts. So the multiethnicity of the community is now quite pronounced. Bahá'í has been strengthened considerably outside the Greater Copenhagen area with half of the Bahá'ís now living in the provinces, and there are permanent local assemblies in several provincial towns. The spirit of the brotherhood is still felt among the early Bahá'ís, but the feeling of professionalism produced by the use of paid secretarial assistance and by the installation of a computer at the *Ḥaẓíratu'l-Quds* (Bahá'í centre) is indicative of the ecclesiastical body.

Although the Danish Bahá'í Community is still very small, it nevertheless seems to be a permanent feature of the contemporary religious scene in Denmark. The history of Bahá'í in Denmark demonstrates that religious innovation is possible even in an apparently highly secularized society. It also demonstrates that a new religious community formed around a missionary has many striking sociological similarities with the development which Wach observed as being general for religions founded by one particular individual.

## Acknowledgements

A warm thanks for help and confidence is directed to the National Spiritual Assembly of the Bahá'ís of Denmark and to all the members of the Danish Bahá'í Community. My gratitude is also extended to the Danish Research

Council for the Humanities and the University of Copenhagen for a travel grant which enabled me to do the necessary library and archival study at the Bahá'í World Centre in Haifa, Israel, in January and February 1987. As the first non-Bahá'í scholar, I obtained access to the Bahá'í World Centre collections, for which I thank the Universal House of Justice. I also wish to thank the staff of the Bahá'í World Centre for their great hospitality and invaluable assistance. Research expenses were once again met by the generous support of the University of Copenhagen in September 1987 when I worked at the National Bahá'í Archives in Wilmette, Illinois. I thank the staff of the archives for their kind assistance.

**Notes**

1. Only a few of the sources for the history of the Danish Bahá'í Community are publicly available. I have made use of unpublished material from the following Bahá'í archives, cf. the bibliography:
   - Bahá'í World Centre Archives, Haifa.
   - National Bahá'í Archives. Bahá'í National Center, Wilmette, Illinois.
   - The archives of the National Bahá'í Centre in Denmark, Copenhagen.
   - Kaya Holck's private archive, Copenhagen.
   Furthermore, I have drawn on the results of an extensive interview survey (120 completed interviews), carried out as part of my ongoing study of the Danish Bahá'í Community. These interviews constitute a major source to the history of the Danish Bahá'ís, and unless otherwise stated the presentation is based on the general conclusions drawn from the interviews. The publicly available archival material is from the archives of the Danish Ministry of Ecclesiastical Affairs and from Professor Arthur Christensen's personal files at the Royal Library, Copenhagen.

2. The role of the charismatic individual in the foundation of a new religion was originally described by Max Weber in the 1920's in his sociology of religion (1972, 268-279). The concept of charisma has since been frequently utilized in the sociology of religion. Of particular relevance to the present work is Peter L. Berger's early study on the Bahá'ís of North America where he introduces the term "charismatic field" (1954, 161). The theme is taken up by Peter Smith in his discussion of religious leadership in the Bábí religion (1987, 24-41).

3. One of the most pertinent reviews of the concept of charisma in the study of religion is found in Peter Worsley's analysis of the millenarian cargo cults of Melanesia which in many respects displayed the features of charismatic movements. In two large sections of his book, *The Trumpet Shall Sound* (1970, 274-280, 285-297), he gives a clear and thorough presentation and critique of the concept of charisma, from Weber to contemporary, popular uses of the term as a synonym for a particularly attractive personal appeal. In order to give it a sociological

meaning, Worsley stresses that charisma must be interpreted as an interactional phenomenon between the leader and the followers. The leader is ascribed charisma only if he is successful in striking emotional chords in his audience and in giving proofs of his ability to fulfill their aspirations.

4. Interview with Johanne Høeg (née Sørensen) 11 March 1980. Cf. [Alexander, A.B.] 1974, 29.

5. The following three publications by J.E. Esslemont resulted from these efforts: Esslemont 1926, [1926], and 1932.

6. This is clearly reflected in the extensive correspondence between Johanne Sørensen/Høeg and Shoghi Effendi, cf. Shoghi Effendi to Johanne Sørensen, 2 February 1928. Bahá'í World Centre, Haifa. Research Department, GCI/84/184.

7. Johanne Sørensen to Arthur Christensen, 26 June 1932. The Royal Library, Copenhagen. Utilg. 319. Johanne Sørensen to Arthur Christensen, 10 November 1932. The Royal Library, Copenhagen. Utilg. 319. Johanne Sørensen to Arthur Christensen, 2 April 1935. The Royal Library, Copenhagen. Utilg. 319.

8. A bibliography covering most of Arthur Christensen's published works is included in Barr 1946, 65-102. Unfortunately, several of Arthur Christensen's minor papers on Bábísm and Bahá'í are not included in this bibliography. See Christensen 1903; 1911; 1912; 1914a; 1914b; 1918, 127-143; 1930, 82-89, 109-114; 1932; 1933; 1935; and 1937, 79-105. Christensen *et al.* 1928-30, contains his Danish translations of extracts of the *Bayán* by Báb, and *The Hidden Words*, by Bahá'u'lláh.

9. Cf. Barnes 1979, 169-188. Using the case of the Danish Bahá'í Community, I have discussed the question of communicating results of sociological research to the group under investigation in Warburg 1983.

10. White 1981, 399. The first missionaries to arrive were Anders and Helga Nielsen who came 16 October 1946 (*Bahá'í News* 194, 104 B.E., April 1947, 7). Of more importance were Dagmar Dole, who stayed in Denmark from 1947 to 1951, Eleanor Hollibaugh, who spent a year in Copenhagen in 1947 and 1948, and Nancy Gates, who was a missionary between 1948 and 1950 (interview with Jean Deleuran 13 March 1980). Amelia Bowman stayed for a short while in the autumn of 1947 (I. Hjelme, "Strejflys", *Bahá'í Nyhedsbrev* 19, 134 B.E., 2 March-20 March 1978, 7), and Alice Dudley for a few months in 1948 (Dudley, *Unfinished Journey*, vol. 1, 1-8).

11. Two of the early travelling teachers were Etty Graeffe and Marion Little, who visited Denmark in October 1946 and early 1947 respectively, (*Bahá'í News* 194, 104 B.E., April 1947, 7, and 199, 104 B.E., September 1947, 7). A further travelling teacher was the later "Hand of the Cause of God", Dorothy Baker, who spoke to the Women's International League for Peace and Freedom in Copenhagen, January 1948 (I. Hjelme, "Strejflys", *Bahá'í Nyhedsbrev* 19, 134 B.E.,

2 March-20 March 1978, 8, and interview with Inger Hjelme, 10 April 1980; the twelve, later twenty-one, "Hands of the Cause of God" ranked next to Shoghi Effendi, cf. White 1981, 320-323). Dorothy Baker also gave a speech in the Danish Council for Peace which was reported in a leading women's journal, "Set og sket", *Tidens Kvinder* 26 (8), 24 February 1948.

12. Interview with Tove Deleuran, 11 March 1980.
13. *Ibid.*
14. Interview with Lise Raben, 3 May 1986. One of the early Bahá'ís wrote to the European Teaching Committee and told the chairman, Edna M. True, that "...Dagmar is wonderful to convince people of, that the Baha'i Faith and teachings are the only and right things to believe in and to live up to." (Lilly Quistgaard to Edna True, 26 June 1949. National Bahá'í Archives. Bahá'í National Center, Wilmette, Illinois.) Eleanor Hollibaugh, however, suited the Danes just as well. "Eleanor is very greatly loved here, by all of the Baha'is and by a good many other people also. She has an unusual personality and approach to the Cause, that appealed greatly to the Danish people." (Dagmar Dole to Edna True, 22 October 1948. National Bahá'í Archives. Bahá'í National Center, Wilmette, Illinois.)
15. Interview with Inger Hjelme, 10 April 1980.
16. Some semantic aspects of this phenomenon are discussed in Lienhardt 1982 and in Rivière 1981.
17. *Riḍván*, meaning paradise, is the twelve-day Bahá'í festival commemorating the days when Bahá'u'lláh declared that he was the prophet foretold by the Báb. According to Bahá'í tradition, this took place 21 April to 2 May 1863 in a garden outside Baghdad.
18. European Teaching Committee, "First Bahá'í Chirldren's Class in Denmark", *Bahá'í News* 228, 106 B.E., February 1950; E. Steinmetz, "The Third European Teaching Conference Copenhagen, Denmark July 24th through 27th, 1950", *Bahá'í News* 236, 107 B.E., October 1950, 10-12; C. Stirratt, "The First Bahá'í European Summer School Copenhagen, Denmark July 28 through 30, 1950", *Bahá'í News* 236, 107 B.E., October 1950, 12-13; I. Hjelme, "Strejflys nr. 3", *Bahá'í Nyhedsbrev* 2, 135 B.E., 9 April-27 April, 1978, 16; *idem*, "Strejflys nr. 4", *Bahá'í Nyhedsbrev* 3, 135 B.E., 28 April-16 May 1978, 15-16; and idem, "Strejflys nr. 5", *Bahá'í Nyhedsbrev* 4, 135 B.E., 17 May-4 June 1978, 11.
19. Interview with Johanne Høeg (née Sørensen), 11 March 1980. Her difficulties are illustrated by a minor controversy over the publication of an Inuit (Greenlandic) translation of J.E. Esslemont's *What is the Bahá'í Movement?* Johanne Høeg wrote to the European Teaching Committee in Wilmette, Illinois explaining that in agreement with Shoghi Effendi she had initiated a translation of the pamphlet, but that she was willing to let the Local Spiritual Assembly handle the

publication if the European Teaching Committee decided that she should do so. (Johanne Høeg to Edna True, 10 April 1949. National Bahá'í Archives. Bahá'í National Center, Wilmette, Illinois.) In May 1949, when the assembly had been formed, Edna M. True wrote to Dagmar Dole and recommended that the matter should be held in abeyance. (Edna True to Dagmar Dole, 26 May 1949. National Bahá'í Archives. Bahá'í National Center, Wilmette, Illinois.) Eventually it was solved by Shoghi Effendi who in a letter of 25 December 1949 informed Johanne Høeg that she could personally handle the publication independently of the Local Spiritual Assembly (Shoghi Effendi through R. Rabbání to Johanne Høeg, 25 December 1949. Bahá'í World Centre, Haifa. Research Department, GC1/106/157.) The pamphlet was published in Hjørring in 1950 under the title *Baháp ajokersûtânik maleruainiarnek sunauna?*

20. I. Hjelme, "Strejflys nr. 6", *Bahá'í Nyhedsbrev* 8, 135 B.E., 1 August-19 August 1978, 14.
21. *Ibid.*
22. I. Hjelme, "Strejflys nr. 7", *Bahá'í Nyhedsbrev* 9, 135 B.E., 20 August-7 September 1978, 16.
23. I. Hjelme, "Strejflys nr. 9", *Bahá'í Nyhedsbrev* 11, 135 B.E., 27 September - 15 October 1978 (unpaginated).
24. The number of Iranian Bahá'ís in Denmark until 1961 appears from Kaya Holck's list.
25. Explanations of the apparently larger acceptance of Bahá'í among Danish women than among Danish men are yet on the level of hypothesis and will have to await a more detailed analysis of the material of my study of the Danish Bahá'í Community.
26. *Naw Rúz* is the Iranian New Year which is celebrated by all Iranians at the vernal equinox on the 21st of March. However, it is also part of the Bahá'í calendar.
27. The individual reasons for converting are known for those of the new members who remained in the community and who could therefore participate in my interview survey of 120 Danish Bahá'ís, but whether there is a particular pattern different from the general sociological trends during those years can only be answered after a more thorough analysis of the interviews.
28. The recognized communities are the Reformed Congregations (i.e., the Danish Reformed, French Reformed, and German Reformed), the Roman Catholic Church, the Jewish Community, the Methodist Community, the Swedish 'Gustav' Congregation of Copenhagen, the Orthodox Russian Congregation of Copenhagen, St. Alban's English Church of Copenhagen, the Danish Baptist Community, and the Norwegian Congregation (Roesen 1976, 353-355).
29. Kamma Jørgensen, the National Spiritual Assembly of the Bahá'ís of Denmark to the Ministry of Ecclesiastical Affairs, 31 August 1972; file

1. kt. 661, archives of the Ministry of Ecclesiastical Affairs, Copenhagen.
30. Roesen 1976, 347-353. Roesen states that size, organization, the existence of institutions for educating the clergy, permanency of the community, and its international affiliation are important aspects to consider in questions of recognition.
31. Ole Berthelsen, Bishop of Copenhagen Diocese to the Ministry of Ecclesiastical Affairs, 26 July 1976; file 1 kt. 6629-4, archives of the Ministry of Ecclesiastical Affairs, Copenhagen.
32. The Ministry of Ecclesiastical Affairs to the National Spiritual Assembly of the Bahá'ís of Denmark, 16 March 1979; file 1. kt. 6629-4, archives of the Ministry of Ecclesiastical Affairs, Copenhagen.
33. Cf. Warburg 1985. After an introductory chapter, the book contains documentary material from Iran, mostly governmental letters, verdicts of the court, and newspaper articles. The material, which clearly shows that Iranian Bahá'ís are persecuted solely because they are Bahá'ís, is brought in facsimile together with a translation into Danish.

## Unpublished material

*Bahá'í World Centre, Haifa*
Correspondence to Shoghi Effendi from Bahá'ís resident in or passing through Denmark, 1925-1957, Archives Department.
Correspondence from Shoghi Effendi (or his secretaries) to Bahá'ís resident in or passing through Denmark, 1925-1957, Research Department.
Dudley, A., *Unfinished Journey*, vols. 1-2, unpublished manuscript, [between 1974 and 1979], Bahá'í World Centre Library.

*National Bahá'í Archives. Bahá'í National Center, Wilmette, Illinois.*
Correspondence between the European Teaching Committee and the American missionaries in Denmark, 1947-1951.
Correspondence between the European Teaching Committee and Bahá'ís resident in Denmark, 1947-1959.

*The archives of the National Bahá'í Centre in Denmark, Copenhagen.*
Card index of members of the Danish Bahá'í Community except for 10 persons who requested anonymity, 1980.

*Bahá'í Nyhedsbrev* 1968ff.

*Annual reports of the National Spiritual Assembly 1962ff.*

*Semi-annual statistical reports to the Universal House of Justice 1962ff.*

*The Ministry of Ecclesiastical Affairs, Copenhagen.*
Correspondence between the National Spiritual Assembly and the Ministry of Ecclesiastical Affairs 1972-1979, file 1 kt. 661 and file 1 kt. 6629-4.

*The Royal Library, Copenhagen.*
Correspondence between Johanne Sørensen and Arthur Christensen, 1932-1935, Utilg. 319.

*Kaya Holck's private archive, Copenhagen.*
Card index of members of the Danish Bahá'í Community, 1925-1962.

*Interviews*
8 personal interviews with the most senior Bahá'ís on the early history of the Danish Bahá'í Community.
120 personal extensive interviews with members of the Danish Bahá'í Community.

## Bibliography

[Alexander, A.B.], 1974: *Forty Years of the Bahá'í Cause in Hawaii 1902-1942*, The National Spiritual Assembly of the Hawaiian Islands, Honolulu, (rev. ed.).
Anonymous, 1947: *Bahá'í News* 194, 104 B.E., April, 7-8.
Anonymous, 1947: *Bahá'í News* 199, 104 B.E., September, 7.
Anonymous, 1948: "Set og sket", *Tidens Kvinder* 26, (8), 24 February, 20.
Bahá'u'lláh, 1947: *Tre daglige Pligtbønner*, Hjørring.
Bahá'u'lláh, 1948: *De skjulte Ord*, Hjørring
Barnes, J.A., 1979: *Who Should Know What? Social Science, Privacy and Ethics*, Harmondsworth.
Barr, K., 1946: "Arthur Christensen. 9. Januar 1875-31. Marts 1945", *Oversigt over Selskabets Virksomhed Juni 1945-Maj 1946, avec un résumé en français*, Copenhagen.
Berger, P.L., 1954: From Sect to Church. A Sociological Interpretation of the Bahá'í Movement, Ph.D. thesis, The New School of Social Research, New York.
Christensen, A., 1903: "Babismen i Persien", *Dansk Tidsskrift*, 526-539.
Christensen, A., 1911: "En moderne orientalsk Religion", *Nordisk Tidsskrift för Vetenskap, Konst och Industri* 5, 343-360.
Christensen, A., 1912: Review of Herman Roemer: *Die Babi-Beha'i, die*

*jüngste muhammedanische Sekte* (Potsdam 1912), *Le Monde Oriental* 6, 242-243.

Christensen, A., 1914a: Review of Herman Roemer: *Die Babi-Beha'i, die jüngste muhammedanische Sekte* (Potsdam 1912), *Der Islam. Zeitschrift für Geschichte und Kultur des islamischen Orients* 5, 389-390.

Christensen, A., 1914b: Review of *L'Épître au Fils du Loup par Behaōu'llāh*, translated by Hippolyte Dreyfus (Paris 1913), *Der Islam. Zeitschrift für Geschichte und Kultur des islamische Orients* 5, 390-391.

Christensen, A., 1918: *Hinsides det kaspiske Hav. Fra en Orientrejse ved Krigens Udbrud*, Copenhagen.

Christensen, A., J. Pedersen & F. Pullich, eds., 1928-30: *Religionernes Bøger*, Copenhagen [1929].

Christensen, A., 1930: *Det gamle og det nye Persien*, Copenhagen.

Christensen, A., 1932: "En moderne Verdensreligion", *Berlingske Tidende Aften*, 7 November, 7-8.

Christensen, A., 1933: "Babisme", *Illustreret dansk Konversationsleksikon*, Copenhagen, Bind 2, 185.

Christensen, A., 1935: "Bābier", *Salmonsens Konversationsleksikon*, 2nd ed., Copenhagen, Bind 2, 458-459.

Christensen, A., 1937: *Kulturskitser fra Iran*, Copenhagen.

Esslemont, J.E., 1926: *Bahá'u'lláh og hans Budskab*, Copenhagen.

[Esslemont, J.E.], [1926]: *Hvad er Bahá'í Bevægelsen?*, Copenhagen.

Esslemont, J.E., 1932: *Bahá'u'lláh og den nye Tid*, Copenhagen.

[Esslemont, J.E.], 1950: *Baháp ajokersûtânik maleruainiarnek sunauna?*, Hjørring.

European Teaching Committee, 1950: "First Bahá'í Children's Class in Denmark", *Bahá'í News* 228, 106 B.E., 9.

Lienhardt, G., 1982: "The Dinka and Catholicism", in: J. Davis, ed., *Religious Organisation and Religious Experience*, London, 81-95.

Peel, J.D.Y., 1977: "Conversion and Tradition in Two African Societies: Ijebu and Buganda", *Past and Present* 77, 108-141.

*Principles of Bahá'í Administration. A Compilation*, 1976, London, 1950 (4th ed. 1976).

Rivière, P., 1981: "'The Wages of Sin Is Death'": Some Aspects of Evangelisation among the Trio Indians", *Journal of the Anthropological Society of Oxford* 16 (1), 1-13.

Roesen, A., 1976: *Dansk Kirkeret*, 3rd ed., Hillerød.

*Saga Bahá'í trúarinnar i megindráttum. Stutt samantekt um uppruna, thróun og megininntak Bahá'í trúarinnar*, 1985, Andlegt thjódrád Bahá'ía á Islandi, Reykjavik 1981 (2nd ed., 1985).

Said, E.W., 1978: *Orientalism*, New York.

Shoghi Effendi, 1947: *Messages to America. Selected Letters and Cablegrams* addressed to the Bahá'ís of North America 1932-1946, Wilmette, Illinois.

Smith, P., 1987: *The Babi and Baha'i Religion. From Messianic Shi'ism to a World Religion*, Cambridge.

Steinmetz, E., 1950: "The Third European Teaching Conference Copenhagen, Denmark July 24th through 27th, 1950", *Bahá'í News* 236, 107 B.E., 10-12.

Stirratt C., 1950: "The First Bahá'í European Summer School Copenhagen, Denmark July 28 through 30, 1950", *Bahá'í News* 236, 107 B.E., 12-13.

Wach, J., 1971: *Sociology of Religion*, Chicago, 1944 (12th impr. 1971).

Warburg, M., 1983: "Formidling som en del af forskningsprocessen - om et religionssociologisk forskningsprojekt: Bahá'í i Danmark", in: K. Krarup & O. Rieper, eds., *Formidling og anvendelse af samfundsforskning. Røsnæssymposiet 1982*, Copenhagen, 129-141.

Warburg, M., 1985: *Iranske dokumenter. Forfølgelsen af Bahá'íerne i Iran*, Copenhagen.

Weber, M., 1972: *Wirtschaft und Gesellschaft. Grundriss der verstehenden Soziologie*, I, Tübingen, 1921-22 (5th ed. 1972).

White, R., ed., 1981: *A Compendium of Volumes of the Bahá'í World. An International Record I-XII 82-110 of the Bahá'í Era (1925-1954)*, Oxford.

Worsley, P., 1970: *The Trumpet Shall Sound. A Study of 'Cargo' Cults in Melanesia*, London, 1957 (2nd ed. 1970).

# Contributors

# Contributors

*Lourens P. van den Bosch* was born in England in 1944 and studied theology, history of religions, and Indonesian languages at the University of Groningen, The Netherlands. He took his degree in Indian Languages and Culture at the University of Utrecht. His thesis entitled: *Atharvaveda-pariśiṣṭa, Chapters 21-29*, appeared in 1978. Articles of his are published, among others, in *Indo-Iranian Journal, Numen, Nederlands Theologisch Tijdschrift*, and in several volumes with essays, among others, in H.G. Kippenberg, et al., eds., *Concepts of Person in Religions and Thought*, Berlin/New York 1990. Presently he is associate professor in the history of Islam and Indian religions at the Faculty of Theology, Department of Religious Studies, the University of Groningen.

*Monica Engelhart* received her graduate degrees at Stockholm University, Sweden in 1970 and her post-graduate degree under Professor Åke Hultkrantz at the same university. She has been teaching methodology and theories of comparative religion and native religions since 1986. She is presently teaching on the religions of the Near East, Greece, Rome, and Old Norse. Her publications include articles such as "Religionsstudiet i Australien och studiet av australsk religion" (The Study of Religion in Australia and the Study of Australian Religion, *Svensk Religionshistorisk Årsskrift* 1985), "Vcms är landet?" (Whose Land Is It?, *Fjärde Världen* 1986), "Dubbelt så många urinvånare då Australien koloniscrades" (Twice as Many Aborigines When Australia Became Colonized, *Fjärde Världen* 1987), "De första australiernas levnadssätt" (The Lifeways of the First Australians, *SANZFU Newsletter* 1988), "Australiska urinvånare i modern tid" (Australian Aborigines in Modern Times, *Chaos* 1988), and an essay collection entitled *Studier i religionshistoria, tillägnade Åke Hultkrantz* (Studies in the History of Religions, Dedicated to Åke Hultkrantz, in press).

*Armin W. Geertz* was born in the United States in 1948 and received his degrees in the history of religions at the University of Aarhus in Denmark. He has done fieldwork among the Hopi Indians of Arizona and is presently associate professor at the University of Aarhus, Chairman of the Danish Association for the History of Religions, and Honorary Treasurer of the International Association for the History of Religions. He is also editor of a number of journals in Europe and the United States. In addition to a number of articles and books on various indigenous cultures and on methodology, his publications include *Hopi Indian Altar Iconography* (Leiden 1987), *Children of Cottonwood. Piety and Ceremonialism in Hopi Indian Puppetry* (together with Michael Lomatuway'ma, Lincoln 1987), *A Concordance of Hopi Indian Texts* (Aarhus 1989), and *Mystik - den indre vej?* (Mysticism: the Inner Way?, edited together with Per Bilde, Aarhus 1990).

*Pieter F. Goedendorp* was born in 1957 and studied the history and religion of ancient Israel, of social anthropology, and of the history of religions at the State University of Groningen, The Netherlands. Since 1984, he has been attached to the Department of the History of Religions at the Groningen Theological Faculty as a research assistant. He is presently preparing a doctoral dissertation on the usage of the so-called messianic title "The Standing One". Since 1990, he has been employed by the Dutch Reformed Church in Deurne.

*Durk Huite Hak* was born in 1944 and studied human geography and cultural anthropology at Groningen University, The Netherlands. At the moment he is dean of the Department of Sociology at the same university. He has published, among other things, on Dutch agriculture in the nineteenth century, on Dutch maritime (fishing) cultures, and on Dutch religious fission and fusion processes in the nineteenth century.

*Jeppe Sinding Jensen* was born in 1951 in Copenhagen, Denmark. He received degrees in Semitic languages and the history of religions at the University of Aarhus. He is presently associate professor at the Department of Philosophy, Section of the Study of Religion at Odense University. His publications include *The Amyclean Apollo and Reshep MKL* (University of Aarhus 1982), articles and essays on methodology and theory in the study of religions such as "Ritual between Art and Control" (*Temenos* 1986), "History of Religions without an Object?" (in W. Tyloch, ed. *Studies of Religions in Context of the Social Sciences*, Warsaw 1990), and "Towards Contemporary Islamic Concepts of the Person" (in H.G. Kippenberg et al., eds., *Concepts of the Person in Religion and Thought*, Berlin 1990). He has also written numerous articles and essays in Danish on the study of Islam, on various aspects of culture theory, and on the history and methodology of the history of religions.

*Yme B. Kuiper* studied sociology and cultural anthropology and is presently associate professor in anthropology and the history of religions at the Faculty of Theology, Department of Religious Studies, the University of Groningen, The Netherlands. His publications concern theory and method in the humanities, religious movements, and historical elite groups. He co-edited *Struggles of Gods* (with H.G. Kippenberg and H.J.W. Drijvers, Berlin/New York 1984) and *Concepts of Person in Religion and Thought* (with H.G. Kippenberg and A.F. Sanders, Berlin/New York).

*Niels Peter Lemche* was born in 1945 and became a theological candidate at the University of Copenhagen, Denmark, in 1971. He was research fellow at the University of Copenhagen from 1972 to 1978, associate professor at the University of Aarhus 1978-1986, visiting professor at the University of Hamburg 1986-1987, and professor of theology (Old Testament) at the University of Copenhagen since 1987. He is also founder and editor of the *Scandinavian Journal of the Old Testament*. His major publications are *Israel i dommertiden* (Israel in the Time of Judges, Copenhagen 1972), *Det gamle Israel* (Ancient Israel, Aarhus 1984), *Early Israel* (Leiden 1985), *Ancient Israel* (Sheffield 1988), and *The Canaanites and their Land* (Sheffield 1991).

*Poul Pedersen* was born in 1949 in Denmark. He is associate professor in anthropology at the Department of Ethnography and Social Anthropology at the University of Aarhus. His publications are on general anthropological theory, history of anthropological theory, and British and Danish colonial and missionary history in India. His publications include "The Racial Trap of India: Reflections on the History of a Regional Ethnography" (*Folk* 1984), "The Nature of Anthropology: From Description to Action" (*Folk* 1989), "Khatri: Vaishya or Kshatriya. An Essay on Colonial Administration and Cultural Identity" (*Folk* 1986), and "Anxious Lives and Letters. Family Separation, Communication Networks and Structures of Everyday Life" (*Culture and History* 1990).

*Jan G. Platvoet* is associate professor at the Katholieke Theologische Universiteit Utrecht, The Netherlands. He has taught the history of religions at this university as well as at the Faculty of Theology at the University of Utrecht from 1969 to 1991. He also taught at the University of Ghana in 1980 and at the University of Zimbabwe from 1985 to 1989. He is presently teaching at the Faculty of Theology, University of Leiden. His publications include *Comparing Religions, a Limitative Approach* (The Hague 1982) as well as articles in English and Dutch academic journals and essay collections on Akan traditional religion, the study of African religions, the study of religions, the analysis of rites, spirit possession, and the general traits of pre-literate religions.

*Michael Pye* was born in England in 1939 and studied at Cambridge University. He has spent many years travelling and studying in Japan. He has held teaching posts at Lancaster University, the University of Leeds, Philipps-University in Marburg, Germany, and is presently Professor at Lancaster University. He is also General Secretary of the International Association for the History of Religions. His major publications are *Skilful Means. A Concept in Mahayana Buddhism* (London 1978), *The Study of Kanji. A Handbook of Japanese Characters* (Tokyo 1971, 1984), and *Emerging from Meditation* (London 1989).

*Steven Vertovec* received degrees in anthropology and religious studies from the University of Colorado and the University of California, Santa Barbara, U.S.A., before obtaining his doctorate in social anthropology from Oxford University, The United Kingdom. Currently he is a research fellow at Oxford University's School of Geography. He is author of several articles on the Indian diaspora, editor of *Aspects of the South Asian Diaspora* (Delhi, 1991), co-editor of *South Asians Overseas: Migration and Ethnicity* (Cambridge, 1990), and his book *Hindu Trinidad: Religion, Ethnicity and Socio-Economic Change* is forthcoming from Macmillan.

*Margit Warburg* was born in 1952 in Copenhagen, Denmark. She holds her degree in the sociology of religion from the University of Copenhagen. She is presently associate professor at the Department of the History of Religions at the University of Copenhagen. Her main area of research is religious minorities, in particular Bahá'ís and Jews. She has published *Iranske dokumenter. Forfølgelsen af bahá'íerne i Iran* (Iranian Documents. The Persecution of the Bahá'ís of Iran, Copenhagen 1985) and coedited *Der var engang...amol iz geven...Jødisk kultur og historie i det gamle Østeuropa* (Once Upon a Time...amol iz geven...Jewish Culture and History in Old Eastern Europe, Copenhagen 1986).

*Hans Witte* was born in 1928. He was a contemplative monk from 1954 to 1968 and studied philosophy, theology, and the science of religion. He was curator of the Afrika Museum, Berg en Dal, from 1971 to 1981, and associate professor in African religions at the State

University Groningen, The Netherlands. His books include *Yoruba Symbolism of the Earth* (1982), *Ifa and Esu. Iconography of Order and Disorder* (1984), *L'oeuvre à l'oeuvre: Pierre Borgue et Maarten Beks* (1986), and *Earth and the Ancestors. Ogboni Iconography* (1988).

# Index of Authors